TALKING WOMAN

Also by Shana Alexander

The Feminine Eye

Shana Alexander's State-by-State
Guide to Women's Legal Rights

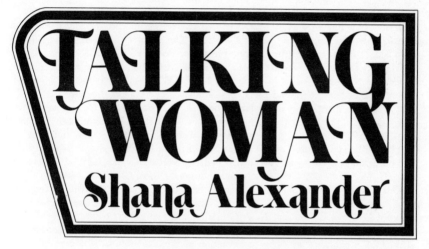

TALKING WOMAN
Shana Alexander

———— DELACORTE PRESS/NEW YORK ————

ACKNOWLEDGMENTS

"Good creatures, do you love your lives" by A. E. Housman: From THE COL-
LECTED POEMS OF A. E. HOUSMAN. Copyright 1936 by Barclays Bank Ltd.
Copyright © 1964 by Robert E. Symons. Reprinted by permission of Holt, Rinehart
and Winston, Publishers, The Society of Authors as the literary representative of the
Estate of A. E. Housman, and Jonathan Cape Ltd., publishers of A. E. Housman's
COLLECTED POEMS.

Acknowledgment is made to the following publications in whose pages the follow-
ing material first appeared. *Life*: "Judy Garland," "On the Lookout for Lurleen,"
"The Zero-Calorie Diet," "Nell J.'s Letter," "Decision to Die," "Shana Talks About
Shana," "The Fine Art of Marital Fighting," "Images of Patty," "Helen Gurley
Brown," "Marlon Brando," "Editor's Note," "The Elephant's Child," and "The
Rich Kid." *McCall's*: "Splashing Around in Other People's Lives" and "Here I Am.
Hello. This Is Me." *Newsweek*: "Alabama in the Afternoon: George and Cornelia
Wallace," "Cagney," "*Life* Magazine: R.I.P.," "What Is a Marriage?," "Dinty
Moore's Restaurant," "Beyond the Doll's House," "The Girl in the Box," "Water-
gate Overture: Love Song to Martha Mitchell," "Nixon's High Command: The
Crazy Gang," "The Seven (New) Deadly Sins," "Watergate Metamorphosis: Nixon
into Nixxon," "The Need (Not) to Know," "Perfect Secretaries: Sally and Rose,"
"Big Graffiti: The Nixon Tapes," "Watergate Finale: Good Guys and Bad Guys,"
"At the Sexual Delicatessen (Last Tango in Deep Throat)," "Hanging Out in Sexual
Space," "Out of the Closet: Masters and Johnson," "Kids' Country," "Getting Old
in Kids' Country," "And Now . . . Infants' Lib!," "Children of Vietnam," "Operation Baby Lift: A Sentimental Binge," "Prisoners of Peace," "Eagleton's Saintly
Revenge," "Breast Cancer and News Overkill," and two Letters to the Editor. *Redbook*: "Real Gardens, Real Toads: Some Speculations on Secrecy and the Dark Night
of the CIA" (published as "The Assassination of President Kennedy"), copyright ©
1975 by Shana Alexander.

Copyright © 1976 by Shana Alexander

Manufactured in the United States of America
First printing

Designed by Leo McRee

Library of Congress Cataloging in Publication Data

Alexander, Shana.
 Talking woman.

 1. Alexander, Shana. I. Title.
PN4874.A36A37   070.4'092'4 [B]   76-25137
ISBN 0-440-08595-0

For Cecelia and Milton, who
taught me how

Contents

Section Three: Thumbsucking—The Feminine Eye on Watergate

Section Four: At the Sexual Delicatessen

Section Five: Kids' Country

Section Six: Deep-water Diving, Unbuttered Truth

TALKING WOMAN

Introduction

Autobiography was never intended, only vaudeville. But *Talking Woman* has turned out to be a bit of both. I had set out to collect and republish some favorite old pieces. The surprise in rereading them was that many were almost as much about me as they were about the people I had spent my life talking to. As I prepared the pieces for publication, a faint outline of my own life began to appear to me, like an astral projection, or a blurry stone rubbing, over the piles of old magazines. Perhaps this happened because I always of necessity wrote out of myself, not talking from any solid political or philosophical or aesthetic position (though I often wished it otherwise), but only about whatever interested me personally. In any event, much of my stuff over the years now seemed to constitute a kind of shadow autobiography. I was talking *to* others, but very often *about* myself.

I wanted to add some new material, talking back to my former self. This back talk became *Diary: 1976*— today's comments on yesterday's news, and yesterday's me. Why did I bother? I think because heretofore my work had always seemed to me entirely random, unplanned as a doodle, and so had my life. The unexpected appearance of the stone rubbing showed me my life and my work as two doodles, interrelated, symmetrical, one mirroring the other. You would have to have lived it to understand how reassuring this was.

The *Talking Woman* label comes from show business, as I do; father a songwriter, mother a movie critic. George Burns told me once that in vaudeville a talking woman was something special, rather like a horse that could count, I imagine. Most vaudeville women were silent smilers

—coat-holders for magicians, targets for knife throwers, dancing partners. If, like Gracie Allen, you could actually open your mouth and
say something, you got paid extra.

I got paid $24.50 a week—New York Newspaper Guild minimum
—when I started out during World War II as a talking schoolgirl on
summer vacation, hired as a cub reporter on the Sunday magazine of
the New York newspaper *PM*. Assigned on my very first day to go see
Gypsy Rose Lee and interview her about her pregnancy, I went to
pieces instead (start of lifelong habit) and could scarcely dial the phone
to make the appointment. I was sure she could tell that I had never
interviewed anybody, had never even *seen* a stripper. The truth was I
had never seen a pregnant woman up close.

She invited me to lunch, and so a terrified sixteen-year-old arrived
at Miss Lee's splendid town house in mid-July wearing white gloves.
The questions I planned to ask her were written out and tucked into
the gloves. I resolutely refused to unglove through the sherry, even
during the omelette. What could the majestic lady have made of the
trembling young glove fetishist seated on her divan? In retrospect I see
she understood, because when I finally blurted out, "Miss Lee, after the
birth of your child, do you intend to resume your career?" she favored
me with the one thing she knew could save me—a good quote.

"Honey," she said, "I can't have everything going out and nothing
coming in."

That's how the doodle began.

As a lifelong working reporter and working woman, I have found
little time for reflection, and little inclination. I *knew* my life was a
doodle; no need to examine it. I was also aware that Socrates would not
have approved of this attitude (I didn't much approve of it myself) but
I had followed another philosopher, Satchel Paige: "Don't look back
. . . it may be gaining on you."

I have not looked back immoderately here; just enough to tie up the
pieces into loose bundles, and to comment from time to time on how
something came to be written, or on what was running through my
mind at the time.

Today talking women are everywhere; under federal employment
guidelines for press and broadcast media, we have become a legal
imperative. We are also box office. I have always considered us a moral
imperative as well, even back thirty years ago when I was still a novelty
act, like a bear on ice skates. When I signed on at *Life* magazine in

January, 1951, the only other (nonclerical) women on the staff were "researchers," like myself. Only men could become writers. To get my job I had had to agree to a drastic cut in salary as well as station, from glamorous $125-a-week entertainment editor of *Flair* magazine to $65-a-week *Life* researcher. The blithe unconcern with which I accepted the humbler station astonishes me today. But back then I didn't care a fig. I was planning to get married soon, hey-nonny-nonny, and subside professionally into permanent wife-and-motherhood. But I stayed at *Life* eighteen years (divorced after fourteen) and lifetime pension and retirement benefits were calculated from that $65 base. I tell this story to college students now, and tell it here for the same reason. Even today, liberated as she may fancy herself to be, a young woman tends to underrate her marketplace value relative to men. Don't.

Life was a joy, a delirium, nonetheless, and my deepest friendships grew out of the giddy, fizzy, delicious atmosphere of *Life*'s show business department, which was led by two dazzling people, Tom Prideaux and Mary Leatherbee. Mary was a brilliant (and nonstop) talking woman, a beauty, and the most gallant, vivid creature I have known, male or female. She was also the most resolute. After Mary became movie editor, she once conceived the mad notion of restaging a full-scale Mack Sennett comedy for *Life*'s cameras, with a dozen modern movie stars playing all the bathing beauties and Keystone Cops. By then, I had been transferred from New York City to *Life*'s Los Angeles bureau, and one day I got a cable from Mary asking me to round up twelve top movie stars, plus props, funny costumes and funny cars, and get everybody out onto the beach at the same time. I can't believe we did this except that the picture is right there in *Life Goes to the Movies:* Rock Hudson, Paul Newman, Buddy Ebsen, and three or four other fellows in cop suits leaping off the rocks in hot pursuit of Debbie Reynolds, Shirley MacLaine, Kim Novak, et al.

This was my DeMille pinnacle as a researcher/photographer's assistant. Shortly after, in 1961, I wrote the piece on Judy Garland which appears here on page 15, and became *Life*'s first woman staff writer. Three years later I was invited to write a signed column. This notion was similar to, but scarier than, having to interview Gypsy Rose Lee, but the honor was so great I didn't know how to refuse.

"Demand a $5,000 raise," Mary suggested, but the editor offered exactly that as I walked into his office, and modesty sold out on his doorstep.

I called the column "The Feminine Eye," because the editor wanted it clear that the writer was a woman, and my own name offered no clue as to gender. I used to get fan mail addressed to "Dear Mr. Mrs. or Miss Alexander. Please check one." Writing "The Feminine Eye" over the next four years gave me a new clue as to my own gender. A few years later, someone would coin the term "consciousness raising" to explain what was happening to me. I only knew that, before the column, I had always been, and felt like, a talking woman in a man's world; a novelty act; your basic bear on ice skates. Calling myself "The Feminine Eye," I finally began to develop one.

I also developed into enough of a mini-celeb so that, for the first time ever, other people occasionally wanted to interview *me*. The first was Pierre Burton. ("The Johnny Carson of Canada" is the way he was described to me. Or was it "The Jack Paar"?) I arrived in front of Pierre's TV cameras, the first I had ever faced, and he said to me, reading from a Time, Inc. publicity handout, "Mrs. Alexander, it says here that you were *Life*'s first woman reporter, first woman staff writer, and first woman columnist. . . . Doesn't that make you feel a little like the house nigger?"

I told the Johnny Carson of Canada that there was nothing wrong with being a token woman, provided you didn't stay in the job too long. I tell this story to college students today, too. I don't tell them much about the next phase in my life though, when I left *Life* to become editor of *McCall's*. Only after I got there did I discover that it was the world's largest women's magazine, and I was to be the magazine's first woman editor in fifty years. I had become a big-time token woman, a sort of female totem pole to which the management hoped to moor a sinking ship. It was an uncomfortable position for me, but it didn't last long. I was expected to talk and act like a lady editor. I didn't and I got fired.

Then came a weird period as an executive talking woman, running out my contract with Norton Simon, Inc., the giant food conglomerate which then owned *McCall's*. At Norton Simon I had acquired a Dickensian benefactor in the person of company president David J. Mahoney, and when *McCall's* dropped me, Mahoney lifted me up and sent me around to talk to the presidents of his various Norton Simon Companies (Hunt Foods, Canada Dry, McCall's Printing, and so on) on behalf of sexual equality in the board room. So far as these business-men were concerned, I might have been talking in tongues. Neither one of us understood what the hell the other was talking about, and doubtless they were as relieved as I when I managed to talk my way back into a business I knew something about.

Talking my way into *Newsweek* was not outstandingly difficult. I went to see editor Osborn Elliott about possibly publishing my column again, and it turned out that, although I didn't know it, he had my name in his pocket—on a list of possible future contributors. Two days later he had me there too. My three years at *Newsweek* were happy times. I was my own woman again, talking once more in my own voice, and not as Baby Snooks, Fannie Farmer, Mother Bloor, or Betty Crocker, as had from time to time been necessary in the high food-biz days. People around the Washington Post Company, which owns *Newsweek*, warned me that inasmuch as Katherine Graham was our proprietor, I would also have to be her surrogate talking woman. Not so. Around *Newsweek* I was never made to feel anything but my own woman; everything printed as written, and not a comma changed without my okay. When I left, I thanked Kay and Oz for treating me not only like a lady but like a gent.

A year or two before fetching up at *Newsweek*, during the dainty *Götterdämmerung* that was *McCall's*, I salvaged some journalistic self-respect by becoming a regular commentator on *Spectrum*, a CBS News radio program which offers hot and cold dabs of highly personal opinion to spice up the twenty-four-hour news format. I like radio. *Spectrum* was short, breezy, and you didn't have to get your hair done to appear on it. I had to give it up when the *Newsweek* job began, but I missed it, so it was a happy morning a year or so later when the telephone rang and Don Hewitt, executive producer of *Sixty Minutes*, told me he had an unusual idea for the Point-Counterpoint segment of his TV show. "Guess what, Shana? We've been thinking of having a man argue with a *woman!*"

I said the novelty of his idea certainly appealed to me. I auditioned, and won, and—for ninety seconds a week, at least—found myself CBS' talking woman, back on Gracie Allen's old network.

One major difference between women and men in my generation is that women have to be more people than men, or to play more roles. Wife, mother, mistress, and housekeeper are distinctly different personalities. Husband, father, lover, son, and breadwinner are pretty much the same fellow, seen at different ages and stages of his life, but temperamentally little changed. So women are accustomed to talking in many voices, and women writers like myself find it natural to write in many voices. I am no Mel Blanc, but looking back over my own work, I can distinguish perhaps a dozen. The number of *subjects* available to write about is infinite (and, with practice, one can learn to deal with any subject in 1,100 words, the size of a one-page magazine column, or even in ninety seconds) but the repertoire of *voices* is limited. Some of mine are D. Alexander (M.D.); Herr Doktor Alexander (eminent shrink); Granny Alexander (folksy wisdom); Miz Shana (gossip, as in Miz Rona); Pollyanna; Funny Lady (wryly self-critical); Ms. Alexander; Cassandra; Sob Sister; Kid Sister; The Wife of Bath (very difficult), and a few others. Interested readers can readily find and identify them here.

Rereading the old pieces, I also heard an autobiographical progression in these developing voices, and that interests me more. I began at *Life* in 1951 as an invisible Talking Woman. Ten years later I had become a staff ventriloquist. But I only found my own voice as a writer as I was approaching my fortieth year.

My first voice at *Life* was entirely anonymous, not merely unsigned. It spoke only in picture captions and "text blocks," as we called them, and I myself was not permitted to write even these bland, turf-squares of prose. My job was to write up my interview notes with, say, Lucille Ball, for the writer, and he (it was always a *he*) carved out the captions and text blocks from those notes. Afterwards I checked his captions and text blocks. I learned to put a tiny red dot over each word as the copy was being processed, to show it was accurate as to spelling and fact, that *he* had not taken too many liberties with my notes. The penalty for a false red dot was an "errors report," to be filed in triplicate. Three errors reports, and you got fired. I received one errors report for the sin of calling something in a caption a "suitcase." (Seaman Jenkins packs suitcase for weekend leave.) Somebody wrote to our publisher that this object was properly an "overnight bag." The complainant thus attempting to slam the lid on my First Amendment rights was the Associated Luggage Manufacturers' Association of America.

Later, in 1954, when I was sent to California, my job was to compose teletype files for the writers back in New York so that he—it was still always, only, *he*—could use them to compose captions and text blocks.

Life's writers always composed their copy on special, maxi-erasible, ruled paper—twenty lines to a sheet, triple-space, eighty characters to a line, using an elite typewriter. *Life's* editorial offices contained oo such typewriters, and oo half-crazed writers, of whom the looniest was KOMING. ("oo" was *Life's* code for a number unknown to the writer, to be looked up and filled in later by his researcher. "KOMING" indicated an unknown word. I still write in that same code today.) When I became a *Life* writer in 1961, I proudly used the same thick, expensive white graph paper. We got so we couldn't write without the stuff. We were paper-trained, like puppies, conditioned to do it on *Life* paper and nowhere else. The morning *Life* folded, nearly four years after I had quit, my first act was to telephone the survivors, commiserate, and say for God's sake save all the special training-paper they could. Without it, I was certain I could never write another word. The *Requiem for Life Magazine,* published in *Newsweek,* and reprinted here on page 77, was written on old *Life* paper.

My second voice was an attempt to adapt the ventriloquist's art to paper. As a staff writer whose specialty was the "personality piece," my hope was to sound, and even to think and feel, like Streisand, Brando, or whoever my subject might be. The more I could submerge my own ego and "become" my subject, the more immediate the "personality" would seem to the reader. I did this first with Garland. Indeed I identified with her to such a degree that when she lost her voice on tour, I lost mine, and one day when she complained of an earache, a trickle of blood ran out of my own ear. Writers are set apart by strange stigmata. One dark night of despair and what felt like terminal writer's block, I inadvertently stabbed myself with a pen and bled all over my beloved editor and mentor, Ralph Graves, who dryly recounts that incident on page 168. It was Ralph who had encouraged me to try to become a writer some years before, who promised me that, if I would attempt a major piece on Garland, he would himself attempt the impossible and get bureau correspondent Alexander promoted to exalted staff writer status. Eventually, it all happened. The same week in June, 1961, that Fidel Castro liberated Cuba, Ralph Graves liberated himself from *Life* articles editor up into the assistant managing editor's slot, put Fidel on the cover, put my Judy Garland story inside, and liberated me into staff writer status.

Then came "The Feminine Eye," and at the age of thirty-nine I learned to use a new word. I learned to write "I" for the first time, to say "I think," or "I feel." Stepping into the first person for the first time, and talking as myself was the hardest thing I have ever tried to make myself do, far more difficult than stepping in front of a television camera for the first time. On TV one has make-up, lighting, coaching, kind friends. On the printed page, "I" stands naked as a bare stick. The distance from third person to first is the longest throw in journalism.

Only with "The Feminine Eye" did I learn to speak in my own voice at last—though still on *their* paper. The challenge in writing a column of personal opinion is not so much to *say* what you think as to be sure you *know* it. Often I wasn't. The deadline helped. The imminence of a deadline almost invariably clarifies the brain, though often not before it has teased and tenderized that poor organ almost beyond bearing. At such times, the clock and your fingers tell you what you think. If it sounds wrong after you've read it over, you throw up and try again.

When the *McCall's* offer came, I bit hard. I would speak not just for myself but for all women, *to* all women, in an up-to-date, sisterly voice they would understand. (And love me for.) So I moved bag, baggage, cats, daughter, and nanny back to New York City . . . and in fairly short order lost job, voice, self-confidence, self-respect, and nearly all the rest. But I learned my limitations. In short, I grew up. About time. I was over forty.

Newsweek beckoned. The week before the 1972 Democratic convention, I checked in, *with* my stack of *Life* paper, and filed my first column. Leaner, more rakish, closer-hauled than *Life*, the smaller news magazine thrived while *Life* foundered. I confess it now: I wrote all my *Newsweek* pieces on *Life's* pilfered paper.

I carried on with the columns for nearly three years, until I heard still another voice, another talking woman—this time, my own voice, on *Sixty Minutes.* To be able both to talk at length on paper, and to talk for a few moments each week on TV, is finally to have the best of both worlds. I have loved learning a new trade in middle life: television is writing for the ear, and speaking for the eye. I love being in vaudeville. I adore my gentleman-adversary, Jack Kilpatrick, and relish the long phone conversations each week between his farm in Virginia and my orchard on Long Island in which we pick out the subject on which we can agree to disagree. Each week we alternate positions, Point and Counterpoint. Whoever is Point writes out his argument and reads it on the telephone to the other, so he can write an answering Counterpoint. To show me what a gentleman he was, Jack let me go last, first.

Best of all, a year after I joined the TV show, the show entered prime time. I do not claim credit. And in truth, I am on camera only ninety seconds of the time. But it's an exhilarating ninety seconds, a great work-week, even if it does take me two days to prepare (one to write, and one to rewrite, get my hair done, go to the studio, and tape). Nobody I had ever known worked as hard as the *Life* editors did on closing night, until I met Mike Wallace and Morley Safer. My first year on the show, I sometimes noted in the corridors of CBS a new complexion shade: mikeanmorley gray. The only way you can achieve it naturally is through extreme fatigue. As David Niven said of Truman Capote when he decided to become an actor, "He'll do fine, until he discovers how hard it is." Good work is always very hard. Hard work is always the only way.

I am happy on *Sixty Minutes* for a multitude of reasons, not least because once a week Franny Arvold, our resident make-up genius at CBS, makes me look like the talking woman I used to be. But I am happiest of all because a show composed of journalists talking on TV in prime time means that I haven't been talking in vain for thirty years. Somebody out there *was* listening. The meaning and the triumph of *Sixty Minutes* as TV's first news show in prime time is that a whole lot of people out there have been listening. The public cares about what is happening in the world. Public affairs have become box office. The news biz has become show biz. The two main themes of my own life have come together, in Counterpoint, if not in harmony. That's good enough for me.

SECTION 1

Splashing Around in Other People's Lives

1

Splashing Around in Other People's Lives

This country has gone mad for gossip. TV, newspapers, radio, movies, books, magazines, all our media are obsessed with private lives. Prying, spying, eyeing—the hounding of public figures has reached such proportions that we may have to declare open and closed hunting seasons. A Kennedy head on every wall. WHAT IS JACKIE REALLY LIKE? looks out from a thousand newsstands. Strange, this new spawning of what is essentially housemaids' gossip, the low keyhole peeping of servants at their masters' lives. For it comes at a time when there *are* no more servants. Does no more servants mean that there are also no more masters?

Personally, I am not against gossip. I enjoy it hugely. But I am for privacy, too. More and more, I prefer my gossip anonymous. Dear "Dear Abby." No names, please, and long may she wave. It's when real names get into the act that I begin to squirm. Once I wanted to know all about other people's lives; now that I know some delicious personal gossip, I have lost my taste for it. (This may be one definition of maturity.)

I think our new national craving for gossip is related to the terrifying assault on privacy, and the erosion of intimacy, which characterize the way we live today. It is a vicarious age. Our lives are too much lived for us by other people's shadows. But passions on paper and love by tube are not enough to sustain life. The Medium Is the Message is no message. Although the media pander to voyeurism and exploit it, they do not cause it. An insatiable appetite for gossip betrays great hunger for real feeling, but affords only vicarious feeding. It is a Chinese meal for the heart.

The best word on gossip comes to us from Jonathan Swift: "Lash the vice, but spare the name."

Today in America we disregard Swift's counsel. It is the name we lash, and with appalling savagery. The gossip columnists are the ghouls of the fourth estate. They live by leaning heavily on the First Amendment. The quarrel in the bedroom is what brings them swarming; the rage at night—not the kissing but the slugging. They feed on dead love. High bitchery is their art. Gossipists poke and rake into areas where other people have the decency to look away. Not all gossipists are evil. Some are merely clumsy and kill badly, like amateur matadors.

Since I have written about other people for years, I suppose it was inevitable that sooner or later people would begin to write about me. Still the change from author into character is an awful shock. I was not in the least prepared a year or so ago when my own name began to turn up in gossip columns. To find oneself lied about in public for the first time is surprisingly nasty. Lawyers advise you not to sue; you will only spread the stain. One's sole recourse is silence. But silence cannot be.

Communications in the innuendo industry are instantaneous. Gossipists swarm like wasps and sting out of the same place. Denials only increase their frenzy. Within hours, they zoom in on neighbors, parents, employers, friends. Schoolmates one hasn't seen for thirty years are interviewed as bosom pals. Rumor and gossip, like sound itself, appear to travel by wave-effect, sheer preposterosity being no barrier. And once the first stone, or word, is cast, it is already beyond recall.

Medieval satirists liked to draw Rumour as a thin beast of many slobbering mouths. They were right. At my own door I have seen the beast. Even when he is shot down or topples over in his own wind, he does not die without giving birth to another. Denial causes a counter-rumor to arise from his ashes. (Counterrumors are, of course, carried by countercolumnists, a new gang of gossipists who now appear out of nowhere, scavengers of the scavengers.)

When Harold Ross invented *The New Yorker* and its signal adornment, the magazine profile, his entire idea was that writer and subject never meet. The article was to be a kind of shadow-picture drawn by the writer after talking to as many of the subject's friends, and enemies, as he could find. An elegant idea, I think, but alas as extinct as the housemaid.

Having plunged headlong into the age of personal journalism, we

seem now to be joyously splashing around in other people's lives without any rules at all. What *is* the dividing line between gossip-monger-
ing and good personal journalism? I think it is this: gossipists are figures
outside the window peeking in. When a journalist knocks and is admitted, the situation changes. You are in a close consultation which you
cannot abuse. You're involved. You have a relationship, hence a responsibility not to betray. The responsible journalist solemnly swears to tell
the truth and nothing but the truth. But "the whole truth" is not in
his contract.

I do not mean to suggest that the figure at the window always lies.
Gossip is often true. Sometimes it *becomes* true. People get hooked on
their own bad press and begin to act out the new roles being written
for them. But mostly, gossip is half-true. Between the two poles of
whole-truth and half-truth is slung the chancy hammock in which we
all rock.

McCall's—February 1970

2

Judy Garland

Up a dark alley to the stage door hurries a strange little creature
bundled in mink from ears to ankles. In the dim light it looks like a
fur shmoo wearing a topknot of hair curlers.

Inside the jampacked theater, tension hangs like a net between the
audience and the big orchestra on stage. The overture begins, and one
by one all the familiar hoped-for melodies come flooding back. Each
time the musicians launch a new one across the footlights, fans send
back salvos of applause, and with every volley the emotional pressure
inside the hall rises a few more degrees. Finally the vast space above
the audience shimmers with visions of clanging trolley cars, men that
got away, and birds flying over the rainbow. At this point in the series

of identical musical evenings which have taken place recently in four-teen major U.S. cities, a plump little thirty-eight-year-old woman hiding behind furls of dusty curtain knows it is again time to go to work, and to deafening billows of applause that drown out the orchestra's final crashing chords, Miss Judy Garland trots cheerfully to center stage.

The uproar subsides, the songs begin. ". . . So keep on smiling, 'cause when you're SMILING . . ." At first the audience cannot believe it will last. "You *go* to my head. . . . I could cry—salty tears—" The big, sobby voice flows out unrestrained across the footlights, rich as caramel, solid as lava. This is the *old* Judy Garland voice. ". . . Who cares what banks *fail* in Yonkers, long as you've got a kiss that CONquers?" She's strutting now, balancing on the slender legs and prancing like a pony. At the end of Act I comes a performance of "San Francisco" so brassy, so sassy, delivered with such a full head of steam that one expects the whole theater to pull away from the levee and start churning downriver under its own power.

More than a concert is under way in this hall now; it is a tribal celebration. "I—can't—give—you—anything but love, baby . . ." After the first four notes, everybody recognizes the song at the same instant, and 4,000 people gasp with pleasure. The hot, solid voice speaks personally to each listener until the entire audience has been hypnotized into one huge multicelled organism. The tribal celebration takes on overtones of a mystical experience. "I'm gonna love you like nobody's loved you . . . I'm gonna *love* you, I'm gonna *love* you . . ." Then the Vesuvius of torch songs, "Stormy Weather," sung with tears in her voice, her eyes, her throat, running down her neck. By the end of Act II (*"Zing* went the *strings* . . . Clang, clang, clang! Rock-a-bye your bay-BEE! . . ."), she has the crowd on its feet, shouting and swaying down the aisles, reaching up over the footlights to touch her hand. Comes the final heart-stopping cry of innocence and unbearable longing, "Why then, oh why . . . can't I?" and on some nights the true believers come swarming up onto the stage like lemmings.

It is over. The tribe staggers homeward to sleep off the magic spell. When they awaken, they are a tribe no longer, just individuals, tinker, tailor, soldier, sailor, and nobody can quite say what the uproar was all about. Yet the next time Judy Garland walks out onstage in another town to face thousands of different people, the same thing will happen again. And if she doesn't appear for five years or ten, they will still remember and still pack the theater in hopes that the magic will come again. And if she can't sing another note, they will stand in the aisles and shout, "We love you, Judy!" and "Just stand there, Judy!" For Judy Garland today is more than the most electrifying entertainer to watch on stage since Al Jolson. She has moved beyond talent and beyond fame to become the rarest phenomenon in all show business: part bluebird, part phoenix, she is a legend in her own time.

Sometimes in the evangelical frenzy of her finale, as the crowds scream hoarsely for "More! More! We love you! We want more!" one gets the feeling that Judy Garland may be about to cut a vein. By temperament she is incapable of holding anything of herself in reserve. This gives her performance an old-fashioned theatrical excitement, as if a shower of Roman candles were coming over the footlights. It is a style marvelously florid in this cool electronic era of entertainment. For Garland fans, her great warmth and responsiveness generate the enormous emotional identification that each listener feels for Judy personally. It is what Spencer Tracy is talking about when he says, "A Garland audience doesn't just listen, they feel. They have their arms around her when she works." It is an all-out, go-for-broke performance that takes everything to give.

Seen from backstage, Judy sometimes suggests a Calliope that has been mortally wounded. At intermission she staggers to her dressing room, gasping and clutching her middle, panting that she cannot possibly finish the show, she is too exhausted, too hot, there is a dagger in her throat. She tears off her soggy costume and sips a glass of white wine as her hairdresser blows icy air over her heaving back and shoulders with a portable dryer. But ten minutes later, the streaked makeup restored, the limp hairdo repuffed, she is zipped into the next costume and ready to go back to work. Often visitors comment on Judy's powers of physical recovery. "Well, you know, I'm like Rocky Graziano," she says amiably, and with a little giggle she scampers back toward the stage.

When she comes off at the end of her show, she sometimes must be helped to her dressing room. Sprawled on a couch in her fuzzy blue robe (a sentimental talisman from her daughter, Liza), waiting for enough strength to flow back so that she can dress and make her way through the huge crowd gathering now at the stage door, Judy talks about what it feels like to face the kind of frenzied, revivalist receptions she has been getting.

"You stand there in the wings," she reflects, "and sometimes you want to yell because the band sounds so good. Then you walk out and if it's a really great audience, a very strange set of emotions can come over you. You don't know what to do. It's a combination of feeling like Queen Victoria and an absolute ass. Sometimes a great reception—though God knows I've had some great receptions and I ought to be prepared for it by now—can really throw you. It kind of shatters you so that you can lose control of your voice and it takes two or three numbers to get back into your stride. I lift my hand in a big gesture in the middle of my first number and if I *see* it's not trembling then I know I haven't lost my control.

"A really great reception makes me feel like I have a great big warm heating pad all over me. People en masse have always been wonderful to me. I truly have a great love for an audience, and I used to want to prove it to them by giving them blood. But I have a funny new thing now, a real determination to make people enjoy the show. I want to give them two hours of just *pow!*"

This all-out quality, this determination to give everything she has, is a trait that Judy was born with. It is the secret of her success as a performer and it lies at the heart of the Garland legend. But it has taken a lifetime in show business for Judy to learn how to give a maximum of *pow!* with a minimum of blood, and in the course of her thirty-five-year-long lesson in this difficult art, the woman behind the legend has many times come close to destruction.

Judy, whose real name is Frances Ethel Gumm, has been a professional singer since the night she dashed onstage at the Grand Theatre in Grand Rapids, Minnesota, where her family's small-time vaudeville act was booked for Christmas week, and sang two impromptu choruses of "Jingle Bells." She was two and a half years old, and thereafter she toured as the youngest of the Gumm Sisters. "I had great fun as a little girl," Judy says today. "We played games backstage. Then I went on, sang, took bows, came off, and had my mother do my ringlets up again. People always applauded and it was all rather pleasant."

It was very much less pleasant when, at twelve, she became a child movie star at M-G-M. For eleven years, after her triumph in *The Wizard of Oz*, though audiences clung to her image as an innocent child skipping along the yellow brick road without a care in the world, she was in reality keeping pace with the most backbreaking production schedule in Hollywood history. While she was still in her teens, she completed twelve pictures, nearly all of them long, difficult, exhausting song-and-dance extravaganzas. On film the result was wonderful: from *Strike Up the Band* through *For Me and My Gal, Meet Me in St. Louis,* and *Easter Parade,* she was about the nicest, prettiest, most talented minstrel girl a moviegoer could hope to see.

But the making of the movie star very nearly crippled the girl. M-G-M was cashing in as fast and as often as it could, and nobody worked harder at becoming a star than Judy herself. By driving herself mercilessly, by loading up with stimulants to keep going and then with sleeping pills to relax, she managed to make thirty movies for her studio, every one of them with a high professional sheen. But between pictures, instead of the vacations she needed, she began having nervous breakdowns. Before she was twenty-three years old, she had had three breakdowns and two marriages, first to bandleader David Rose, then to Director Vincente Minnelli.

Under the relentless necessity of laying golden eggs for M-G-M, she became a frazzled song-and-dance zombie. She was difficult, impossible. There was a series of suspensions, recriminations, tears, forgiveness, brief rest periods, then more work, more breakdowns. On June 17, 1950, after she failed to report for a Saturday dance rehearsal with Fred Astaire, the studio suspended her for the third time. Despondent and frantic, M-G-M's prize goose dashed into the bathroom and slashed her neck with a broken water glass, and the golden eggs stopped.

A few months later, "for her own best interests," the studio released her from her contract. She was considered unemployable. Her salary had not been high by Hollywood standards, and her frequent breakdowns plus the normal movie star's expenses had taken all she earned. Her second marriage had just fallen apart. She was twenty-eight years old.

"After I was thrown out of Metro, I really went to pieces for a while," Judy says today. "All I wanted to do was eat and hide. I lost all my self-confidence. For ten years I was afraid of stores, planes, cars. When I worked, I suffered agonies of stage fright. People had literally to push me out on stage." The person who did the pushing and at times was able to restore Judy's sagging confidence in herself both as a woman and as a performer was Sid Luft, a onetime test pilot for Douglas Aircraft. Luft became Judy's manager, then her husband.

Under Luft's stewardship, Judy began making more comebacks than a yo-yo. Over a period of nearly ten years, she played the Palladium, the Palace, nightclubs, theaters. Everywhere she went she drew record crowds and large grosses. She and Luft made their own movie, *A Star Is Born*, and some critics called it the finest musical ever to come out of Hollywood. She did a TV show for the biggest audience in history. She already had one daughter, Liza Minnelli, and she and Luft had two more children, Lorna and Joseph.

But between the high points came many lows. She was obviously often ill; she couldn't pay her bills; there were rumors that she was a hopeless alcoholic, a drug addict; she didn't show up for work, she collapsed onstage, she lost her voice, she lost her figure, she fought with everybody. But it was during these same years of violent ups and downs that the public image of Garland as the bluebird really began to take wing. The struggles of the woman, no longer hidden by the smoke screen of studio publicity, were the making of the legend.

By 1958 and 1959, the Garland yo-yo had begun to lose its resiliency. The great voice had perceptibly begun to fail along with everything else, and though people by the thousands still came to see her, all they saw onstage some nights was a dumpy woman singing a quavery lullaby. Neither Judy nor her public knew then how sick she really was. "Sometimes I felt as if I was performing in a blizzard," she says today. At other times she would suddenly feel nauseated or dizzy in the middle of her performance. This was a new terror. "You are never so *alone* as when you are ill onstage. The most nightmarish feeling in the world is to suddenly feel like throwing up in front of four thousand people."

By autumn of 1959, Judy was unable to work at all. She felt frightened, sick, and mentally confused. In late November, she was admitted to a hospital in New York City. She looked awful. Her face was a puffy white mask. Her eyes were glazed, she felt faint, she couldn't remember things. Her whole body was grossly fat and bloated. Her limbs were so stiff and swollen that sometimes she could barely move, and at other times she trembled uncontrollably. She was clapped into bed at once, and batteries of tests were begun.

All her alarming symptoms, including the mental ones, turned out to have a real physical basis. The doctors said she had hepatitis and that it was due, at least in part, to the combined effects of certain tranquilizers and diet pills which previously doctors, treating previous breakdowns, had prescribed for her. The new doctors guessed she might have been walking around with hepatitis for as long as three years. The patient admitted she had swallowed a great many drugs over the past fifteen years, careening and ricocheting between sleeping pills and pep pills, diet medicines and nerve tonics, in her struggle for physical and emotional stability.

There were many puzzling symptoms to her latest collapse, and as the weeks dragged on, platoons of specialists were summoned to review her case. Finally one day the chief specialist appeared at her bedside. Behind him stood Sid Luft, looking equally grave. "Miss Garland, you are still a young woman and I wish I did not have to tell you this," the doctor said. "But I have no choice. For the rest of your life all your physical activity must be curtailed. Everything you eat and drink must be strictly regulated. You must learn to accept the fact that you are a *permanent* semi-invalid. It goes without saying that under no circumstances can you ever work again."

Up to that moment it had been a classic Hollywood bedside scene. Then the patient spoke. "Whoopee!" she cried weakly and fell back among the pillows.

After five months of hospital care, she spent four more months convalescing at her home in Beverly Hills. She appeared publicly for the first time in July to campaign for her friend Jack Kennedy, and then rather suddenly she flew off to England alone.

This flight was the first sign that Judy Garland might have recovered from something more than hepatitis. Her fear of airplanes had once been so severe that she could not go near an airport without trembling. As Judy herself tells the story today, "When the doctor told me that work was out of the question for me forever, I felt greatly relieved. The pressure was off me for the first time in my life. Physically I recovered rather well because I'm a terribly strong woman, but I knew I had to get out of California. I was liked in California but nobody needed me. The phone never rang. In Hollywood I was somebody who *had been* a movie star."

In England Judy told the British press she hoped to settle there permanently. Her husband was detained in the United States but would join her in a few weeks. So would her three children. She took a town house, bought a dog, took steps to enroll the children in English schools, and put her Beverly Hills house up for sale. She shopped in Mayfair and fed the pigeons in Trafalgar Square. Life as a nonworking semi-invalid was turning out to be every bit as pleasant as she had hoped. She still looked chubby but the unhealthy bloat had almost disappeared. By early autumn of 1960, she was feeling better than she had in years.

One sleepless night in London (she still suffered, as she has all her life, from galloping insomnia), she got out of bed, locked herself in the bathroom, turned on the hot shower full blast—both to drown out the sound of her voice and to pamper her long-unused throat with live steam—and began to run through some of her old arrangements. Twenty minutes later, she flung open the door, shook her groggy husband awake and, still steaming faintly, read him a list of some thirty-odd songs. "Are you sure it isn't too much?" he inquired, recalling the doctor's warning.

"Too much?" repeated Judy in a newly steamed voice that could carry to the second balcony. "If I die we'll know it's too much! That specialist! Where'd they import *him* from, Transylvania?" It must have been clear to sleepers for blocks around that Judy Garland was ready to go back to work.

Judy played her new show at the Palladium on August 28, 1960, and, in her words, "It was a pistol!" She played the show in the provinces thereafter and a few times on the Continent. "My work was not going in any particular direction," she says now, "but I didn't care. I seemed to have a brand-new life." In her new life Judy Garland the performer was for the first time playing second fiddle to a high-spirited housewife with the horrible name of Frances Ethel Gumm Luft. As F. E. G. Luft, "I was terribly happy personally. I immensely enjoyed taking my kids to Battersea Park. I looked forward to the days. It sounds so corny to say it, but I felt reborn."

At the same time that Judy was being reborn in England, a Music Corporation of America talent agent in New York named Freddie Fields decided it was time to get reborn himself. Fields cut loose from MCA and went into business on his own as a combination personal manager, business manager, and agent for "a few select clients." Judy Garland, he knew from the show business grapevine, was in England, semiretired, personally happy but professionally drifting. What a challenge for a fledgling impresario! He obtained an appointment with Judy and flew to London.

The meeting was a pistol, too. "With Freddie, something clicked," Judy says. "He seemed to know how to do exactly what I could not do: channel my work." Returning to New York, Fields cut back the underbrush of a lifetime of managerial untidiness:

• He settled his new client's three-year legal battle with CBS and negotiated a giant new TV spectacular.

• He got her a starring role in a big new Hollywood movie, *Judgment at Nuremberg.*

• He booked her for a fourteen-city, six-week U.S. concert tour, which was the quickest way simultaneously to prove to both the singer and her public that no one in the business could create as much pure theatrical excitement as Judy Garland, and also to begin paying off a huge pile of old bills.

Four months ago in Dallas, the phoenix aspect of the Garland legend was revealed to a U.S. audience for the first time. She gave the same show she had programmed in the shower. It lasted two and a quarter hours, left her shaking with fatigue, earned her two standing ovations and a newspaper review that began, with Texas grandeur and simplicity, "No entertainer has ever given such a show in Dallas . . ." Two nights later in Houston she gave the same show, got four standing ovations and, except for the geographical change, the same review: ". . . unquestionably the greatest show ever given in Houston."

Buoyed by Texas, Judy Garland went before a Hollywood camera this spring for the first time in six years to play the most un-Garland role ever invented—a drab little German *Hausfrau* and onetime victim of Nazi persecution who returns to Nuremberg to testify against her former tormentors. Any actress would think twice before accepting the *Hausfrau* role: it was totally unglamorous, technically demanding and she would be playing against such giants as Spencer Tracy, Burt Lancaster, Richard Widmark, and Maximilian Schell, all of whom had important assignments in the same scene. For Judy in particular, the part seemed an insanity: she would not sing a note, she would be on screen for only nine minutes, and the salary was $50,000, a tiny fraction of what she used to be paid. Yet despite all obstacles, Judy and Fields realized that Hollywood needed fast, dramatic proof that Garland was a dependable, professional actress after all.

On her first day on the *Nuremberg* set, in the first scene of the day, *Hausfrau* Garland was required to burst into tears. As the cameras ground away, the actors did the scene once, twice, a third time. Finally in the middle of the sixth take Judy suddenly scowled, stamped her foot angrily and walked off the set. The entire crew froze: so it was just like the old days at M-G-M.

But it was not like the old days at all. As Judy explained to Director Kramer, "Damn it, Stanley, I can't do it. I've dried up. I'm too happy today to cry." Kramer called a ten-minute break, Garland retired to her dressing room to discompose herself, and when shooting resumed she was able to weep.

The night before she left Hollywood Judy went to a small party given by old friends. During the evening, Kramer telephoned from his office at the studio. He, Tracy, Widmark and screenwriter Abby Mann had just viewed the completed footage of her scenes for the first time. When the sequence ended, Kramer told her, the four men had stood up all alone in the little projection room and burst into applause. At this news Judy shed her first real tears since coming back to her hometown. She was now completely ready in every way for the brutal but profitable concert tour.

Judy's financial objective these days is to pay off her old debts, then establish some trust funds for her three children. Alan Jay Lerner and Richard Rodgers hope to write a Broadway musical version of *Roman Holiday* for her. She is working on an autobiography of her first thirty-eight years, and Capitol Records will soon bring out *Judy At Carnegie Hall*. She will tape a TV spectacular in the fall and has scheduled more concert dates. But that's not all: among those negotiating for her services is, of all companies, M-G-M. Her total earnings for this year should be approximately a million dollars. After taxes, expenses, and old bills are paid, she will begin to see some of what managers call "keeping money" for the first time in years.

From then on, the chief beneficiaries of the Garland legend will be the three people in the world who are least interested in that legend and most interested in the woman herself: namely, Liza, Lorna, and Joe. This state of affairs is just fine with Judy, a devoted and skillful parent who, despite her own troubled past, has managed to raise a trio of remarkably untroubled and charming children. Sometimes when work forces her to be away from them, Judy says, "I have *no* ambition to be an actress, *no* ambition to be a singer, I have absolutely no drive. I just want to be a mother." But Judy does not envisage complete retirement, even when her debts are paid and her children provided for. She simply would prefer to work less often and under circumstances that she could control. So far, such control is a luxury she cannot afford.

The most grueling form of show business ever invented is the one-night stand, whether the performer is a third-rate juggler or a big star like Judy Garland. As the tour progresses, the physical wear and tear tends to increase. In addition to the intense physical exertion on stage (Judy works so hard that her heavy clothes drop to the dressing-room floor at the end of each act like suits of soggy armor), there are all the normal offstage touring problems of getting star, Manager David Begelman, conductor, three musicians, a hairdresser, and a secretary all transported from city to city every second day, on and off trains, in and out of hotels, taxied back and forth to theaters, seeing that everybody is fed, housed, rehearsed, and paid, and keeping track of a mountain of luggage packed with everything from tom-toms to chicken soup. The logistics of all this are carefully planned well in advance of the tour, and none of it is supposed to worry Judy. Her job is to sing, which is like saying that Sir Edmund Hillary's job is to climb.

Actually she becomes involved in everything. One night when the entourage arrived at the railroad station, a strip of red carpet was stretched across the tobacco-stained marble floor. The proud stationmaster was on hand to greet Miss Garland and invite her to wait in his private office until train time when he would personally escort her to her compartment. Judy said she would be delighted. A short while later the dispatcher wandered by and complained that he was having an awful time announcing trains lately. His throat hurt all the time.

"You're probably not using your voice right," Judy said. "Take a deep breath and I'll show you." The mink-coated star took hold of the startled dispatcher and pushed hard against his belly. "Feel it? *That's* where your power comes from." She gave him a light punch in the diaphragm. "And be very careful of those loud *eee* sounds. They'll give you a bleeding throat unless you keep your teeth open."

Judy copes with her own professional problems with equal efficiency and not much can happen in front of an audience that will faze her. Musically, she depends on her conductor, Mort Lindsey, and three permanent musicians (a jazz drummer, a bongo player, and a first trumpet) to weld the twenty-five-man local orchestras into a unit during the meticulous six-hour rehearsals that precede every concert. The orchestral surprises that do occur are usually caused by Judy's own sudden, powerful impact on the local musicians.

In one city, right in the midst of her blood-vessel-bursting final chorus of "Swanee," the brass section was so astonished by Judy's lung power that several men stopped playing and listened. In Buffalo a musician rose in the middle of a number, opened his coat, focused a camera dangling against his chest, clicked, wound, buttoned up, sat down, and got his viola back under his chin in time for his next passage.

If there are surprises during a performance, Judy lives through them.

One night during "Over the Rainbow," standing on a blacked-out stage in front of 8,000 people, many of them sniffling audibly, her face illuminated by a single dramatic pin-spot, her eyes brimming with tears, she got as far as ". . . way up high—There's a land that I heard of . . ." when a rather large moth flew into her open mouth. With a flick of her tongue, she tucked the moth into her cheek, sang her way perfectly through the next twenty-eight bars while waiting for the blackout, then coughed, spit and stomped. When the lights came up she was seen bowing and smiling through her tears like a seraph.

Naturally enough Judy has occasional sore throats, and she knows from experience that the only balm and restorative is live steam. This commodity being sometimes hard to come by in a hotel room, she travels with a hot plate and a steam kettle for emergency treatments. But if a hotel does have good hot water in its pipes, she likes to take advantage of it. Before a performance, she often spends an hour or more in a steam-filled bathroom, reclining on a pile of sofa pillows like some small Turkish odalisque, writing postcards to her children and tidily steaming out her collection of knitted travel outfits which hung from the shower rod like a frieze of misty banners.

Her hotel room is also the setting for her continuing and incredibly complex battles with insomnia. The strain of giving people two hours of "just *pow!*" every other night makes it very difficult for Judy to unwind afterward, and her main problem on tour is to get enough rest or, on many nights, to get any sleep at all. Dinner may last until 1 A.M. and there is always *The Late, Late Show* but then, as any insomniac knows, come the desperate hours.

On tour Judy is no ordinary insomniac. She cannot take sleeping medicines because, when she awakens, she would be too "down" to perform, and if she then took a pep pill to get "up," her vibrato would go. Sometimes during the desperate hours, despite the steamings, despite all care, she can feel her throat closing up *right now!* What to do? Strong magic is needed. At these times Judy the woman must force herself to become the abject handmaiden of Judy the insomniac singer. Ah-ha, she will take the singer for a nice invigorating walk in the beautiful dawn! She dresses and goes outside. She returns invigorated, almost sleepy, but now hungry too. Suddenly she is positive she could fall asleep if only she had a nice hot bowl of Chinese egg-flower soup. She has arrived at the true black magic stage; she knows it, she has been here before and she is rather niftily prepared.

"The main problem when practicing witchcraft in strange hotel rooms," as Judy said later when telling this story, "is not to let room service notice anything unusual." At 6:30 one morning she plugged in her bathroom hot plate, rummaged in her luggage until she found a can of chicken noodle soup, found a beer can opener, and went to work. After half an hour's intense concentration, she got most of the noodles through the holes in the can lid. She sprinkled in some seasoning, also from her luggage, and set the soup to simmer. Now she needed only a raw egg and a soup bowl. This was easy. She telephoned room service and gave a very precise breakfast order: "This is Miss Garland speaking. I would like a glass of orange juice and some dry cereal please. Any kind. No, nothing else . . . Oh, I almost forgot. I like a raw egg in my orange juice, but I will put in the egg *myself.*" When the order arrived, Judy discarded the orange juice (which gives her hives) and the cereal (which she has not tasted in twenty years), assembled her soup, drank it, and drifted off at last to sleep.

The amount of sleep she is able to get varies, but the ritual of getting ready for the show does not. By the time she has to leave the hotel for the theater, Judy has already been fed (lamb chops and tea), coiffed (by her traveling hairdresser), meticulously made up (by herself—short, medium, or long eyelashes, depending on the size of the theater), and soothed by a manager who says the acoustics are superb and by a conductor who swears that *this* band really swings. Her secretary has packed the giant suitcase with two complete changes of clothes, several spare pairs of sheer black nylons in the smallest size made, and a stack of towels for mopping up. Another bag holds a sack of ice cubes, tumblers, and a bottle or two of chilled white wine. The only alcohol Judy is now permitted to drink is diluted Liebfraumilch, and she likes to keep a supply in her dressing room. While she is on stage, a friend stands by in the wings with an emergency glassful in case her throat suddenly should go dry between numbers.

By 8:50 P.M. at the theater, the overture is pounding forward and the star is dressed and waiting edgily in the darkened wings, borrowing a drag on somebody's cigaret, nibbling a mint, taking a last sip of Liebfraumilch-on-the-rocks and chattering inanely: "Well, what'll we all *do* for the next two hours?" The orchestra cannonballs toward its climax and just a few feet away the bass drum pounds its portentous rhythm: ". . . the road gets *rougher,* it's lonelier and *tougher . . .*" Without warning, Judy Garland suddenly turns her back on the watchers in the wings, sets her shoulders, takes what seems like a ten-gallon deep breath, and then—astonishingly, as one looks out from the darkness directly into the footlights' glare—she appears to glide away onto the bright-lit stage like a child's pull toy, powered by the rising wave of the applause itself.

Life—June 2, 1961

3

Ms. Abzug

I like people with funny names. Newspapers make good hunting grounds, and so do movie main titles, where one may discover such marvels of nomenclature as U. B. Iwerks and Slavko Vorkapitch. A less dependable hunting ground—the Halls of Congress—this year yielded up a rare treasure in the new Representative from New York, Bella Abzug, a name of such euphonic discord that it starts off evoking Puccini, and ends by evoking gesundheit.

This dramatically labeled Congresswoman Bella Abzug has just proposed legislation to change the label on every other woman in the United States, or anyway to change it on all government documents, records, and correspondence. Mrs. Abzug objects to classifying women by marital status, which is what happens when we address them either as Miss or as Mrs., though we allow men to take refuge in the protective neutrality of Mr.

Women should be regarded, and treated, as individuals in their own right, as well as wives of individuals, Mrs. Abzug points out, and I agree. I also agree with her that women really are subject to double discrimination: discrimination because they are women, and discrimination because they are, or are not, married. A woman is often denied employment or promotion or responsibility or some other benefit solely because she is or isn't married.

But I'm not convinced that label-changing is the way to deal with this problem, except in the symbolic sense. The proposed new label for all women is Ms.—which I guess is logically derived from Miss plus Mrs. But it has two things wrong with it: the spelling, since Ms. is already the abbreviation for manuscript, and the sound. Ms. is pronounced "Miz," and that doesn't have a very liberated ring, at least not to my ear.

Perhaps I'm dubious because of my own curious name which, containing no built-in clues as to gender, sometimes brings me strangely disturbing letters which begin: "Dear Miss, Mrs., or Mister Alexander (Please check one)."

But if names and titles are easily changed, gender is certainly not, and neither is habit. Our minds tend to run in old grooves. For example, when I looked up the full text of Mrs. Abzug's proposed bill, I found the clerk had made this traditional insert in the *Congressional Record:* "Mrs. Abzug asked and was given permission to extend his remarks at this point . . ."

CBS "Spectrum"—August 25, 1971

4

The Smile on the Face of the Candidate's Wife

Every first lady goes veiled in public. Usually she wears a mask of improbable serenity, buttoned on by two rather blankly smiling eyes, and crowned by a nimbus of freshly coiffed hair. But still I enjoy trying to see through to the woman inside.

What first hooked me on first-lady watching was a certain stricken facial expression I call the smile on the face of the candidate's wife. There's a lot of Irene Dunne in the look: a gallant lift of chin, a mute, appealing desire to please.

I first identified the stricken look on Mrs. Nixon's face back in 1960, as she faced the TV cameras and listened to her husband concede victory to John Kennedy. "What did *she* do to deserve this?" I found myself thinking. I've thought the same thing since, watching the stricken smile appear occasionally on Mrs. Kennedy's face, and even Mrs. Johnson's. Also Mrs. Eisenhower, Mrs. Agnew, Mrs. Khrushchev, Mrs. Reagan, and many others. Essentially it is the look of a wife, attempting mutely to radiate loyalty, interest, and aplomb while trapped in the spotlight's glare.

One first lady who does not wear this look, ever, is Jovanka, the wife of Marshal Tito of Yugoslavia. Mrs. Tito can smile all right, she can practically blind you with it. But she never looks trapped. Mrs. Tito held a press conference in Washington, and it turns out that while Mrs. Nixon was a small town school teacher, and the present Mrs. Onassis was a society reporter, Mrs. Tito was a Yugoslav guerilla fighter. At age seventeen, she joined the Partisans and fought in the front lines, first against the Italians, then the Nazis. In one engagement, her all-female brigade killed or wounded 159 enemy soldiers. Considering what American candidates' wives must go through, a guerilla girlhood may be the ideal first-lady background.

Asked about Women's Liberation, Mrs. Tito mentioned an old Yugoslav saying which hangs over her family's front door, back home: "The house is not built on the ground, but on the woman."

Mrs. Tito told reporters that she intends to throw the sign out, "because it does not go with the times." Maybe not, but it goes with the house, even the White House.

CBS "Spectrum"—November 4, 1971

5

Diary: 1976

The smile on the face of the candidate's wife really was the saddest sight I'd seen in politics, maybe even in all of television, and I have never been able to get Pat Nixon's staunch, stricken look out of my mind. The tear I'd seen rolling down her cheek in 1962 as her husband conceded defeat in California to Governor "Pat" Brown, or its ghost (yes, tears have ghosts, ask any woman), literally haunted me; it seemed to reappear over and over on the cheek of each new political wife as she stood beside her husband, mute and frozen as a rabbit in the spotlight's glare, and always, always that sprayed helmet of hairdo.

I think the look comes mainly from being forced to stand there, from not knowing quite what her job is except to smile, and probably from tight shoes. I'd had the smile in mind again in 1968 when I was writing a farewell piece to the outgoing first lady, Lady Bird Johnson.

"Roughly speaking, the President of the United States knows what his job is. Constitution and custom spell it out, for him as well as for us. His wife has no such luck. The first ladyship has no rules. Rather, each new woman must make her own. It is as if we hand her hammer and nails, gold leaf and bit of bunting, and say, 'Here. Build the thing yourself.' What was handed to Mrs. Lyndon Johnson was something even less: a wrecked and blasted Camelot haunted by our special vision of its dazzling, martyred queen."

Come to think of it, the only political wife who doesn't always wear the frozen smile is one who has least to be cheery about: Betty Ford. I think that must be because she knows who she is, her own woman, and she knew it before the awful spotlight snapped on.

All of which is how I came to begin the next piece, on George Wallace's second wife, with exactly the same words I'd used to start out talking about Mrs. Marshal Tito a couple of years earlier. One good thing about a job like mine—in a crunch, you can borrow from yourself. I don't regard this as stealing, more like personal recycling, like giving the old stalled car a push downhill on a cold morning. It was a mighty cold morning the day I sat down at the typewriter to describe my recent expedition to darkest Alabama. Something was spooking me, and I had even more trouble getting started than usual. I just sat there mute and motionless and plenty sad-faced myself, writer's block holding me frozen in its claw, until suddenly I remembered my old line about the buttoned-on smile. What spooked me, I realize now, must have been the shadowy, half-conscious recollection of my meeting with the first Mrs. Wallace, Lurleen, seven years before. Lurleen was really a sad-faced wife and, though we didn't know it at the time her husband was running her for governor in his stead, she was mortally ill. At the time I interviewed her, she had just recovered from one cancer operation, and was probably still in considerable pain. Twenty-two months later she was dead. I've put in the piece about Lurleen, who gave her life to political wifehood, after the one about Cornelia and George.

There is one reference in "Lurleen" which I would have omitted if I were writing the piece today. Though I didn't know it then, Alabama is not Dogpatch. But I still think the Wallaces—all three of them— could have been Al Capp inventions.

6

Alabama in the Afternoon: George and Cornelia Wallace

Every first lady goes veiled in public. Usually she wears a stout mask of improbable serenity, buttoned on by two smiling eyes and helmeted in hair spray. So does Cornelia Wallace, but she is no ordinary first lady. At thirty-four, she is beautiful, brainy, shrewd, and certainly the best thing that could possibly have happened to Alabama's Governor George Wallace. I met her last week in the bedroom of the governor's mansion in Montgomery. The governor was still downtown at his office, but his presence loomed: an enormous color portrait of him hangs over their bed and is reflected in the mirror opposite.

Cornelia Wallace is warm and cool at the same time, relaxed, tan, tall. Throughout the long afternoon, children wandered easily in and out, hers and his. Sounds of a piano lesson filtered upstairs.

The governor's young wife gives one the feeling she can cope with anything life throws her way. She hunts, flies a plane, and has been a professional pianist and water skier. But these days she is busy running the mansion and caring for her family and injured husband. By custom, the mansion is staffed with convicts, mostly murderers from the state prison, and this crew of silent, gliding black men in white kitchen fatigues lends a surreal quality to domestic life.

Cornelia Wallace is instinctively political. The adored niece of Alabama Governor Kissin' Jim Folsom, she grew up in the governor's mansion. "What you do as a politician arises out of the needs of the people. Farm-to-market roads—that was my uncle! Rural people elected him. They were *his* people. When George became governor, he started our vocational- and trade-school programs. He saw that was the need of *his* times. Now those people are George's people."

In the corner is a huge floodlit desk marked: GOVERNOR OF ALABAMA. Gesturing toward it, she says, "When I was in college I used to wonder what could motivate people when they reached that stage of ambition. You couldn't enjoy the glory that much. It can't be to satisfy your personal needs, and certainly not your financial needs. It could only be a need to serve.

"You know, the life of a politician is short, especially in the governor's office. George has already lost his legs because of his job. Sure, he could have lost them in a sawmill, I suppose. . . . Sometimes I try to discuss our future with him, but George won't even talk about it. I could be speaking Greek. Politics is the only thing that excites people like him."

Waiting through the long Alabama afternoon for George to come home from his office, Cornelia thinks a lot about her two governors, her uncle Big Jim, a vague old man now living in sleepy retirement, and George, downtown in his office, struggling to recover his strength, overcome the pain, beat back despair, and reassert control of himself, his state, his national constituency. Both men lost their fathers at a young age. "That gave each of them an extra push. If they assert themselves overly, it's because of that, it's not just raw ambition," Cornelia says.

It is time for the TV news. The governor makes a fighting speech calling for reinstitution of the death penalty. "See that!" Cornelia shouts. "See him jabbin' with that finger? He hasn't done that since the accident. That's one of those little things only a wife notices." She is thrilled. Then a phone call from the kitchen; the governor is home. We and the children troop downstairs. Seated at the end of the table in the small, private family dining room, Wallace looks small, indrawn. He says the blessing, and we begin. Fried chicken, peas, mashed potatoes. The children are polite, speak only when spoken to. Conversation is difficult. The governor seems to fade in and out like a distant radio station, to be both there and not there. The fading effect is complicated by a hearing aid that he puts on and off without apparent change.

Finally you realize that his mind is running on a separate track from yours, that he hears what he wants to hear, and that what he wants to hear about is George Wallace. He answers *his* questions, not yours. Mention other politicians and he tells you how much he beat them by, or names the ones who came to see him in the hospital. He tells how much it hurt, how clearly he recalls the ambulance ride, how they drained the abscesses, how the acupuncture is going, how he has recovered from the prostate surgery, how he knows now that he will never walk again.

The only good thing about being in the hospital was that it gave him time to read. What books? "Biographies mostly. That English fellow, Lord Nelson. He got shot in the spine too, you know. William of Orange got shot twice."

You listen, patiently—knowing that he is speaking on his wave length, not yours—wanting to be polite, hoping you can lure him into talking about America, or that part of America that he knows better than any other politician. But he will not take the bait. Meat boycott? We got a lot of cattle raisers in this state. Watergate? That's national affairs. Equal rights amendment? That's nothin' the governor has to sign. Wounded Knee? The Indians in Alabama endorsed me in the last election.

"*Newsweek* said I was under sedation all the time. Do I look sedated to you?"

No, he does not. He looks like a man who has shrewdly, drastically narrowed his area of concern. He will only speak on matters of direct concern. "For twenty-five years, I been saying we should find ways to keep the rural poor on the farm, not force them to go to the big cities. Where you live, New York City? Bet you cain't walk down the street there now, right?" I tell him yes. "Twenty-five years ago they used to 'lectrocute fifty, sixty people a year up there," he says. A convict waiter silently serves us homemade cake.

Of paramount concern is his own body. From time to time, Cornelia is able to offer him some newly recovered crumb of recollection—how they tried to rip his $10 shirt off him, but it was too good to tear; how carefully they rinsed out his peritoneal cavity—and then he almost smiles. But the mental depression appears heavy, the effort huge.

Cornelia says, "I saw you walk in my dream the other night, George. Out of the corner of my eye I saw you get out of bed, draggin' one leg a little, and change the TV channel when you didn't think I was watchin'." Wallace looks bleak, says nothing.

Wallace is an original, full of odd quirks and winks, repulsively engaging. This charismatic egocentrism is what got him this far in life and it will probably save him. Little men never quit.

Cornelia asks if I have heard of a place called Buck's Pocket? Buck's Pocket is an Alabama expression meaning the place that politicians go when they are defeated. "Sort of a happy hunting ground?" I ask.

The governor looks up sharply. "No, not when they *die*," he says. "When they're *defeated*." He holds my eye with a stare like an icicle. Then suddenly, astonishingly, he winks.

George Wallace has spent his entire life dodging Buck's Pocket, and he's not about to fall into it now, not if he and Cornelia have anything to say about it. That, as they say in Alabama, is for damn sure.

Newsweek—April 16, 1973

7

Lurleen

Having visited Alabama myself only briefly, I do not know to what degree that state actually does resemble Dogpatch. But ever since Governor George C. Wallace announced that this year his thirty-nine-year-old wife Lurleen would run for governor in his stead, the suspicion has lingered in my mind that the real power behind the scenes in Alabama state politics is Al Capp.

When Governor Wallace said Lurleen was to be the candidate, a Southern newspaper commented, "It's as difficult to imagine her running for governor as it is to imagine Helen Hayes butchering a hog." Not, evidently, for the people of Alabama. And not for us *Li'l Abner* fans, either. Who else but Daisy Mae would campaign on a promise to keep liquor out of the governor's mansion for the next four years? Or consider Lurleen's big campaign promise that if elected she will "make my husband my number one assistant." Shades of Sadie Hawkins Day!

At this point in the rally, according to the newspapers, Governor

Wallace usually takes over the microphone and says something like, "I went up to Harvard University the other day—you know, where all the smart folks is supposed to be—and I made them a speech like they never heard before. I told them the people of Alabama were just as cultured, just as refined, just as educated, and just as *righteous* as the people of any other state—and they should never forget it!" Draw a balloon around this speech and you hear the authentic voice of Jubilation T. Cornpone. Even the Alabama campaign jokes—"bedfellows make strange politics"—sound straight from the pen of Al Capp.

Since I know that in reality all this is just a fantasy of my own horrible brain (sob!), I was pleased to open my newspaper the other morning and read that the real Mr. and Mrs. Wallace were here in California attending the fifty-eighth meeting of the National Governors' Conference. Sounding confident of victory in November, Lurleen had told a reporter that although she had no particular administrative projects in mind for Alabama right now, "I'm sure I probably will have some ideas of my own after the inauguration in January. Once you get into office you see things."

I wondered what Mrs. Wallace would choose to see at the governors' conference. Would she bone up on matters gubernatorial with her future colleagues, the men, or would she take part in the busy round of sightseeing that was offered to her present colleagues, the governors' wives?

When I arrived at the Century Plaza Hotel, the governors were in one great hall listening to a speech by Hubert Humphrey, and on another floor their wives were assembling in a flurry of finery for a fashion show that featured at-home costumes for *"après* election." Although 600 reporters were said to be covering the conference, the press room was deserted and the rows of silent telephones had a forlorn look of wallflowers at a dance. The national conference is "chiefly for show," a friendly first lady told me later. The real work goes on at the smaller, regional governors' conferences.

The official doings in Los Angeles bore her out. Real news was scant, and the Wallaces were among the most sought-after news figures there. But whereas George Wallace was extravagantly approachable, Lurleen remained tantalizingly invisible. Small and rather mousy, Mrs. Wallace is not an easy woman to spot in a crowd. One caught an occasional glimpse of her across a crowded lobby—in contrast to the finery of some other women she looked defiantly drab, a peahen in a tropical aviary. But when reporters attempted to speak to her, she politely suggested they make appointments through what turned out to be a phantom press secretary with a nonexistent phone.

When the other governors' wives spoke of her, their comments were impeccably first-lady-like and always came in two parts. Mrs. Wallace was perfectly charming personally was everybody's part one. Then came the pause, the warm, practiced, governor's wife's smile, followed by part two: "I feel if you can't say what you really believe, it's better to say nothing at all." Or: "If she's duly elected I would not presume to comment." A veteran first lady said, "A man has a terrific ego. It's in his nature to be governor. But for a woman it's—it's just not feminine!" Another wife added, "I know she's supposed to be just a figurehead. But suppose she wakes up some morning in that mansion and says to him, 'Look, who's governor around here?' " Nobody laughed. Finally the freshman wife of a western governor said, "It looks so bad for *us*. For the other governors, I mean. Ever since it happened I've been searching for exactly the right word to describe how I feel. It's on the tip of my tongue, but I can't get it." Al Capp, I thought, could give her the word.

Still looking for Lurleen, I checked out the final session of the actual governors' conference. A resolution in favor of Fourth of July bell-ringing was just going through. "We haven't seen her in *here* all week," someone said. Then, just outside the door, I saw an agitated little man spouting off in the lobby to a merry crowd of tourists, Boy Scouts, and little old ladies. Everybody was in high spirits. "Being governor don't mean a thing any more in this country," Governor Wallace was shouting happily. "We're nothing. Just high-paid ornaments is all. I'm thinking of running for President myself."

I asked his help in meeting Alabama's next governor. "Sure thing, honey," he said, "soon as she gets out of the beauty parlor."

Alas, life is no comic strip, not even in Alabama. In real life, Mrs. Wallace turned out to be a frail woman in a rough spot doing a good job. When I asked her where she had been all week, she looked surprised. "Disneyland," she said. And the Movieland Wax Museum, and Knott's Berry Farm. But her favorite place was Marineland. "I just love anything of, or pertaining to, water," she said, in what by then we both hoped was a gubernatorial turn of phrase. She said she also enjoyed being kissed by a seal and "seeing the tremendous whale that weighs so much and jumps so high."

In person, Mrs. Wallace seemed more at ease and sure of her ability to be governor than she had last spring on TV. "It wasn't being governor that bothered me then," she explained. "I knew I was fortunate enough to have an experienced man as my assistant. It was those TV cameras.

"You know," she whispered in a suddenly intimate, girl-talk tone of voice, "I *still* don't like those cameras. But about being governor, I have no reservations about that at all."

Life—July 22, 1966

8

The Zero-Calorie Diet

Noonday diners at a Los Angeles cafeteria looked up in some astonishment one day last January to see an enormous woman wedged amidships in the doorway. Though not without its comic aspects, the scene was the ultimate humiliation in the life of a thirty-eight-year-old housewife named Elaine Johnson. The nightmarish experience capped Mrs. Johnson's seventeen-year-on-and-off eating binge, a period in which the weight of her 5-foot 6-inch frame has risen from 135 to 315 pounds. When finally she managed to extricate her tremendous bulk from its prison of jamb and lintel, Mrs. Johnson heaved herself aboard a bus, headed for the nearby Wadsworth Veterans/Administration Hospital, and begged for help. "There must be something you can do," she tearfully told the admitting physician. "I think I'm a foodaholic."

Foodaholic or just plain fat lady, Mrs. Johnson was so overweight she could not tie her shoes, cross her legs, visit a lunch counter, or go to the movies—she was too big to fit in the seats. When she visited friends' houses, she never sat down for fear of breaking the furniture. In church, a special chair had to be set up for her. At home, when her eight-year-old daughter asked to sit on her lap, Mrs. Johnson had to say, "Sorry, honey, but Mommy doesn't have a lap any more."

Her severe obesity caused dangerously high blood pressure and a constant headache. She could not walk across a room without feeling exhausted. She gasped for breath and dreaded suffocating in her sleep. She always felt groggy and slightly nauseated. Yet in some horrible way, she was *always* hungry.

Mrs. Johnson felt emotionally unstrung too. Her marriage had broken up. She wept a lot. She was understandably fearful of leaving her house; mostly she remained at home, watched TV, cared for her three children—and ate. Her one source of emotional strength was her piety. She went to church every Sunday no matter how rotten she felt, and she taught a Sunday school Bible class. In fact, it was her zeal not to be late to a luncheon appointment with the new pastor that accounted for Mrs. Johnson's getting stuck in the cafeteria doorway.

All things considered, it was a lucky day for Mrs. Johnson, for the hospital, and ultimately perhaps for all the twenty-six million overweight adults in the U.S. that, instead of crawling into a cave, Mrs. Johnson waddled into Los Angeles' huge Wadsworth VA Hospital. For four years, Dr. Ernst Drenick, section chief of internal medicine there and a member of the faculty at nearby UCLA Medical School, had quietly been engaged in an extremely detailed study of obesity and human metabolism. His guinea pigs must be human beings; rats, monkeys, and other usual laboratory fauna are useless. What is needed is people, and the fatter the better. Accordingly, Dr. Drenick had painstakingly assembled his own private Obese Corps in his research ward. By the time Elaine Johnson showed up, he was studying ten of the fattest war veterans in California—all men so desperately anxious to lose weight that they were happy to submit to any diet or regimen Dr. Drenick could devise. To balance the research, he needed some female patients, a commodity not readily come by in a veterans' hospital. Enter ex-wave Elaine Johnson, breathing heavily and begging for help.

Medical science still has much to learn about the mysteries of obesity, but the doctors are unanimous on one point: those people who get fat do so because they eat more food than their systems can handle. It had taken Mrs. Johnson some 6,200 days of steady overeating to achieve doorway-size proportions. During World War II, she had been a pharmacist's mate in the WAVES, and her Navy discharge shows that in 1945 she weighed a neat, normal 135 pounds. She married the following year and during her first pregnancy, a lonely time of enforced separation from her serviceman husband, she began to overeat. Her weight ballooned to 175, and after her child was born she only got down to 150. After her second child, back down to 165. During her third pregnancy, in 1955, she was still fighting the same old diet battle, but with less success than ever. One day her obstetrician told her she absolutely had to lose five pounds by her next visit. When she next stepped on his scale two weeks later, she had *gained* two more pounds. "Hopeless!" the doctor scrawled across her chart.

"That did it," says Mrs. Johnson today. "I just quit trying. I hated myself for eating, but even after the baby was born I just couldn't stop. It got to be a vicious circle. I wanted to dress in nice clothes and be attractive, so I'd try to diet, and then I'd look in the mirror and feel it was all so impossible that I couldn't think of anything to do but drown my sorrows in more food.

"People picture a gluttonous person as somebody holding a big chicken leg in each hand and drooling. They just don't understand. I would live all day on black coffee, cook three meals for the children, and never even sit down at the table. Then at night I felt so starved I would cook up a plate of spaghetti and have one enormous four-thousand-calorie meal. Then I just wanted to lie down and die. I felt I was falling to pieces. It wasn't only my body. My whole personality was getting out of shape. I wanted to crawl away and hide."

When Dr. Drenick learned that a 315-pound woman had just been admitted to Wadsworth's female ward, he came over at once. "Up until two or three years ago, doctors used to think that all fat people just ate too much—period," he told Mrs. Johnson. "Now we suspect that some individuals, perhaps one in four, may have a minor metabolic aberration, a small genetic difference, which contributes to their obesity. Our experiment—our search for quantitative data—has been designed to try to shed some light on this possibility."

In theory, according to Dr. Drenick, the fatty who swears he doesn't eat enough to keep a bird alive and the bean pole who swears he eats like a horse may both be telling the truth. But the only way to make sure is to make extremely subtle and detailed metabolic observations over an extended period. Subjects of such experiments have to be reasonably healthy and willing to remain for a long time in a hospital where their intimate metabolic ups and downs can be continuously analyzed. Furthermore, the patients must be willing, and capable, to eat nothing at all. Pure metabolic research in obesity requires total starvation. A starving man, existing solely on his body's own stored food reserves, enables the physician to calculate the exact rates at which the body uses up its supply of fat, proteins, vitamins, and so on. The doctor can measure these depletion rates by extremely detailed urinalyses and other techniques, and he does not have to adjust his calculations to allow for extraneous supplies of nutrients added to the body by eating.

Unfortunately, the average person is likely to starve to death before the necessary metabolic data can be amassed. About forty days is considered the outside limit for "normal" human starvation, provided the subject has water and other creature comforts. A rigidly supervised continuing experiment in marathon starvation thus requires gargantuan volunteers with huge reserves of stored food in their bodies.

The average weight of the eleven members of the Obese Corps was 311 pounds. All were people for whom long-term starvation was not only possible but downright therapeutic. In severe obesity, some patients cannot expand their lungs sufficiently to supply enough oxygen to their tissues. Unless they stop putting on poundage, they eventually may be killed by their own bulk.

Dr. Drenick outlined all this in his first meeting with Mrs. Johnson. After reassuring her that her own obesity was far less severe than that of some of his male patients, he invited her to join his experiment. She readily agreed.

"Every time Dr. Drenick said the word 'experiment,' all I could hear was the word 'help,' " she has since explained. So Mrs. Johnson's two youngest children were temporarily placed in foster homes and she moved into Wadsworth.

For a few days, Elaine Johnson prepared herself for the coming ordeal with a low-calorie diet, and lost 10 pounds. After that, for the next 117 days, she lived exclusively on plain water and vitamin shots. When she craved solid food, she chewed ice cubes. At the end of her marathon fast, the former morose fat lady was in high spirits, excellent health, 116 pounds lighter, and famous. She had shattered the all-time human starvation record of seventy-four days set by Terence McSwiney, an Irish patriot and Lord Mayor of Cork, who in 1920 died in a British prison on the seventy-fifth day of a hunger strike. But, to Mrs. Johnson, the best part of the whole incredible experience was that her insatiable appetite appeared to have vanished along with 116 pounds of flesh.

During her record term of noneating, Mrs. Johnson lived in the women's ward of the VA hospital and her metabolic processes were measured in detail. One measurement required a weekly trip to the "counting house," a total body-radiation counter which aids in determining the exact body composition of fat, lean body mass, and water. These and other measurements, incidentally, make cheating instantly detectable—in the event a patient is tempted by an occasional forbidden snack, which Mrs. Johnson was not.

Though hospitalized, she did not feel ill or weak, and after the first few days, her appetite vanished for good. She eventually developed a distaste even for plain water, and by the end of her fast, she was drinking less than a pint a day.

While she was in Wadsworth, Mrs. Johnson also received regular psychiatric counseling, and both she and her doctors now feel that she has gained considerable insight into the emotional aspects of her weight problem. She realizes that during her childhood she had come to think of food as far more than just something to eat: a rich dessert was a bribe, a tasty snack was a reward, food itself became an expression of love. When she was an adult, food came to mean companionship too. Often, with her husband away, her children asleep, she would sit alone in front of her TV set, surrounded by mountains of bonbons, salted nuts, and other goodies, and mindlessly munch the night away. Food was her only friend.

This old habit of experiencing food as companionship was confirmed during her stay at Wadsworth. Evenings when the other ladies gathered around the ward TV set, Mrs. Johnson felt a powerful urge to nibble, despite the fact that her actual appetite had vanished weeks before.

Between visits to the counting house, the laboratories, and her psychiatrist, Mrs. Johnson kept busy during the months of enforced idleness by helping out in the ward. One of her favorite recreations was preparing and serving meals for other patients. One day she received a sort of edible poison-pen letter. In the wake of the widespread publicity attending her metabolic experiment, an anonymous cake, two feet long and smothered in pink frosting, was delivered to her. Mrs. Johnson hacked up the huge pastry and invited the other ladies in the ward to a party. Sometimes she amused her wardmates by answering the wall telephone with a cheery, "Hello, Baby Blimp speaking." When outside visitors asked if she needed anything, she would reply airily, "Bring me a big box of doughnut holes." She was losing a pound a day now, and was euphoric a good bit of the time.

At the counting house, Elaine Johnson often met and compared notes with the male obesity patients who lived together in a special metabolic balance ward in another hospital building. After a tour of this grotesque place, the visitor will never again be able to laugh at a circus fat man, or doubt the truth of Cyril Connolly's remark that "imprisoned in every fat man a thin one is wildly signaling to be let out."

Dr. Drenick's largest patient is Leland Poe, a 6-foot 7-inch former Marine and computer operator, who weighed well over 500 pounds when he was rushed to the hospital. His lungs could no longer supply his huge body with the oxygen needed, and he was semicomatose and "blue as a plum." The fainting giant had to be dumped onto a tarpaulin on the doorstep and dragged inside by eight sweating orderlies. Poe lost twenty-six pounds in his first week on the zero-calorie diet, and continued his fast for eight more weeks before switching to a semistarvation regime of 300 calories daily. His weight is now down to a mere 315 pounds, and his spirits are soaring.

Poe's best friend in the ward is Bert Goldner, thirty-three years old, 5 feet 7 inches, who arrived at the hospital in heart failure. Goldner weighed 425 pounds at the time, and was so spherical he could neither sit nor lie down without fainting from lack of oxygen. He even had to sleep standing up or kneeling. Once he toppled over during a stand-up catnap and broke his leg.

Goldner lasted only two weeks on the zero-calorie regimen, then gave way to intense emotional irritability. When a nurse turned off the TV set he was watching, he burst into tears and announced that he was going to march right over to the rib joint across the street and eat some barbecue. His devoted buddy, Poe, restrained him by force until Dr. Drenick could be notified.

To some extent, all of Dr. Drenick's patients could be described as "compulsive eaters"—that is, people who eat to gratify an emotional need rather than to satisfy their physical hunger. Psychiatrists call such people "oral-dependent characters," individuals who react to conflict, frustration, depression, boredom, anxiety, or almost any emotion by seeking solace in food. Sucking, kissing, chewing, smoking, and drinking are other oral gratifications, and most compulsive eaters employ them all. But so do noncompulsives; it is a tricky field in which little is known and generalities are to be avoided. Dr. Sidney Cohen, chief of psychiatry at Wadsworth, has kept close watch on the obesity studies and characterizes oral-dependent persons as "unweaned sucklings." But he is quick to point out that obesity is not a single disease. According to one gorgeously circular medical definition, "Obesity is a psycho-somatic syndrome of emotional and genetic factors, the cardinal symptom of which is hyperphagia." Hyperphagia, it turns out, is insatiable appetite.

Dr. Drenick employs a more practical rule of thumb. To him a compulsive eater is somebody who gets up in the middle of the night to raid the icebox after a full day's normal eating. Bert Goldner, for example, once listed this menu of a single nocturnal food binge: one lemon meringue pie, one half-pound can of cashews, one-half pound shrimp, one-half pound lobster, one pound assorted cookies, one pound of candy—either fudge or peanut brittle—one quart of chocolate ice cream, one jar of pickles, and one dietetic soft drink. Dr. Drenick estimates this particular orgy at approximately 8,000 calories, and Goldner readily admits that on other occasions he had surpassed even that incredible total.

"The terrible thing about severely obese people is that they can assimilate all the food they eat," the doctor says. "If you have a tendency toward obesity, you actually accentuate the metabolic defect the heavier you get. So it becomes easier and easier to gain, and harder and harder to lose."

Fortunately, not all of the Wadsworth volunteers were so morbidly addicted to food as the unfortunate Goldner. Benjamin Laskow, for example, is the different type of fat man Dr. Drenick terms a "hobby eater." Hobby eaters have no particular emotional problems; they just love food and don't care how they look. Laskow, 5 feet 10 inches, has permitted his affection for cheese blintzes with sour cream to run riot; as a result, he weighed 236 pounds and, at seventy-one, was in grave risk of a coronary attack. After four weeks of starving, and five more weeks of semistarvation, he got his weight back down to 185, and it is indicative of the salubrious effects of his treatment that, the week of his discharge from Wadsworth, he challenged the ward's twenty-six-year-old orderly to a judo match and slammed the daylights out of him.

Many experts believe that obesity is becoming one of the nation's more serious public health problems. Already 23 per cent of our adult population is overweight, and the figure is rising. The enormous excess poundage unquestionably contributes to the rising death rates from hypertension, coronary disease, and diabetes.

In spite of the severity of the problem, medicine has yet to come up with any satisfactory method for returning dedicated eaters to normal weight and keeping them there. Such eaters fall into a classic dieting pattern of two steps forward and one step back. Strenuous dieting eventually gives way to discouragement at the slow results. The discouragement produces weakening resolve, the diet is gradually or abruptly abandoned, and the poor dieter gains back everything he has so painfully lost, and usually adds a few new pounds. As Mrs. Johnson says, "You name it, I tried it—the five-day juice diet, the Mayo Clinic egg diet, patented food substitutes, laxatives, Epsom salt baths, psychotherapy—everything but pushing myself away from the table."

Doctors and scientists around the country are developing many ingenious schemes to, in effect, help push their patients away from the table. There are artificially processed nonfoods in a dozen delicious flavors. Attempts have been made to develop a denutrifying powder which can be sprinkled on food to render it nonabsorbable. For desperate cases, there is the new "blind loop" operation, an experimental surgical procedure which reroutes the alimentary canal so as to make food absorption mechanically impossible. But no matter what the doctors dream up, their patients almost always prove capable of outeating the effects of the treatment.

The only hope for chronic obesity, mild or severe, Dr. Drenick believes, is to retrain the appetite. The eating habits of a lifetime must be abolished and replaced with a totally new eating pattern. The work at Wadsworth indicates that such retraining is possible, providing that first the old, overstuffed appetite is given time enough to wither away under competent medical supervision. This withering away takes at least three weeks. Starving for shorter periods is usually useless, either for appetite-reconditioning or for permanent weight loss. (Up to 70 per cent of anybody's initial weight loss is water. This "weight" inevitably starts to return the instant even limited refeeding begins.) Starving for longer periods without proper medical supervision can be extremely dangerous.

Mrs. Johnson was a unique subject in many ways. Last March, when she had been on the zero-calorie diet for more than two months, Dr. Drenick told a visitor, "She shows no significant physical or emotional ill effects whatever. An only moderately overweight person would have become extremely irritable by now. A normal-weight person would be dead. You see, Mrs. Johnson is, in effect, eating. She still has a good seventy or eighty pounds of lard on her to devour."

Dr. Drenick's prediction proved accurate. His prize patient continued to lose weight slowly and steadily for eight more weeks. But then one morning Mrs. Johnson awakened with a terrible pain in her big toe. Tests revealed it was gout, or something very much like gout, brought on by the high proportion of animal fat and protein in her "diet" of her own flesh. Although Mrs. Johnson was only down to 189 pounds, still 40 pounds overweight, Dr. Drenick decided it was time for limited refeeding to begin. His new objective was to give his patient just enough food to maintain her energy requirements but not enough to reawaken her sleeping appetite. On May 25, he ordered her first meal —a tablespoon of cottage cheese, with a quarter cup of eggnog chaser. Mrs. Johnson could barely get it all down.

Although she obliged her doctor after that by dutifully swallowing 300 to 500 high-protein calories a day (mostly eggs, meat, cheese, skim milk), this much food still remained far below her appetite threshold. She still felt no hunger. "Food tasted like medicine to me. I only ate because the doctor told me to," she says.

Six weeks later, Mrs. Johnson still weighed 186 pounds, despite the fact that she had been sticking faithfully to her bare-subsistence 500-calorie regimen. Regretfully, Dr. Drenick decided it was time to discharge her from the hospital. Her remaining pounds of overweight contained very little fat, he explained. It was solid muscle which she had unwittingly built up in order to tote around all her excess weight. Although the fat was gone, getting rid of the armor of muscle would require many more months, perhaps even years, of strict dieting.

Mrs. Johnson today is in better shape physically and emotionally than she has been for years. She even has a job—as a solderer in an electronics plant. But her future will not be free of strain. A portent of what she may expect occurred last June. Dr. Drenick had given his prize patient a one-day pass back to the "outside world" so that she could attend her son's graduation from junior high school. She marched proudly to an aisle seat, down front, savoring in her mind the many friendly compliments she was about to receive on her dramatically remodeled contours. She got the compliments of course, but what she remembers most about that day was the man who sat beside her. As he squeezed past her to reach his own seat, he muttered, "Gee, lady, why don't you go on a diet?"

Life—October 1, 1963

9

Diary: 1976

I am often asked how I can think of something new to write about every week. My stock answer is that subjects abound; one can write about anything; the difficulty is in deciding what you want to say about it, and how much. Of course, once in a very great while the subject finds you. That is what happened the day in midsummer 1963, when I got a letter from a Seattle housewife telling me she had handpicked me to write up the story of her suicide attempt.

The result was "Decision to Die," which later became the movie The Slender Thread, *with Anne Bancroft playing the housewife's role. For purposes of winding up the dramatic tension even tighter, the movie people changed the identity of the person who saved the housewife's life by keeping her on the line until the phone company could trace the call. In real life, the heroine was a middle-aged night nurse in a Tacoma psychiatric ward, who knew a cry for help when she heard one. But the movie savior was Sidney Poitier, playing a medical student who worked nights in Seattle's Suicide Prevention Center. Thus does art—Hollywood art, anyway—imitate life. But there are a great many levels of reality in this particular story, and not surprisingly they get realer the deeper down you go. To descend just one more level, Poitier was not only playing the real night nurse. He was also in a sense playing the real housewife, Nell J. After Nell recovered from her suicide attempt, she dreamed up the idea of establishing Seattle's Suicide Prevention Center, and she used to help out answering phones there herself. Perhaps she still does.*

Life introduced the piece with an "editor's note."

10

Nell J.'s Letter

"Dear Mr. Alexander," the letter began. "Would you consider doing an article on the aftermath of a suicide attempt?—the heartbreak, the financial burden, the social stigma? I would like to think that something constructive could come from the nightmare of the last six weeks."

The well-written letter went on to outline how its author, Nell J., felt her story should be told. Clipped to the letter was the evidence that this Seattle housewife had, indeed, tried to take her life: an ambulance bill for $16, involuntary hospitalization papers listing suicide as the reason, a Tacoma motel bill for $9.14 with Nell's penciled-in comment "where 'it' happened," a police list of the clothes she left behind at the motel—"one dress, one coat, underclothing, one pair black shoes, one white scarf."

Life staff writer Shana Alexander wrote back that yes, she was interested. "But before we go any further, I would like to know how you happened to write to me. Did you see my name in the magazine? Did you write to a lot of magazines? In other words: why me? By the way," she concluded, "I should tell you that I am not Mr. Alexander but Mrs.—a housewife like yourself."

Here is Nell J.'s reply:

Dear Mrs. Alexander,

I shall enjoy telling you how I came to write you, and I look forward to meeting you.

A couple of weeks after leaving the hospital on July 9, my husband and I spent a weekend camping up on the south fork of the Stillaguamish River. . . . I made a lot of notes and among them was the outline included in my letter to you. There in the quiet of the great Mt. Baker National Forest the stark reality of the past few weeks of our lives seemed so very wasteful.

After the outline had been drawn I couldn't get it out of my mind—yet, only the right person could write this article. I thought of a dear friend who has some writing experience and several articles to her credit, but she is too close to the family to be truly objective. . . . I then went to a newsstand and selected the current issues of six magazines that I read regularly and felt would be interested in the outline.

Nell J. glanced through *Look* magazine but concluded that "in the past year or two the flavor of it has changed for me." She discarded the *Reader's Digest* because it ruled out a pictorial approach, a third and fourth and fifth magazine because they "do not encompass the reader's breadth and depth as does *Life*. So I chose *Life* and started my search for *the* writer—for what I actually was looking for was a *writer*, not a publisher."

Here Nell J. listed eleven *Life* authors whose stories she had read, but the writer who kept coming back to mind was Shana Alexander. Her short article on "The High I.Q. Frat" had been the very first one Nell had read, but now she read it again, put it aside and came back to it several days later. Even though it was a light, humorous piece, something about the approach appealed to her.

"I sat down and wrote you my letter. And I'm glad you are a housewife. I haven't written anyone else, and if in your judgment there is no story here, then I shall let it rest there."

There was a story.

Life—May 29, 1964

11

Decision to Die

Good creatures,
    do you love your lives
And have you ears for sense?
Here is a knife like other knives,
that cost me eighteen pence.
I need but stick it in my heart
and down will come the sky
And earth's foundations will depart
And all you folk will die.
                    —A. E. HOUSMAN

The day that Nell J. attempted to murder *her* world broke clear with the fresh, rain-washed feeling that can make the Pacific Northwest one of the most pleasant places on earth to live. In the swirl of early morning workers, Nell stood out as a pretty woman in her thirties, trim in a black linen coat and a pillbox hat. She wore just enough makeup, a touch of mascara, lipstick to match her coral print dress. In her left hand she carried a pair of immaculate white gloves, swinging them in rhythm with her brisk step. It was nearly 7 A.M. when Nell entered the large pancake house where she worked as breakfast manager. She carefully hung up her coat, tied on a fresh gingham apron and picked up an armful of menus.

Nell moved confidently through her demanding chores, greeting customers, pouring coffee, making change, gently scolding the busboys, assisting waitresses—and through it all, always, always smiling. Nobody at the pancake house remembers anything unusual about the manager's appearance or behavior on this particular Monday, nor does Nell herself.

When her shift ended at 8:30 A.M., Nell put on her pillbox hat, went outside into the sunshiny July morning, and walked seven blocks to the Seattle regional office of a nationwide accounting firm where, from 9 to 5:15 every day, she worked as a bookkeeper and an executive secretary. She badly needed both jobs to help support her family. When overtime was necessary at the pancake house on weekends or at the accounting firm evenings, Nell's work week sometimes stretched to 90 or 100 hours.

Punctually at 9, Nell was at her immaculate desk in the alcove outside her boss's corner office. Behind her was a huge picture window overlooking Puget Sound; in front of her was the quiet, carpeted corridor. The regional office had twenty-eight employes, but most of them worked in individual cubicles behind heavy rosewood doors. Save for occasional strollers in the corridor, Nell was alone.

On this Monday morning, Nell anticipated a busy, tiring day. Her boss had been on vacation for the past two weeks and a thick stack of correspondence was waiting for him on his desk. With her remarkable memory for detail, Nell today recalls carefully sorting the mail and then reviewing the queries and messages she wished to bring to his attention. But at 10 A.M., Nell received word that her boss would not be back from vacation until Tuesday.

Her first recollection of any feelings of disturbance that Monday is of the sharp letdown at this unexpected news. She had braced herself to handle a huge load of back work; now there was nothing to do. She felt suddenly empty. "I knew I had been doing a good job in both places," she says, "yet now I felt I had just been running around like a squirrel in a cage."

Nell's mind turned inevitably to the problem—or, rather, the accumulation of problems—that had been pressing down on her for months. She thought about the three teenage children she was supporting—a son and daughter in high school and a younger son in junior high—and about her husband, who had spent the past six months in a Veterans Administration hospital, unable to work. While she brooded, she picked up the correspondence and began mechanically to re-sort and recheck the letters.

The family fortunes had hit bottom last winter when her husband, John, a barber, had been hospitalized for anxiety and excessive drinking after a series of violent family quarrels. As the debts increased, Nell's health had begun to break down and, worst of all, she had to face the fact that her marriage was smashed. In despair, she had gone to a lawyer to discuss a divorce. Recently, when her parents, who lived in Texas, had come to visit her for a few days, Nell had, despite great tension, succeeded in keeping most of her problems from them.

A perfectionist, Nell placed the restacked correspondence in the exact center of her boss's huge teakwood desk. Back at her own desk, she reached into her handbag and hauled out the clanking set of eighteen keys which she used as manager at the pancake house. She got some clean key tags from a supply cupboard and began inking a fresh set: "Pantry . . . Manager's Office . . . Linen Room . . ." Despite her extreme weariness, Nell was pleased with the clarity of her secretarial school handwriting.

The sudden physical and mental exhaustion had hit her at a time when she had every reason to be encouraged at the way things had improved at home. John had responded well to the VA's psychotherapy program. During his recent visits home, he had seemed almost like the "old." John of their honeymoon days. A few weeks ago, she had dropped her divorce action. Before the weekend, John was going to be discharged from the hospital and would be able to resume his work in the barber shop. Tomorrow, Nell was going to quit her early morning restaurant work: that was why she wanted to return her keys in perfect order.

"My double life is ending at last," Nell thought as she finished labeling the keys and dropped them back into her neat black pocketbook. Nell's latest domestic problem had been posed by her sixteen-year-old daughter. When the girl learned that John was coming home, she said she wanted to move out. His homecoming promised a renewal of old family wrangles. Anyway, she was reluctant to live in the same house with a man who once beat up her mother. Nell had therefore arranged for her daughter to board, at least temporarily, with a schoolmate who lived nearby.

As she did every noontime, Nell ate a sandwich lunch in the company of three other secretaries at the long table in the office conference room. She carefully hid her growing fatigue, and there was nothing else in her attitude or appearance that seemed out of the ordinary.

At 1 P.M., she returned to her small alcove and stared out at the sun-blazed Seattle skyline, fringing the water of the Sound. She thought she had never been so tired. Reviewing her boss's correspondence for the third time, she tried to rearrange it so that each letter was graded in descending order of importance—the most urgent on top. But Nell was finding it harder and harder to concentrate. She fought desperately against the urge to put her head down on her desk and sleep. By 4 P.M., she was chilled and trembling. She ate a candy bar for energy, but it didn't help.

By 4:30 P.M., Nell J. was fighting tears. All the problems she thought she had taken care of—the money troubles, the family fights—seemed not to be solved at all. Most unsettling to her was her "solution" to her problem with her daughter. Had she done her a kindness by making the boarding arrangements, or had she done her a grave wrong? In order to take her husband back, hadn't she in fact kicked her own daughter out of the house? Husband or daughter, which should she choose, and how *could* she choose?

She felt engulfed by despair. The bright and smiling secretary had suddenly begun to fall apart. She was terrified that her co-workers might notice, and yet she was just as terrified of not being noticed. She wanted deeply to be told what to do. "I was scared stiff," she says. "I knew I was coming all unglued inside."

At 5 P.M., Nell telephoned John's VA psychologist in Tacoma. He knew more about the family's emotional troubles than any other person. He was not in, so she left an urgent message for him to call her back. The psychologist was the first of eleven persons Nell would call on for help, either directly or indirectly, before the night was out.

Though dissolving inside, Nell was still able to maintain outward control. Waiting for the doctor to return her call, she typed out a cheery note to her boss and put it on top of the restacked mail on his desk: "Welcome home. I'll see you tomorrow. Nell."

At 5:15, the office closed for the night. With mounting anxiety Nell listened to the muffled footfalls and door-clicks of the other employes going home. At 5:30, she walked to the deserted switchboard and rearranged the lines so that any incoming call automatically would ring in the rear conference room. She wanted to take the doctor's call there so that if she did break down and cry, she would not be seen by anybody who might be working late.

Nell sat alone in the conference room for fifteen minutes, seeing nothing, thinking nothing, numb with fatigue. At 5:45, the doctor's call came and she immediately broke into tears. "I'm going to flip," she sobbed over the phone. "I've got to talk to somebody right away!"

The VA psychologist told Nell to get hold of herself. He pointed out that he was in Tacoma, more than thirty miles away, and suggested that if she needed to talk to somebody, she choose a person nearer at hand. He also reminded her, as gently but firmly as possible, that he was John's doctor, not hers.

To Nell, the psychologist seemed cynical and remote. The thought of trying to confide in a friend, someone like Jim, her assistant manager at the pancake house, or perhaps Kay, her son's devoted English teacher in high school, seemed absurd.

Suddenly Nell heard herself shouting at the psychologist over the telephone: "You can't talk to just anybody about something as horrible as this!" But, as abruptly, she regained her composure. She thanked the doctor profusely for his time and apologized for bothering him. Then she hung up.

On her way out of the office, Nell stopped at her desk and watered her philodendron plant. She took the elevator to the street and walked quickly back to the parking lot near the pancake house, where she had left her car.

It was approximately 6 P.M. when Nell got into her blue and white Ford and began driving toward Tacoma. Highway 99 was still gorged with homebound traffic and she drove with particular care. She became increasingly worried that she might have an accident and hurt somebody before she got where she was going. And where was she going? She knew only that she was going for help.

Nell's careening, chaotic state of mind was not unfamiliar to her. She had come unglued this way before. Five years ago after the first big fight with John, she had dashed dramatically into the bathroom and swallowed a handful of pills. Her husband rushed her to the hospital and she then spent several weeks in the state mental institution, classified as suicidally depressed.

Suddenly Nell saw what seemed to be a police car in the traffic up ahead. She abandoned her careful driving policy and pressed the accelerator to the floor. She thought that if she could get herself arrested, perhaps the police would tell her what to do. She was doing over ninety mph as she overtook the dark blue car and swerved sharply in front of it. Then through her rearview mirror she saw the other car turn off the highway at a truck weighing station. She realized that the uniformed driver was not a traffic policeman but a weighmaster.

Now trapped in the ambivalence—typical of most suicides—of wishing to kill herself and wishing someone would save her, Nell made more pathetic attempts to attract attention. She waved at passing drivers and even timidly honked her horn, but nobody seemed to notice the odd behavior of the woman in the blue and white Ford. Finally she settled down and concentrated on getting where she wanted to go.

Since John's doctor wouldn't see her, she would go back to the state hospital on the other side of Tacoma, where she had been confined after her 1958 suicide attempt. The psychiatrist at that hospital had told her that, despite the effort to kill herself, she was not crazy; now she desperately wanted the same reassurance again.

Terror seemed to be closing in from all sides. She was terrified that her collapse would put her right back in the hospital, and at the same time she was terrified she might *not* reach the hospital in time. If she couldn't get someone to stop her, she feared she would try suicide again. Once more, inside her neatly coiffed head, the old deadly game of to-be-or-not-to-be was under way.

When she left the highway, Nell did not drive directly to the state hospital. Perhaps she never intended to. Her next clear memory is pulling into the beautifully landscaped grounds of the VA hospital where John was a patient. She knew that her husband often played golf on the hospital course in the afternoon and she drove slowly along the edge of the fairway, hoping to spot his red-checked golf cap. She wanted John, more than anybody, to tell her what to do.

He wasn't there. For a time she drove aimlessly around the grounds, afraid for some vague reason to go to the desk and ask to see him. The buttoned-up part of her mind realized that John couldn't help her with her problem; indeed, this part of her mind knew that his imminent homecoming *was* her problem. But the confused and depressed thoughts were continuing to assert themselves more and more. "I didn't know whether I belonged to my daughter or my husband," Nell says now. "I didn't know anything, really, except that I had to have professional help, or I would go out of my tree." She decided to drive on to the state hospital.

Although she had driven the road between the two hospitals many times, Nell had a hard time finding her way. The struggle to maintain emotional control seemed to be taking every ounce of her strength. Afraid to trust herself on the highway, she kept to the back roads now. When she came to a traffic signal, she could not remember whether a red light meant to stop or go. She had to watch the other cars to find out what to do.

As Nell followed the other cars, she prayed one of the drivers would stop her and shake her back into her senses, but nobody did. She pulled into a gas station and asked the attendant for directions, hoping that he would notice her distress, but all she got was directions she already knew. She stopped at a roadside market and bought a container of milk, hoping the clerk would "save" her. He handled the purchase without a word.

By the time she arrived at the grounds of the hospital, Nell was convinced that here lay her final chance to be "saved": "I felt I was playing a game of Russian roulette with a gun that had five bullets instead of one."

Nell walked into the deserted waiting room—prim and erect beneath her pillbox hat—at 7:45 P.M. The nurse on duty, accustomed to dealing with tearful women begging for help, dealt with Nell on a coolly professional basis.

Nell was vague and confused about names and dates, and the nurse could not find the records of her previous hospitalization. Finally Nell remembered the name of Dr. Marlowe, the psychiatrist who treated her before, and asked to speak to him. The nurse said Dr. Marlowe had since resigned. Then Nell recalled that a Dr. Richards had presided over the sanity hearing which had preceded her release from the hospital five years before. The nurse said she was sorry but Dr. Richards had died. Would she like to see the O.D.? Wearily Nell said yes and sat down to wait in one of the nearby wicker chairs. Beside her was a glass case which was intended to display handicrafts made by patients. The case was empty—just as it had been when Nell had been a patient five years before. On top of the case was a dead plant.

The doctor on night duty was having dinner at his home on the hospital grounds when the O.D. nurse called to tell him there was a weeping woman in the lobby. The nurse said that, although she could not find Nell's records, the woman claimed to be an ex-patient; that she refused to sign into the hospital and voluntarily commit herself; that she just kept saying she wanted to talk to someone.

When the doctor walked into the waiting room, Nell started crying so hard she was almost incoherent. "I tried to tell him I was going to pieces," Nell remembers. "I tried to tell him about my daughter and John, but I completely lost control." When Nell asked him if there wasn't something he could do, the doctor said he could commit her. Nell asked how long she would have to stay. "You know I can't tell you that," the doctor said. "It could be two days or two months or two years. If you want to go into the hospital, sign in with the nurse. She'll be glad to admit you. Do whatever you want."

In despair, Nell listened to the doctor's tires crunch on the gravel roadway as he drove away. His brusque professional attitude seemed final proof to Nell that there was no way out. If she agreed to be hospitalized, her husband would have no home to come home to and her children would become wards of the court. Now, in her mind's eye, the children were the toddlers they had been years before, not the strapping high schoolers they had become. "I guess by then I was really out of my tree," Nell says.

She remembers the wave of resentment she felt toward the doctor after he left. "He could have done *something.* If he'd given me any encouragement, or just let me rest overnight, it would have helped. Even if he'd only talked to me about the weather or given me a hot cup of coffee. He didn't even offer to call somebody to drive me home."

The logical reasons why none of these moves was available to the doctor on duty did not occur to Nell. There was no coffee in the waiting room, or any drivers available, and there is no official procedure that permits helping a person who is unwilling to commit himself for admission.

For twenty minutes after the doctor's departure, Nell remained in the waiting room, sobbing and staring at the black and white linoleum floor. "I felt so foolish and so ashamed," she says. "This is a real hard thing to tell anyone, that you want to kill yourself. It's like being an alcoholic—you try to cover up so people won't know. Then you tell someone your big secret, and it makes no difference to him! That's when I felt I *had* to do it—if only to prove to him that I was right."

Gradually Nell's sobs quieted and she became calm. At last she knew what to do. "I had so many problems I decided what I wanted was an absence of problems. I decided to check out."

In Nell's purse, under the heavy bunch of pancake house keys, was an envelope of miscellaneous pills scavenged from the family medicine chest. She had been carrying the envelope around for weeks, not really thinking about it, not telling a soul it was there, yet in some way drawing comfort from its presence. As the confusions and guilts of her life weighed heavier, she had come to think of her envelope the way a diabetic thinks of his insulin. So long as she had the pills with her, she could never be caught unprepared.

Nell walked out of the state hospital waiting room dry-eyed, her head held high. She felt as if the curtain were just rising on an absorbing play

in which she was to be the central shining star. Tugging open the
hospital's heavy oaken door and returning down the red brick steps was
like making her first dramatic entrance on stage.

Nell got into her car and headed back toward Tacoma. Driving was
easy now. Her mind was preoccupied with the scenes to come. She had
the pills, but she needed a place to die and time to make sure the pills
would work. "I didn't want to goof it up and fail at this as I had failed
at everything else."

She had less than $5 inside her purse, not enough to pay for a hotel
room, but she did have a credit card to the Doric Motel chain. Coming
into South Tacoma, she noticed a restaurant, The Gay 90s, where she
and John had once spent a happy New Year's Eve. She went in and
telephoned ahead to the Doric Tacoma and reserved a single room.
Because of the credit card, she had to give the clerk her real name. She
asked him for detailed driving instructions from The Gay 90s; it was
quite dark now and Nell did not know her way around Tacoma very
well.

As she drove on, she still felt tired but her mind was not thrashing
or groping any longer. She decided that, although she seldom drank
hard liquor, she would spend her last few dollars on a pint of vodka,
to give her courage. First though, she thought she had better drive
directly to the motel and check in.

The clerk's instructions took her straight to the Doric's impersonal
glass-and-pink-cement facade near Tacoma Avenue. When she got out
of her car, she carefully smoothed the pleats of her silk dress and drew
on the pair of fresh white gloves she always carried in her glove compartment. Having no luggage, she wanted to appear completely proper
when she registered. "My mood was almost gay. I was an actress
putting on white gloves."

The register of the Doric Motel shows that Nell J. checked in at 9:17
P.M. She went directly to her room, on the fifth floor, switched on the
TV, and sat down on her bed. She dumped her envelope of pills onto
the green tweed bedspread. It was a colorful little arsenal and Nell
checked it carefully.

There were forty-one pills in all. Fifteen were bitter yellow sinus
decongestant tablets which had once been prescribed for her husband;
seventeen were slick yellow pain-killer pills which had been prescribed
to Nell for migraine headaches; nine were large, glossy blue and white
capsules which Nell knew were sleeping pills. She thought that the nine
sleeping capsules alone might be lethal enough, but she determined to

swallow the entire conglomeration just to be sure. (Actually the sleep-ing pills alone would only have produced a deep barbiturate coma. The weird, three-drug combination was far more deadly.)

Nell put her pills back in the envelope, the envelope back in her purse, and looked up liquor stores in the yellow pages. She found one with the same phone prefix as the motel and decided it would be closest. She called and asked how to reach the store.

After getting directions from the clerk, she drove the few blocks to the liquor store for the vodka. On her way back, her attention was caught by the blue neon sign of a funeral home two blocks from her motel. Suddenly it occurred to Nell that she should leave her car parked under this brightly lighted sign and walk back to the motel. Then she could somehow get word to John where the new car was without having to betray her own location and thus "goof up" her suicide.

She stopped the car, turned off the engine, and thought: everything was taken care of. Her insurance was paid up, and it would bring $7,000 or $8,000—enough to send her daughter to college. Her older son already had a college loan; her younger son could go back to Texas with her parents. John would be free to marry again. All this was set forth in her will. A deeply religious person—she is a lifelong, devout Baptist —Nell had never feared death. She thinks of it as "a transition to peace and quiet, the opening of a door." As she sat parked in front of the funeral home, everything seemed neatly buttoned up—everything ex-cept the one annoying problem of disposing of the car.

Then Nell gave herself a little lecture: "Nell, you're being stupid. You're doing everybody a big favor by getting out of the way and by leaving them all the money. And now you're worrying about leaving John the car too. You can only do so many favors. *Forget* the car."

With this, she switched on the ignition and drove back to the motel. She parked in the rear so that she could walk up the back stairs and avoid recrossing the lobby with the vodka. In the upstairs hallway she bought a large cola and some ice from a vending machine, and returned to her room. The TV was still on. She filled a glass with ice, added vodka and cola, took a sip, and almost vomited. It was the vodka, she thought. She got a fresh glass from the bathroom, filled it with straight cola, sat down on the bed, and methodically began to swallow her pills, two and three of them at a time.

As she sipped and swallowed, she idly watched TV. It took her half an hour to swallow all the pills. The last few were almost impossible to get down. She finished the drink, took off her dress and hung it carefully in the closet next to her coat. She arranged her shoes side by side beneath the bed and lay down. She was wearing a bra, panties, and a slip. She felt tired but completely calm.

It was 10:30 P.M. and the television programs were changing. She watched a show about fishing and enjoyed the peaceful country scenes. She did not feel at all drugged. At 10:55, she decided to leave a final message for John. She reached for her bedside phone, called the VA hospital, and asked the nurse to tell John in the morning to get a pass and go straight home to see the children. She was careful to keep her voice under control.

Finally she turned off the TV. She drew back the bedclothes and crawled into bed. She felt utterly relaxed. Her last memory is of "pounding one pillow down, the way I like it, and pulling the other pillow over. I can remember seeing that stupid vodka bottle on top of the TV set, and almost laughing. I couldn't even succeed in getting drunk. . . ."

A very few moments after Nell slipped beyond the conscious act of arranging her pillows for her last sleep, the world began to react to her predicament. Though she recalls nothing of the ensuing twenty hours, there is no question that the person who alerted the world to her plight was Nell herself.

The first one to realize something was badly wrong was Mrs. Joan Smith, night nurse at the VA hospital where John was a patient. Nurse Smith is gray-haired, crisply competent, and a veteran of ten years of psychiatric nursing. Her post was the fourth-floor nursing station. Night calls to the hospital come in directly on the fourth-floor phone, not through a switchboard. Nurse Smith was just arriving for duty at 10:55 P.M. when she overheard the evening nurse taking the message for John. Both nurses knew him.

About twenty minutes later, the night phone rang again and Nurse Smith answered, "Veterans Hospital." A woman's voice said that she would like to talk to someone. For the next hour and fifteen minutes, Nurse Smith never stopped talking.

"At first, all the woman would say was that there should be a place where you can call when you need help," Nurse Smith remembers. "Then she mentioned John J., and I knew him, and I realized this must be his wife."

The nurse offered to call the doctor on duty. Nell said, "No, I don't want to talk to any more doctors. I want to talk to you."

"Well, what's happened?" Nurse Smith asked.

Nell said she had taken some pills. Mrs. Smith kept talking and at the same time sent a nurse's aide scurrying to get the nursing supervisor, Althea Hutchins. In a few moments, Miss Hutchins hurried up to the desk and Nurse Smith scribbled on the duty-report pad: "Mr. J.— patient in 81C—wife taken overdose of sedatives."

Miss Hutchins went to another phone and called the doctor serving as O.D. for that night. He had been asleep in his room on the first floor. The doctor called the men's ward and told someone to awaken John and send him down to the lobby switchboard right away.

At her fourth-floor station, Nurse Smith kept trying to find out from Nell how many pills she had taken. But throughout their long, rambling conversation Nell never revealed what she had swallowed nor where she was.

By the time John arrived in the lobby in his pajamas, the O.D. already had notified the police and the telephone company, and he had set up the main hospital switchboard with three open lines. Upstairs, Miss Hutchins huddled next to Nurse Smith. Each time the nurse scribbled a clue on her pad, Miss Hutchins relayed it on another phone to the doctor and he, in turn, passed it on to the police and to the telephone company, which was trying to trace the call.

Nurse Smith has encountered many would-be suicides in mental hospitals, but she says, "I never had an experience like this before. It was like a Hitchcock movie. This woman didn't need a lot of encouragement. She really *did* just want to talk to someone. Her voice was anxious—real anxious—but otherwise she sounded normal. She talked about her children, and how upset they were about her husband's coming home, and how she'd made arrangements for them to be taken care of in Texas. But through it all she kept coming back to her idea of setting up a suicide rescue center.

"She told me, in a real bitter way, that she had already called a psychologist and a psychiatrist that night and that neither one would listen to her. That was heartrending, because I could tell by the way she said it that she wasn't making anything up. It really struck home with me because I know better than anybody how callous you can get in psychiatric work. I could have just said: 'Here's another nut. Let her ring somebody else's phone.'

"I don't care how often a person cries wolf. Anyone who gets close enough to suicide to talk about it, or make any overt act, I consider them a potential suicide until the day they go."

After Nell had been on the line about twenty minutes, the phone company was able to determine that hers was not a long-distance call, that Nell was somewhere in Tacoma. The phone company gave this information to the O.D., and Nurse Smith began pressing Nell for her location. She asked her what she could see from her window. Nell finally said she could see a funeral home sign, but she refused to give the name. She talked a lot about the car, too, and said it was parked on the street where John would know where to find it. But she wouldn't say where.

"I felt she really wanted to be found very badly," Nurse Smith says. "The trouble was, she just could not bring herself to say, 'Come and get me'—even though she knew that, unless she said it, she was probably going to die."

John pleaded to speak to his wife himself, but the doctor said no, fearing that if Nell actually got through to John, she would feel her call was completed and hang up. About midnight, the phone company determined that the call was coming from someplace near Tacoma Avenue. The police sent Officers Herbert Wood and James Thornberg to that street to search for the blue and white Ford that John had described for them.

Also at about midnight, Nell started urging the nurse to speak louder; she said she couldn't hear very well. Nurse Smith noticed that Nell's respiration was becoming more and more labored. The deafness and changing respiration showed that the drugs had begun to take effect. At 12:15 A.M., Nell passed out, still clutching the open telephone.

Nurse Smith listened helplessly to the shallow breathing for ten or fifteen more minutes. Then suddenly the telephone man's voice broke in on her line. "Don't hang up, lady," he shouted. "I think I've found her!"

"Where the dickens have you been?" Nurse Smith cracked back in momentary relief. "On TV they trace calls in five minutes!"

It was 12:36 A.M. when Officers Wood and Thornberg received word that the suicide call had been traced to the Doric. In the Dick-and-Jane prose of their police report: "We checked the register and found a Nell J. in Rm. 527. The hotel mgr. went with us to Rm. 527 and let us in. We found Nell J. lying in bed with phone in her hand. Nell J. was unconscious in bed. We called for an ambulance and sent her to Mt. View Gen. Hosp."

When she was wheeled into Mountain View, Nell was very nearly dead. First efforts to save her occupied the hospital's five-man emer-

gency staff for two frantic hours. Her chances of regaining consciousness—and life—seemed doubtful through the early morning hours. At
noon, the doctors finally told John, who had spent a sleepless night at
Mountain View, that his wife would probably recover. He drove back
to the VA hospital and secured his final discharge papers a day ahead
of schedule. Then he drove to Seattle to tell their children what had
just happened.

Nell returned to consciousness Tuesday afternoon, some twelve
hours after she had passed out. She had no recollection of her lifesaving
talk with Nurse Smith. "The first thing I knew I was in a knock-down-
drag-out battle in a hospital somewhere, kicking a nurse, ranting and
raving, tearing tubes out of me. I woke up fighting."

Attendants swiftly moved to tie Nell down. As she wrestled in a vain
effort to get free, Nell shouted, "Get away from me. You're supposed
to help people to *live,* and I want to *die!*" The struggle lasted until John
returned to the hospital. As soon as she heard his voice, she stopped
fighting and fell into a deep sleep.

The following day, Nell was rational but extremely depressed. She
was ashamed to face the children. She was sickeningly aware that she
had compounded all the family's problems. She couldn't manage her
life; she couldn't even stage-manage her own death.

Nell's slow recovery from this depth of self-loathing began in a bare
6-by-9 cell in the psychiatric ward at Mountain View. Here, under the
ever-burning, bare light bulb in the ceiling, her will to live rather swiftly
reasserted itself.

She became acutely aware that in a few days she would have to face
a sanity hearing for the second time in her life. She concentrated all
her energies on making sure she would pass it. She tried to behave like
a model patient, eating well, sleeping, cooperating with the nurses.

"I began to think it wasn't really me in that cell," she says. "Or else
it hadn't been me who poured the cola and took the pills. When I talk
about it to my psychiatrist today, I feel as if I were giving a book
review."

Following the successful outcome of her sanity hearing and her
discharge from the hospital nine days after the suicide attempt, Nell
began receiving regular long-term psychotherapy for the first time in
her life. With the help of her psychiatrist, who has been treating her
regularly for the past three months, she has gained considerable perspective on her effort to kill herself.

She regards her suicidal tendencies as a symptom, like alcoholism, of an underlying emotional disorder, rather than as a unique disease. She knows why she was so deeply depressed during her first few days at Mountain View: "When you try suicide and fail, you gain insight before you gain strength. When you realize how really deep your failure is, that turns you morbid again." She also understands why her will to live reasserted itself: "Attempted suicide is actually good therapy for a very immature, emotionally disturbed person like me. If you live through it, it seems to give you a positive message—you're not the horrible person you thought you were."

A professional insight into Nell's personality and the reasons why she tried to murder her world is offered by her psychiatrist. "When I first met Nell, I thought I was dealing with a severe neurosis," he says, "one which manifests itself most often in immaturity. But as a person, she seemed well above the average in intelligence, a capable woman with a great deal of energy and determination. I saw an idealistic person, a perfectionist—imaginative and creative, too. She seemed quite capable of taking care of herself.

"Gradually, as she showed symptoms of depression and even expressed thoughts of suicide, I saw other aspects of her. She is a Peter Pan type—with a wide-eyed look of expectancy, which she uses to control other people. In our conversations she showed an oversensitivity, and when I ventured into certain interpretations of her own thoughts and actions, she reacted with hostility. Her ego is not strong enough; it tends to be undermined by her feelings. Such a person does not have enough resources available in ego strength to concern herself adequately with the outside world. Most of us can give ourselves to the business at hand. But people like Nell become so concerned with their own feelings that they can have only a partial critical relationship with the outside world.

"There is an analogy here in the geography of the state of Washington. As you go east over the mountains you notice that the vegetation changes; the dense fir forests give way to pine trees—a zone of transition where the pines begin to merge with the firs.

"A person can reach a critical point where he can no longer read his environment. Nell is beyond the firs now and among the pines; if her ego is strong enough for her to recognize the environment—and her motivations—she probably won't try suicide again."

Today, nearly eleven months after Nell's suicide attempt, her family appears to be on a more realistic footing than ever before. John is the manager of a Capitol Hill barber shop, and soon hopes to have enough money saved to buy a part-interest in the business. Nell's daughter is living at home again; she was named chief cheerleader and student body secretary of her high school. Nell has become an enthusiastic supporter of a committee that is trying to establish a suicide rescue center in Seattle. Two and a half months after her discharge from the hospital, she returned to full-time work at the accounting firm, this time as receptionist in the big rosewood and glass lobby. Her mind for a while was too confused by emotional shock—and perhaps from the residual effect of the drugs—to concentrate on the precise bookkeeping and secretarial work she had handled before. But with continued psychotherapy these skills returned, and recently she shifted to another secretary-bookkeeper job.

Her old boss still maintains that "Nell is the best secretary I've ever had." He was forced to hire two girls—a stenographer and a bookkeeper—to replace her. Neither these girls nor her new boss nor any of the other employes in either firm know of Nell's suicide attempt; it is doubtful they would believe it if they were told. Nell's old boss reflected the popular view of her when he remarked recently, "I was sorry to lose her. She was the most stable girl in this office."

Life—May 29, 1964

12

Cagney

Thirteen years ago James Cagney left Hollywood the way I once saw a Chinese illusionist leave the stage. No flutter of silks, no blinding flash, he was just suddenly Not There. The effect was devastating. Now Cagney has hit town again, without really coming back to it. He turned up to accept the Life Achievement Award of the American Film Institute, and to answer questions. The most intriguing one was *why?* Why had he left, and how had he resisted all temptations to make a comeback? "How do you turn down two million dollars?" somebody wanted to know.

"Simple. You just say no," he replied. But of course it wasn't simple at all. Most things in life are easier to get into than to get out of. The rule applies equally to marriage, career, trouble, and politics. Hard as it may be to break into the big leagues, it is harder still to walk away. Failure helps. But success, especially the overnight, heavy-money, American kind, seems to double-lock the exit door. To get out and stay out is most difficult of all. Frank Sinatra retired in 1971 and has already come back twice. He'll be back again in March to emcee the Cagney dinner, a yo-yo pattern of which the award winner is in no way critical. "One of the neighbor's children" is Cagney's term for Frank, meaning he feels very close.

But when Cagney quit show business, he did it with a grace and finality unmatched by any other retiree I can think of, and without so much as a backward glance. For a natural-born backward-glancer like Cagney, this seems a pity. Cagney moved so fast on screen, much of his dialogue was said over his shoulder. His most violent actions had humor. Belting Mae Clarke with the grapefruit was Cagney's own acid touch; the script called for an omelet. His ferocity was fastidious. He would put his fists through his pockets rather than beat up what Hollywood is now beating up. He had lovely footwork. His feet were as important as his fists. He was vulnerable, but not an underdog. Cagney was a small but unmistakable overdog with a tag on his collar: No Surrender.

It's a pity Cagney has hung up his gloves, but a pity for us, not him. He has never regretted it, and is never even tempted to sneak a peek at himself on *The Late, Late Show*.

As Pauline Kael has observed, the good guy has disappeared simultaneously from our society and from our movies, and Cagney today seems like some very rare creature, perhaps an arctic owl—sleek, plump, white-tufted, intelligent, and very much at ease inside his plumage.

"That press conference unfolded like a rose," I said when I visited him at his home in Beverly Hills the next afternoon.

"We gave 'em the hokeypokey pretty good," Cagney replied, "but that was a red-hat audience. We used to say in vaudeville, 'They'd laugh at a red hat.'"

The private, offscreen Cagney was always a painter and—in Alva Johnston's phrase—"an associate of known intellectuals." The walls of his library are lined with paintings, many Cagney's own.

My strong sense that I was visiting a nearly extinct creature was probably heightened because I had arrived on the doorstep of the old Hollywood in headlong flight from the new. That morning I had seen *The Exorcist,* a calculated exercise in disgust of the most infantile kind. This is romper-room orgy; if you are squeamish about having the potty dumped on you, avoid *The Exorcist. Deep Throat* by comparison is clean fun.

Strip off the phony tinsel Hollywood, as the old joke says, and see the real tinsel underneath. I suspect that Cagney must have seen the real tinsel from the start. In any event, he talks readily about his exit, and his answer takes many forms. "I didn't like it," he says. "I was psychologically finished. I'd been at it thirty or forty years. It wasn't fun any more. After a while, it gets down to essential needs. You need a wife, need friends, you need some money, good talk, and you need the laughs. I had it all."

Mr. and Mrs. Cagney, who have been married fifty-one years, met when they were both dancing in the chorus. "I was always a hoofer," Cagney says. "Nobody taught me how. I'd watch a step, then steal it, change it, make it eccentric. I always thought it wasn't showy enough. Here's the Bandy Twist, for example." Suddenly he was up on fast-moving feet. "I did *this* to it!" adding a flashy little hop.

I had read that The Public Enemy was really a shrinking violet, so shy he became seasick before starting a new picture. Was this true? "There's always the driving need to get it done properly, so there's always the butterflies. But you have a professional approach, so you go do it. But one day, I just said fini, that's all. There was not even an awareness of having arrived at anything."

Cagney still tap-dances mornings to shake out the aches and pains, runs 350 yards uphill to his painting studio and jogs during TV commercials. "Never surprise your heart, Pet," he told me.

Do you keep busy, I asked? "There aren't enough hours in the day! In the autumn, you hitch a couple of horses up front and go up into the woods, up through the leaves. Beauty, beauty, beauty! Listen. Think of a full-rigged ship coming around a headland. Think about wild horses galloping in moonlight. What are we talking about? Beauty in motion—that's what it's all about."

In the next room a sound of hammering stopped, and Cagney's sister, Jeanne, came in to say the new stereo equipment was installed. We went to listen to a special tape from the sound track of *Yankee Doodle Dandy*, Cagney's own favorite movie. He propped his feet up on the coffee table and his glasses up on his forehead. As the band played, Cagney began to chuckle almost inaudibly, his body shaking with ho-ho-hos like a silent Santa. "Who says nostalgia isn't what it used to be?" he exclaimed.

Then, "So much more meaningful, those patriotic songs, because of the trouble we're in today. This period in our history is a lot like the years between 1830 and 1860," he said. "A historian of that time called it 'the confusion of the many, and the ambition of the few.'" Then he leaned back and closed his eyes and we listened in silence. Jeanne said, "You're crying, Jim."

"You know it!" he replied.

By now I had a kind of crush on him. Not on the movie character, because I never even saw most Cagney movies, and not on the man, whom I scarcely knew, but a crush on the near-extinct Cagney type—the non-Napoleonic small man.

Cagney attracts people today more than ever because he is the man who has done it all, the man endowed with many talents who has achieved his whole potential. Having done so—at great cost in time and energy—he *can* walk away. He can even tap-dance away.

We shook hands in the doorway in the dusk, and suddenly he tapped out an intricate step, a tiny ruffle and flourish of feet on polished floor. "The Getavasia," he said. I looked blank. "The Getavasia. A step I made up in vaudeville. Before you go off, you do a little something extra, so they'll remember you."

Newsweek—February 4, 1974

13

Chaplin

Charlie Chaplin, the cockney clown who made an art form of himself, has come back to America. Twenty years ago, the U.S. government threw the little fellow overboard in mid-Atlantic. Now, at eighty-three, he comes swimming back alive. Charlie was always the clown with the last laugh.

In the bad old days of the McCarthy era, Chaplin's exile was deemed a matter of "moral worth." It is possible now to wonder whose moral worth was really being tested—was it his, or ours? In those days when innuendo, prejudice, and half-thought ruled our reason, we imagined we could clean our house by evicting Chaplin. All we did was soil ourselves.

We didn't understand that no one can evict Charles Spencer Chaplin. Although he occupies a luxurious Swiss mountaintop, his home is the world. More people love America for its Chaplin movies than will ever love us for our foreign policy, whatever it may be. By putting the bundle back on the little tramp's back twenty years ago, we made him a world hero, as well as a world citizen. We made ourselves the heavy, and as Chaplin himself has taught us, the heavy always gets it in the shins.

For over a week now, we have been watching thousands of people hop and cheer and stomp to welcome Charlie back, and we have seen Chaplin, the artist, respond with all of the old grace and charm. In life, he seems to be imitating his art—happy ending and all. His very presence suggests a silent movie. He blows kisses, he waves, he walks, he gestures. On the rare occasions when he does speak, his words are as blunt and spare as a title card in one of his two-reelers. Chaplin hasn't forgotten the ambiguous power of brevity. A shrug, a silence even, is another way to make something perfectly clear.

If there is guilt mixed in with other emotions in this tumultuous cross-country welcome home party for Chaplin—and I am sure there is—it goes tactfully unremarked on, and we are left free to enjoy Chaplin again in an uncomplicated way. This feels good. For no one has ever meant quite what Chaplin meant. No comic in our times—I might say, "Modern Times"—has stretched his art like Chaplin.

The star is back on Hollywood Boulevard, and he has returned on his own terms. This makes us feel good on many levels. Richard Nixon goes to China. Charlie Chaplin comes to America. Perhaps it is possible to put Humpty Dumpty together again, after all.

CBS "Spectrum"—April 10, 1972

SECTION 2
Requiems and Love Songs

1

Diary: 1976

I only remember crying on a story three times—while I was out reporting it, that is. I've cried scores of times afterwards, at the typewriter, struggling to get the story down. The time I remember best happened without warning when I was writing a piece about Tony Curtis. I had been interviewing him nearly every day for about three months, because for good and private reasons neither one of us wanted to break off the marathon interview and face the other parts of our lives. One morning toward the end of the marathon, I arrived at Tony's house, notebook in hand, and he said, "You know, Shana, I've been thinking. Maybe you should talk to some other *people about me. To get a more rounded perspective." And he handed me a typewritten list of about twenty names.*

At the head of the list was Tony's longtime agent, Lew Wasserman, the powerful head of MCA, and widely considered to be the smartest man in Hollywood. He was also the most inaccessible.

"Jeez, Tony, I know *Wasserman won't see me," I said weakly. "He hates reporters. Fortune just sent a task force out here from New York to do a big takeout on MCA, and Wasserman wouldn't even accept their phone calls."*

Tony picked up the phone. "Lew, there's this girl here doing a big story about me for Life *magazine, and would you . . ."*

A moment later Tony hung up, grinned, and said, "Tomorrow morning, ten o'clock."

MCA agents are famous, among other things, for wearing all-black suits, for furnishing their offices with eighteenth-century English antiques, for keeping spotlessly bare desk-tops, and for being very sharp fellows. Wasserman's desk was grandest and barest of all. I sat down across it from him and forced myself to make up a few stock questions to which I already knew the answers. (After our three-month marathon, I knew more about Tony than his psychiatrist did.) Wasserman gave me stock replies. We were both doing Tony a favor. The "interview" lasted less than ten minutes. But when it ended, Wasserman pushed a concealed button and told a secretary in the outer office that for the next hour he did not wish to be disturbed for any reason, no phone calls, nothing.

Then gravely placing his black-clad elbows on the acre of polished mahogany between us, Wasserman leaned forward and said gently, "Now, Shana. Tell me all about yourself." To my own horror, and utter astonishment, I burst into floods of tears.

Later, I told this story on the phone to Phil Kunhardt, Jr., then, Life's assistant managing editor in New York. "You see, Phil," I said, "that proves Lew Wasserman is the smartest man in Hollywood."

Phil is smart too, as well as kind. "Tell me about yourself," he said, and a few weeks later the following appeared on Life's table of contents page. Nearly thirteen years after I joined the staff, thirteen years of talking about other people, I was talking about myself for the first time. After years of invisibility, my own picture even appeared in Life, feeding a pregnant elephant. A terrific week.

2

Shana Talks About Shana

"All my life it seems I've been interviewing people," says our West Coast staff writer, Shana Alexander. "No one ever asks about me."

So we did and these are some of the things she said.

"I was born in New York City, the same year my father, Milton Ager, wrote 'Ain't She Sweet.' As a child I was very fat and very young.

I went to Vassar and our freshman class gained a ton before Christmas. I majored in anthropology. It was the ideal subject to train for journalism—the study of exotic people in their native habitats. I left college and went to look for a job as an office girl at a newspaper. The guy interviewing me said how old are you and I told him sixteen and he burst into hysterical laughter, and finally when he got hold of himself he said, how would you like a job as a reporter? My first assignment was to interview Gyspy Rose Lee on her pregnancy.

"Many years later I did another pregnancy. I was the only lady reporter on the baby elephant story in Portland. Everybody was very courteous; they gave me hay to sit on. I made four trips up from Los Angeles. They'd call me up and say 'Now!' and I'd race up there and sit in the hay. I had special elephant clothes because of the smell. They knew me so well at the hotel, on the last trip they gave me a room with two baths. I'm still a member of SPOPE—the Society for the Preservation and Observation of Pregnant Elephants. We have secret meetings, handshakes, grunts, and that sort of thing.

"When I'm writing about someone, I have to get to know my subject terribly well. I interview them and interview them until suddenly I find myself thinking just like them. After I did Dr. Bach, the psychologist who promotes battles between husbands and wives, I started throwing wineglasses at my husband. During the no-calorie diet story, I went on a tremendous diet myself. I pinned a picture of me as a fat freshman on the inside of the refrigerator door and I lost seven pounds.

"On the story I wrote about Judy Garland, Judy and I used to talk about how awful it was to be a little fat girl. We agreed that the worst thing in the world was to sit on your bed and look down at three stomachs. I like Judy enormously. She is indestructible. She'd be dead by now if her protoplasm wasn't stronger than other people's. Burt Lancaster? He gave me absolutely straight answers, none of the usual Hollywood phoniness. He's very tough and I like tough people, being such a marshmallow myself.

"I've learned how to be a journalist and a girl, too. All my clothes are specially made to fold flat in a suitcase and they have pockets in them just the size of a small notebook. It's a marvelous life, this life in a man's world. I'd climb the walls if I had to live the feminine mystique."

Life—October 11, 1963

3

Diary: 1976

Six years later, I left Life *magazine. I had gone to work there in 1951, intending to stay only a few months, then get married. I got married, and stayed at* Life *eighteen years. It was in some ways the happiest period of my life. In 1954, the company offered to transfer me to Los Angeles. My husband was in the TV-film business in New York. It seemed a good opportunity, and we took it. I left* Life *in early 1968 when I was offered the editorship of McCall's. It was an offer I felt I couldn't refuse. I had been divorced several years earlier, so now I packed up bags, baggage, cats, eight-year-old daughter, and nanny, and we headed back East.*

The eighteen years at Life *was a kind of protracted adolescence, followed by an extended honeymoon. By the time I became a staff writer, in 1961, the generation of young men who had started out at* Life *when I did were running the magazine. My editor, Ralph Graves, the man who had so long and so patiently encouraged me to write as well as report, was now the editor. Phil Kunhardt, his deputy, now edited my column, "The Feminine Eye." I often stayed with Katherine and Phil Kunhardt, on my frequent trips East. They had become my closest friends, and were the godparents of my daughter, Katherine. The idea for me to do the column at all had come from Loudon Wainwright, another close and old friend, whose own* Life *column, "The View From Here," alternated with my own. When I first went to work for* Life, *in 1951, I was the junior researcher in the* Life Goes To A Party *department. The Party writer was Loudon. When Loudon was promoted to Los Angeles bureau chief for* Life, *in early 1954, he had brought Phil and me to California as bureau correspondents, and all our families had moved out there at about the same time.*

Now these old friends were back in New York editing the magazine, and I was doing a star turn. They were trying to make me look good, and I was trying not to let them down. I felt like Sonja Henie a good bit of the time. It had all gone on so long, and so well, that I didn't know it had been a honeymoon until after it had ended. As editor of McCall's, I finally grew up, fast. Life in the harsh, cold world of ladies' magazines was a painful experience that ended for me with a bang and a whimper; I simultaneously quit and got fired.

Between commenting for "Spectrum" on CBS News, consulting on employment for women for Norton Simon, Inc. (the parent conglomerate that then owned McCall's), beginning work on my state-by-state guidebook to women's legal rights, and helping to found the National Women's Political Caucus, I managed to keep busy until July 1972, when I very suddenly became a columnist again, this time for Newsweek.

At last I was back working at a real, honest-to-God magazine. It felt like a second honeymoon. Five months after the honeymoon began, Life died. Newsweek asked me if I would write its obituary.

4

Life Magazine: R.I.P.

Life magazine is dead, and I don't want to talk about it. I worked there eighteen years. I learned my trade there, and made my truest friends and lived my own best life—1951–1969, R.I.P., as the tombstone carvers would have it. Wild, rich, wonderful years in which I thought I had the best job, and the best editors, in the best possible game in the world.

Tell everybody how wild and rich and wonderful it all was, people say now. Roll out the anecdotes, the memories, all the wacky yarns. I remember—*Life was* my life, after all—but I don't want to talk about it. I can't do a vaudeville turn on a grave.

Most of the old-timers feel this way. For some twenty-four hours now, we have called each other up, looked into each other's eyes, clasped hands. . . . But an extraordinary dumbness and numbness oppresses us; there *is* nothing to say.

We are too sad to talk about it, and too mad. I think we share a dreadful, oppressive feeling that somebody betrayed a trust. *Life* died as a body dies. It died slowly, of creeping old age, progressively enfeebled, yet dragging itself pitifully forward until it just fell over in its traces, a bony, used-up, worn-out old cart horse of a magazine.

I don't believe that this death was inevitable, that *Life* was doomed inevitably by rising expenses, rising postal costs, by television, by changing life-styles of the American public. These are conventional pieties, the cover-ups and tongue-clackings of bad doctors as they decently pull the sheet up over the remains.

Life died because of a failure of management action and nerve. Sure, budgets were cut, and cut again. Sure, circulation was cut and cut again. Not a few little editorial games were played as well. But only editors make magazines. Managers don't make them, nor bureaucrats, nor second- or third-guessers in the executive suite. Once the slide began, it seemed to me that those people never did the right thing to prevent it. The new economic realities of mass magazines required bold, creative steps that they were too timorous to make. Not only did they fail to move; they stopped other people from moving.

Downstairs on the editorial floors they had the best editors in the world, the best writers and photographers, but Upstairs didn't let them move. Downstairs were ideas aplenty—changes in format, changes in page size, changes in approach, and even in the weekly cycle. But always it was the Upstairs boys with the sharp pencils who had the final word. And always the word was no.

The autopsy surgeons now exploring the cadaver say that somewhere, somehow, *Life*'s editors lost touch with America, and that once they lost it, they could never find it again. This is partially true, but it is more true to say that they were never *allowed* to find it again. I speak here as a reader and as a sentimental alumnus, nearly four years gone. I was a working staff member. I never really knew what went on behind closed editorial and business office doors. But as a professional journalist, I do know that, consistently over many years, the *Life* staff was quite possibly the best collection of journalists in the world. I think that in the last years many of these talented writers and reporters and photographers and editors must have been stymied, hobbled, prevented in one way or another from doing what only they could do.

Executive-suite propaganda to the contrary, photojournalism is not dead, and magazines are not dead, and the American people have not stopped reading, nor have they lost interest in the world around them. What died at *Life* was an appropriate relationship between editors and management.

Life's last managing editor, Ralph Graves, years ago was my own editor, the man who received my teletyped files of raw copy and patiently, subtly, with infinite care and not a little sleight-of-hand, slowly convinced me that I could one day become a staff writer like my ideals, Paul O'Neill and Loudon Wainwright. I was a mere correspondent then, in the Los Angeles bureau of the magazine, and the possibility appeared to me as remote as the thought of becoming a tap dancer—the one job in the world I would have preferred.

Later, every time I sent Ralph a first draft, no matter how flawed or blotted, clumsy or contorted, he cabled back the same reply: AS GERTRUDE LAWRENCE TOLD NOEL COWARD WHEN SHE RECEIVED THE MANUSCRIPT OF "PRIVATE LIVES," NOTHING WRONG THAT CAN'T BE FIXED. Ralph was right. With time, patience, and editorial skill, it always *was* fixed. That is what good editors get paid to do.

Six words—"nothing wrong that can't be fixed"—six wonderfully reassuring words. This morning it seems ironic, tragic, and infuriating that the same simple message—so full of confidence, of caring, and of understanding what the editorial process is all about—was never sent from the executive suite where the power was down to the editorial floor where the talent was. That's why I don't want to talk about it. That's why, sad and mad as all journalists today must be, *Life* in the end deserved to die.

Newsweek—December 15, 1972

5
Diary: 1976

I enjoy a good cry. Here are some other requiems . . . for people I loved, for institutions I loved and longed for, like marriage; requiems for terrible ideas and good ones, like cannibal funerals. Requiems for dreams, plans, childhood fantasies; requiems even for myself.

6
What Is a Marriage?

Disturbed by the true-life coming apart on national television of the marriage and family of William and Pat Loud of Santa Barbara, I have been worrying how my own family might look on TV. What is a family, anyhow? What is a marriage, I might add, for I too have been divorced.

The question of what marriage is, or should be, itches at us all. But it particularly troubles people in the Louds' generation and my own, men and women now in their forties and early fifties. We were the last ones who really, fully believed in it. We may even have worshipped it to death. For the sorry truth is that we, the parents of the baby boom, are also the plaintiffs of the divorce boom.

Ours was the Togetherness Generation. We equated togetherness with salvation, and expected so much from it that it was bound to let us down. Companionship, security, lifelong physical and spiritual and emotional warmth—all were to be had for the twist of a ring and the breathing of a vow. *And to be had no other way.*

"Do you know *anyone* today who is really happily married?" an old friend asked as we sat morosely watching the sorrowful Louds. I could name but two couples. Then, last week, I realized I know a third, an utterly astounding pair whom I have known all my life: my own mother and father.

First, a caveat. As an American family we are no more typical than the Louds. In fact, we are quite a lot weirder. Further, I believe that a marriage really is a private affair, and would not presume to explain any one of them, my parents' least of all. And finally, my mother and father are very private people who would never let a TV camera in the door. They have never capitulated to the let-it-all-hang-out life-style, so I hope they will forgive me now. I think their story is worth trying to tell, worth it as much for its mystery as for its triumph. The DMZ is no place from which to analyze a battle, and the egocentrism of childhood distorts the picture on one's parents. The bicker in the bedroom is heard as the clash of giants, and it takes years for the truth of Housman's lines to sink in:

> The night my father got me
> His mind was not on me.

Or, as my own father always put it, "Children don't ask to be born." My father, Milton Ager, is a composer; my mother, Cecelia, a critic. He wrote "Happy Days Are Here Again," "Hard-Hearted Hannah," and hundreds of other enduring songs. She wrote the best movie criticism of her day. I remember my New York City childhood as a series of hotel apartments divided into His, Hers, and Children's areas, with the living room serving as a kind of neutral zone. Mother worked mostly by day, Father by night, and they dined together in restaurants. They both suffered terribly from insomnia, which accounts in part for the floor plan. To this day, my sister and I tiptoe and whisper in the early morning. When we were small children, my father worked at a special noiseless keyboard, actually a portable, folding Salvation Army organ which he refrained from pumping so as not to disturb *us*. He also composed songs in his head. He still does, and my mother is still the savviest critic I know. Physically, they are small, stylish, blue-eyed, and fastidious. My mother has worn the same upswept hairstyle since the early 1930's. As a schoolgirl, I was embarrassed by her Chinese chic. Do I embarrass my own daughter, who is now eleven? What does nine-year-old Soft-Hearted Hannah, my sister's daughter and the youngest of the clan, think of our family, and what will marriage be like for her?

Except for my daughter and me, our family lives in California now. The other day I got a note from my father. "We are having our golden, Thurs. Chantal back room with all the members of both families invited. Have already congratulated her. If you wish to, same address. Love, Milton."

Fifty years! I was flabbergasted. I didn't understand it, but I did want to celebrate it. When I phoned to say I was coming to the party, my father was drafting a speech which indicates the flavor of their relationship. "Some of you may wonder what has held us together all of these years. Well, it is one of the great forces of nature—the force called inertia."

At the airport I ran into S. J. Perelman, an old friend. "Bet Milton can't think of a rhyme for inertia," he said, knowing the right way to torment songwriters.

At the party, I delivered the challenge. "Better-or-worse-ye!" Father shot back. Not much of a rhyme, but it does indicate what was on his mind. That sense of commitment to better-or-worse is one thing missing from today's marriages. Perhaps you have to survive the inertia in order for lasting love to set in.

The party was an entire success. We sang the songs we always sing, and my father remembered a few of his oldies that none of us had ever heard. One, a vaudeville parody of "M Is for the Many Times She Kissed Me," began, "F Is for the Many Times He Flogged Me." My father said he earned $3 in 1912 for writing this, and then he began to reminisce about *his* parents. Ancestry piled on ancestry. "My mother, she made everything. She made the curtains, the shirts, she even made the carpets. We all liked special foods, so she made different things for nine children, and for my father. She was his second wife and about sixteen when she married him; he was nearly fifty. He wore a gold earring and I think he was a gypsy. He always warned me never to sign anything, and it was only after I had left home that I found out he couldn't read."

In a way, my parents are gypsies too. In both the His and Hers bedrooms of their present furnished hotel-apartment, which they have occupied for the past ten or fifteen years, the drawer space is augmented by an open wardrobe trunk standing in one corner, mute reminders that if anybody gets too fed up around here, he/she is equipped to go it alone. If my parents don't make carpets, they have at least woven a rare marriage. In carpet vocabulary I would describe it as tough, vivid, springy, and durable. Since the party, I have been wondering what else besides a tradition of better-or-worse-ye helped pull them through. Strong, immigrant stock, I would say, with a peasant tradition of hard work and an intellectual tradition that respects the life of the mind. Then they had independence, luck, humor, health, pride, and two children who very much wanted them to stay together. Terrific mutual respect was tempered by a fine command of wit, scorn, and put-down. Both worked, each had separate interests. All this may have allowed enough air into the system to keep it from blowing up.

In the end, I must admit that I cannot know what tides returned them always together, no matter what noons and moons pulled them apart. But I don't think we will see many more fifty-year marriages. They are a miracle, nearly extinct. My mother and father are the snow leopards of the social contract. I remember them tugging, fighting, pulling in opposite directions. As antagonists, they were well-matched. My father silently putted a cotton golf ball through the living room neutral zone in his underwear after my mother had been sitting there for some hours interviewing Wendell Willkie.

I cannot know why they did it, how they survived it. I only know that today they are gallant and tough and funny and absolutely, utterly triumphant.

Newsweek—February 19, 1973

7

Dinty Moore's Restaurant

Watergate is full of sudden strokes and surprises. My personal stun-
ner came the day somebody said that thirty years ago J. Edgar
Hoover and Daniel Ellsberg's father-in-law used to dine together in
Dinty Moore's restaurant. At that, Watergate faded and Dinty
Moore's came floating up out of my past, all its lights ablaze, polished brass and mirrors gleaming—a gala, ghostly cruise ship bearing my childhood back to me.

Moore's was the best restaurant in New York City, and I grew
up in it, dining out once a week or so with my parents from the
time I was old enough to hold a fork. Although I often saw J. Edgar Hoover and other famous figures tucking away the corned beef
and cabbage, the "nose-warmers" of oxtail soup, the rice pudding
nonpareil—politicians ate better in those days, and so did crooks—
it was not the celebrities who impressed me but the ionized,
charged-up atmosphere of the place. Anything might happen in
this closed, immaculate world of delicious food and fierce emotions
where once a customer was tossed out the door for ordering a ham-
burger *without* onions; where out on the sidewalk enraged rabbis in
black hats and beards picketed because the menu listed "kosher
calf's liver and Irish bacon."

Moore's was a self-contained, white-tile universe, so Irish that years
later when I landed in Dublin, I felt I had come home. Ireland seemed
a larger, much-diluted, outdoor Moore's. The white-tiled kitchen in the
rear was wide-open to public view, and my sister and I had cooking
lessons there after school. While our classmates were wearing white
gloves and learning the right way to fox-trot, we wore big white table-
cloths tied around us, waiter-style, and learned the right way to cook

carrots and peas (rapidly, with a pinch of sugar) and potatoes (unpeeled, with a handful of salt).

Our teacher was the old man himself. Everyone called him "the old man," including his family. To his face, he was "Mr. Moore" or "Jim." Nobody ever called him "Dinty," not even the cartoonist George McManus, who immortalized him in his abrasive comic strip "Bringing Up Father."

McManus was right about the long-smoldering warfare of the Irish household. In the Moore family, nobody talked to anybody else if he could help it. Mr. Moore and his wife occupied separate floors above the restaurant and had not spoken in decades; the children rarely spoke either, except to borrow some money, or to plot against one parent or the other.

The old man believed there was only one right way to do everything. All food must be young and all ingredients perfectly fresh. The only acceptable canned food is applesauce. The only cooking sherry is Harvey's Bristol Cream. Hamburgers can only be made from prime rib. Female lobsters are sweeter. Cooking is concentration. "Watch everything on the stove," he told us, "the way you watch a piece of toast."

When the old man went to Palm Beach in winter, he sent back daily postcards: "Caught a tuna today; crust on pot pie should not be too thick." "Weather beautiful; put enough barley in soup." Each vacation at least twenty-five postcards arrived, every one a reminder to prepare the food exactly as it had been prepared for a quarter-century.

Mr. Moore had rigid standards. Leaving your mother and gambling were the unforgivable sins; larceny was lower down the scale. When my mother protested that Jim should not waste his time and energy making up elaborate food hampers to send to my sister and me at camp, he told her he had to do the monthly baskets anyway, "for the boys up the river."

He had rigid health standards, too. In hot weather, avoid iced drinks; sip warm soup instead. When my sister visited Jim in Florida and got a bad sunburn, he knew what to do: "Soak a large linen handkerchief in ice cubes in a silver bowl. Wring out in Gordon's gin . . . must be Gordon's . . . and apply to affected parts." She swore it worked like a charm.

In memory, the old man is a wobble of chins, an aroma of bay rum, a shirtfront of creamy pongee, a fine London suit with a cuff of long underwear peeking out, a pink, just-barbered face, and a few long strands of hair plastered on gleaming scalp. From him, I learned inflexible rules about everything that is most important in life—food, sex, death, and deportment. The sex lecture occurred when I was twelve or thirteen. One wintry night he glanced at me sharply, then bellowed, "Moran! Bring me a plate of oysters. Don't open 'em." Moran wore a perpetual poker face. Years before, the waiter had got a $500 tip, for placing a $5,000 bet on the Dempsey-Firpo fight, and surprises after that were anticlimax. Moran presented the bivalves without comment. Mr. Moore deftly opened one with the tiny gold penknife on his watch chain. He rapped his big knuckles hard on the table to rivet my attention, thrust the mucid and cold object under my nose, and said sternly, "Listen here, girlie! An oyster has everything *you* have. So don't leave your mother when her hair turns gray." So much for the facts of life. I was a woman now.

Jim Moore died in his restaurant in his eighty-fourth year. They laid him out in the parlor upstairs, and the next afternoon I saw for the first time in my life the small, rouged face of death. But he had already beat death long ago. He was an Irish Catholic of the most barnacled kind, yet his belief in God had not been unduly calcified by organized religion. When I say he beat death, I am not being fanciful; he smacked it in the face with a flounder.

As he aged, the old man badly missed his departed cronies, and one quiet afternoon the absurdity of their absence grew intolerable. He wrapped two packages in parchment paper and butcher string, climbed into the open, cream-colored, wicker-sided Packard that was always parked in front of the door, and instructed his chauffeur to drive to the Hebrew cemetery. At the grave of his friend Sam Harris, the theatrical producer, the old man placed a beautiful hunk of his own corned beef and reminded Sam aloud how inconsiderate he had been to die young. By the time Jim had driven on to Mount Calvary and the grave of George M. Cohan, he was steaming mad. The other parcel was a fish which he beat against the headstone, shouting "Cohan! In case you don't know, it's Friday, and I want you to see what you're missing!"

Our world very much misses men like Jim Moore. He was more than a man with absolute standards; he was a man who lived up to those standards—publicly. Like his kitchen, his life and his foibles were totally exposed. His cards were always on the table along with the food.

Like his old customer J. Edgar Hoover, the old man had a bottom line below which he would not go. Unlike the Watergate pragmatists, bent on the reelection of their President at all costs, Jim could never believe the ends justified the means. He was too smart. His whole life was a testament that bad means, like bad raw ingredients, positively *guarantee* a bad end.

Newsweek—August 10, 1973

8

The Fine Art of Marital Fighting

In the morning, his secretary quits; in the afternoon, his archrival at the office gets a promotion; when he gets home that evening he finds out his wife has put a dent in the new car. He drinks four martinis before dinner, and then calls his wife a lousy cook. She says how can he tell with all that gin in him, and he says she is getting as mean tempered as her stupid mother, and she says at least her mother wasn't stupid enough to marry a phony slob, by which time he is bellowing like an enraged moose, she is shrieking and hurling dishes, the baby is screaming, the dogs are yapping, the neighbors are pounding on the walls, and the cops are on their way. Suddenly a car screeches to the curb and a little man with a tape recorder under his arm hops out and dashes inside.

This scene is a recurrent dream of George R. Bach, Ph.D., a Los Angeles clinical psychologist and West Coast chairman of the American Academy of Psychotherapy. For him, it is not a nightmare but a rosy fantasy of things to come. His great ambition is to set up a Los Angeles Municipal Fight Center which any embattled husband or wife, regardless of race, creed, or hour of the night, could telephone and get a fair hearing. Trained marriage counselors would man the switchboards, referee the disputes, tape-record the hubub for analysis by dawn's early light, and if necessary, dispatch a mobile referee on a house call.

It is Bach's dream to become that referee. He studies human aggression, and he loves his work. Over the last twenty-five years, he has professionally analyzed 23,000 marital fights, including, he figures, at least 2,500 of his own. Gifted marital gladiators in action thrill him as the sunset does the poet.

Unfortunately, his clinical practice yields so few sunsets that Bach feels the future of American family life is gravely threatened. He recently told a startled audience of newsmen and psychiatrists at the annual meeting of the Ortho-Psychiatric Association that a primary aim of psychotherapy and marriage counseling should be "to teach couples to have more, shorter, *more constructive* fights." Along with a growing number of his colleagues, he says, he has come to believe that proper training in "the fine art of marital fighting" would not only improve domestic tranquillity, it could reduce divorces by up to 90 per cent.

What dismays the doctor is not bloodshed per se; it is the native cowardice and abysmal crudity of American domestic fighting style. Most husbands and wives, he has found, will avail themselves of any sneaky excuse to avoid a fight in the first place. But if cornered, they begin clobbering away at one another like dull-witted Neanderthals. They are clumsy, weak-kneed, afflicted with poor aim, rotten timing, and no notion of counterpunching. What's more, they fight dirty. Their favorite weapons are the low blow and the rock-filled glove.

The cause of the shoddy, low estate of the marital fight game is a misunderstanding of aggression itself, says the fight doctor. "Research has established that people always dream, and *my* research has established that people are always to some degree angry. But today they are ashamed of this anger. To express hostile feelings toward a loved one is considered impolite, just as the expression of sexual feelings was considered impolite before Freud."

What Freud did for sex, Bach, in his own modest way, would like to do for anger, which is almost as basic a human impulse. "We must remove the shame from aggression," he exhorts in a soft, singsong German accent much like Peter Lorre's. "Don't repress your aggressions—program them!"

When primitive man lived in the jungle, surrounded by real, lethal enemies, the aggressive impulse is what kept him alive. For modern man, the problem gets complicated because he usually encounters only what the psychologist calls "intimate enemies"—wives, husbands, sweethearts, children, parents, friends, and others whom he sometimes would like to kill, but toward whom he nonetheless feels basic, underlying goodwill.

When he gets mad at one of these people, modern man tends to go to pieces. His jungle rage embarrasses, betrays, even terrifies him. "He forgets that real intimacy *demands* that there be fighting," Bach says. He fails to realize that "nonfighting is only appropriate between strangers—people who have nothing worth fighting about. When two people begin to really *care* about each other, they become emotionally vulnerable—and the battles start."

Listening to Bach enumerate the many destructive, "bad" fight styles is rather like strolling through a vast Stillman's gym of domestic discord. Over there, lolling about on the canvas, watching TV, walking out, sitting in a trancelike state, drinking beer, doing their nails, even falling asleep, are the "Withdrawal-Evaders," people who will not fight. These people, Bach says, are very sick. After counseling thousands of them, he is convinced that "falling asleep causes more divorces than any other single act."

And over *there*, viciously flailing, kicking, and throwing knives at one another, shouting obnoxious abuse, hitting below the belt, deliberately provoking anger, exchanging meaningless insults (You stink! *You* doublestink!)—simply needling or battering one another for the hell of it —are people indulging in "open noxious attack." They are the "Professional Ego-Smashers," and they are almost as sick—but not quite—as the first bunch.

An interesting subgroup here are the "Chain-Reactors," specialists in what Bach once characterized as "throwing in the kitchen sink from left field." A chain-reacting husband opens up by remarking, "Well, I see you burned the toast again this morning." When his wife begins to make new toast, he continues, "And another thing . . . that no-good brother of yours hasn't had a job for two years." This sort of fight, says Bach, "usually pyramids to a Valhalla-type of total attack."

The third group of people are all smiling blandly and saying, "Yes, dear." But each one drags after him a huge gunnysack. These people are the "Pseudo-Accommodators," the ones who pretend to go along with the partner's point of view for the sake of momentary peace, but who never really mean it. The gunnysacks are full of grievances, reservations, doubts, secret contempt. Eventually the overloaded sacks burst open, making an awful mess.

The fourth group are "Carom Fighters," a sinister lot. They use noxious attack not directly against the partner but against some person, idea, activity, value, or object which the partner loves or stands for. They are a whiz at spoiling a good mood or wrecking a party, and when they *really* get mad, they can be extremely dangerous. Bach once made a study of one hundred intimate murders and discovered that two-thirds of the killers did not kill their partner, but instead destroyed someone whom the partner loved.

Even more destructive are the "Double Binders," people who set up warm expectations but make no attempt to fulfill them or, worse, deliver a rebuke instead of the promised reward. This nasty technique is known to some psychologists as the "mew phenomenon": "Kitty mews for milk. The mother cat mews back warmly to intimate that kitty should come and get it. But when the kitten nuzzles up for a drink, he gets slashed in the face with a sharp claw instead." In human terms, a wife says, for example, "I have nothing to wear." Her husband says, "Buy yourself a new dress—you deserve it." But when she comes home wearing the prize, he says, "What's that thing supposed to be, a paper bag with sleeves?"—adding, "Boy, do you look fat!"

The most irritating bad fighters, according to Bach, are the "Character Analysts," a pompous lot of stuffed shirts who love to explain to the mate what his or her real, subconscious, or hidden feelings are. This accomplishes nothing except to infuriate the mate by putting him on the defensive for being himself. This style of fighting is common among lawyers, members of the professional classes, and especially, psychotherapists. It is presumptuous, highly alienating, and never in the least useful except in those rare partnerships in which husband and wife are equally addicted to a sick, sick game which Bach calls "Psychoanalytic Archaeology—the earlier, the farther back, the deeper, the better!"

In a far corner of Bach's marital gym are the "Gimmes," overdemanding fighters who specialize in "overloading the system." They always want more; nothing is ever enough. New car, new house, more money, more love, more understanding—no matter what the specific demand, the partner never can satisfy it. It is a bottomless well.

Across from them are found the "Withholders," stingily restraining affection, approval, recognition, material things, privileges—anything which could be provided with reasonable effort or concern and which would give pleasure or make life easier for the partner.

In a dark, scary back corner are the "Underminers," who deliberately arouse or intensify emotional insecurities, reinforce moods of anxiety or depression, try to keep the partner on edge, threaten disaster, or continually harp on something the partner dreads. They may even wish it to happen.

The last group are the "Benedict Arnolds," who not only fail to defend their partners against destructive, dangerous, and unfair situations, forces, people, and attacks but actually encourage such assaults from outsiders.

Husbands and wives who come to Psychologist Bach for help invariably can identify themselves from the categories he lists. If they do not recognize themselves, at least they recognize their mate. Either way, most are desperate to know what can be done. Somewhere, they feel, there must be another, sunnier, marital gym, a vast Olympic Games perhaps, populated with nothing but agile, happy, bobbing, weaving, superbly muscled, and incredibly sportsmanlike gladiators.

There is indeed such a place, says Bach. It is full of people doing things like Expressing Emotional Concern, Giving Full Display to Negative Feelings, and Offering Correctional Critiques of Conduct. As a matter of fact, Bach just happens to run such a place. His main training camp is a penthouse suite on "Couch Canyon," the local nickname for Bedford Drive in Beverly Hills, in whose medical buildings roost more psychiatrists and psychoanalysts per frontage foot than any other place on earth. Here Bach trains married fighters one at a time, in couples, and in group therapy of three or four couples together.

To each client, Bach preaches the same simple code: program your aggressions, so as to avoid tedious wear and tear on children, friends, and other innocent bystanders. In the well-fought fight, combatants are taught a creative style whereby both partners can "win." Their prize is "an increased area of relatedness" because the battlers have learned to recognize what the fight was *really* about. Untrained couples, by contrast, remember only the insults and the low blows, and quickly forget the issues. The reason, says Bach, is that "intimate fighting arouses so much shame and guilt that depression reduces memory almost to nothing."

When properly practiced, the fine art of marital fighting puts each patient on more realistic terms with the jungle beast within himself. Or herself. Tame it, says Bach, train it, program its outbursts, and at times even permit it to yowl its atavistic head off—but don't, for heaven's sake, try to pretend the beast isn't there or that violent disagreements do not exist. Repression can be disastrous; since Freud, it has been the dirtiest word in the analyst's lexicon.

Some of Bach's couples have become so enthusiastic about programmed aggression that they reserve one hour a day exclusively for cocktails and fighting. At 6:30 every evening, they get out the ice, shoo the children upstairs, and open fire. One of Bach's simplest cases involved a happily married couple who grew to enjoy fighting so much that if a really good brawl got going at breakfast, the husband came home for lunch. The only fight training this family needed was a briefing course for their children, the maid, and the dog.

Bach himself is a short, scrappy, convivial husband, but one who admits he dearly loves a good fight. Unhappily, he finds Mrs. Bach is "not naturally a good fighter," and has been giving her private coaching for many years in all phases of his gladiatorial techniques. Such training, Bach believes, has done wonders to enrich their family life. Peggy Bach, a statuesque, serene, and level-headed former Spokane secretary who has been married to the doctor for twenty-three years, says she thinks her husband is absolutely right.

Like Mrs. Bach, most people need coaxing and conditioning to reach peak fighting trim. To help them, Bach has stocked his office with every device he and his colleagues can think of to bring out the beast in man under stress-free circumstances. There are blackboards for chalk talks, outdoor terraces for walk-talks in the Greek mode, small indoor chambers for "pair fighting," and a large arena for group sessions. The rooms are air-conditioned, soundproofed, thickly carpeted, and wired with tape-recording equipment. The furnishings are soft and comfortable, the colors subdued, the lighting gentle. A storage wall is stacked with Monopoly boards, Scrabble sets, playing cards, and other devices for "symbolic fighting." The bookshelves include the complete works of Edward Albee. A record collection is heavily weighted with Wagner.

The big arena has a one-way viewing window to give therapists-in-training a safe, concealed vantage point from which to observe the fray. Inside, the active therapist and his patients sit in special padded swivel chairs which can tip in any direction, and also whiz freely about the room on ball-bearing wheels. In this way, the combatants are encouraged to "indicate non-verbally"—that is, by wheeling—the degree of fury or intimacy they feel toward one another as the tides of battle ebb and flow. There *is* one couch in the place, but it is used chiefly for filing, or for resting between rounds. In one corner is Bach's desk, piled high with manuscripts (he is writing a fight textbook called *The Intimate Enemy*) topped by an ornate paperweight: a bronze eight-armed Hindu goddess in furious battle with herself. She seems to be smiling.

When new students first enter this ornate battleground, Bach explains to them that toe-to-toe confrontation is usually preferable to ducking a fight. "It's a cinch to just walk out," he says.

The walkout need not be physical. Slamming the door, going home to mother, falling asleep to avoid a fight, or applying the "silent treatment" are equally hostile acts. A classic case of this sort involved a man who got so mad at his wife that he refused to say one single word to her for eighteen months. (Bach claims that men employ the "Silent treatment" much more often than women, who are partial to the falling-asleep ploy.) During this entire period, the man lived and worked normally, came home on time, ate a silent dinner, and retired with his wife—who must have been a formidable character herself— to a silent double bed. After intensive family counseling, the husband finally broke his marathon silence. His very first words were "I DON'T WANT TO TALK ABOUT IT!"

The Bach graduate, by contrast, *always* wants to talk about it, and the sooner the better. To start matters rolling, the well-programmed wife merely has to say, "John, I want ten minutes," and her husband will recognize his cue to put on a pot of coffee and get ready to go a fast fifteen rounds.

Merely by agreeing to fight, he has already completed the first round. The next five consist of preliminary verbal sparring. The object at this stage is to define what the fight is about, and how deeply each partner feels about his stake in it. Suppose, for instance, the wife's complaint is the familiar female dirge that her husband is trying to do too many things, and is not spending enough time at home. While he listens to the opening blasts, the husband must calculate how deeply he feels about the area his wife is attacking, how much he can afford to yield without sacrificing principle, and where his mate is vulnerable.

Then it is time really to get down to business. Human nature being as elfin as it is, the next nine rounds cannot be expected to conform to any exact sequence, even between champions. But in any complete fight, key elements should always emerge with the same forceful clarity that two skilled lawyers display in court.

Once the wife has summoned all her eloquence to explain *why* her husband should spend more time at home and less, say, on the golf course, his task is to replay her argument in his own words to make sure he has understood it. Then he goes on to present his counterargument ("Golf is important for business reasons. How are we going to put three kids through college if I don't improve my business contacts?"). Now it's the wife's turn to replay *his* case, to be sure no oranges have rolled in with the apples.

Sweet reason is never at more of a premium than at this moment. The next task is to discover where their two positions conflict (differing definitions of an idyllic home life) and coincide (wanting the best for the kids). If neither party has lost his/her head, each should be able to take the long view and try to see how he/she can help the other. "If you permit me to play golf on Saturday," the well-trained husband might say, "I will promise to take you and the kids to the beach on Sunday."

"In that case, dear," the trained wife might reply, "I'll mend those golf socks you've been nagging me about." The final rounds of a Bach-directed fight really aren't a fight at all. They're an orgy of positive thinking in which the reconciled partners compare the "learning yield" of their dialogue against the "injury felt" at blows inflicted in the heat of battle.

Understandably, Bach does not burden already troubled beginning patients with talk of "rounds" and "learning yield." He is content to simplify the jargon in order to get across the basic principles. The first big trick is to get his fighters to quit hitting below the belt, a talent almost all married couples seem to develop by instinct.

This requires that each partner admit to the other that certain places in his psyche are especially vulnerable. An attack in such a region becomes an act of sheer sadism, says Bach, because "in intimacy, a knowledge of your partner's weak spots would make you feel protective, not sadistic. For example, if Mrs. Bach calls me a 'little, sawed-off, runty Kraut,' *that* is a low blow."

The most important rule of all is: recognize the Yablonsky. This is anger without reason, a spontaneous explosion of free-floating aggression named for a friend of Bach's, the criminologist Dr. Lewis Yablonsky, who described the phenomenon in his book *The Violent Gang.* A Yablonsky is just blowing off steam. When it happens, the trained mate waits for it to subside. Above all, she does not "hook in." If her husband suddenly shouts, "I'm going to take this goddam lawn mower and throw it in the swimming pool!" the trained wife does not say, "You and who else, pip-squeak?" She does not say *anything;* she just takes her chances.

When Bach himself feels a Yablonsky coming on, he knows just what to do. Either he telephones one of his "sparring partners"— usually some fellow therapist on Couch Canyon with whom he is having an academic dispute—and vigorously tells him off. Or he dashes off a furious letter to the mayor, or goes about setting up a symbolic fight—preferably a card game. Touch football, a judo lesson, even an evening spent watching the violence on TV, are other useful means of symbolic fighting. In fact, Bach thinks their symbolic usefulness accounts for their great popularity. The most all-round useful symbolic fight is a game of contract bridge, although when a really high-powered Yablonsky strikes, the doctor recommends pinochle.

To program the aggressions of others, Bach first must get his hands on some of the stuff in its raw state. This is a tricky assignment, because a plump, full-blown aggression combines the strength of an alligator with the skittishness of a dragonfly. The best way to catch it is with a tape recorder. Since the Los Angeles Municipal Fight Center of Bach's dreams is still in the distant future, he must for the present rely for raw material on recorded arguments voluntarily submitted by his patients. Accordingly, Bach's basic prescription for most new students is a tape recorder, to be turned on the instant one feels a good, rousing fight coming on. Later the student brings the specimen to the doctor for analysis.

This instruction may itself provoke a flurry of panic. The most savage of self-righteous fighters turn pale at the thought of committing their emotional outbursts to tape. Excuses abound: the fight might break out anywhere, anytime; must one walk about constantly wired for battle? When the uproar starts, won't they be much too mad to flick a switch?

Nonsense, says the doctor. Blind fury does not exist. "In part of your mind, you always know what's going on." As for where to put the machine, long experience indicates that husbands should stash it under the bed, and that wives should keep it in the kitchen. Bach has not yet got around to analyzing *why* women pick fights in the kitchen. "Probably they feel most psychologically secure there, but it may be because knives are handy. We're not sure."

He *is* sure that marital fighting doubles in tempo and ferocity on weekends, holidays, and vacations. "Instinctively, man is a secretive, suspicious animal. Intimacy makes him very nervous." On holidays and vacations, the threat of intimacy and the consequent exposure of one's true self is much increased.

During his training, the student tapes as many spontaneous fights as possible, learns to analyze his style and to calm his intimacy-jitters. A therapist is helpful at first, especially to referee in "deutero-fights," or the fights-about-fights, which usually occupy much of the student's actual time on Couch Canyon.

When the tapes are replayed in the office, the trainee's initial panic fades. The playback actually becomes a useful trigger, or warm-up, for the clinical fight session to follow. Far from being embarrassed by fighting openly in front of the doctor, couples soon come to welcome his understanding presence. Bach's office makes a safer battleground than the bedroom or the kitchen. "They know things won't get so ugly here," says Bach, "and they are touchingly glad that somebody in the world accepts the reality of their conflict."

After a relatively small number of coaching sessions, the adept and not-too-punchy couple can learn to evaluate and "score" its own fights at home without professional help. However, abrupt changes in environment may cause later flare-ups and require a few postgraduate sessions back on Couch Canyon. The most severe threat to tranquillity is buying a new house; fears of losing the old nest, losing the old neighbors, and gaining new debts are all involved. "But the main reason is that people have unrealistic expectations of what a new house will do for them. Even a new car can throw a couple off balance. And vacations—*lieber Gott!*"

Having become trained gladiators, Bach's alumni can indulge in all sorts of tricky, baroque, "in" fight styles not available to the average married stumblebum. But that is not the end of the matter. It is deflating to learn from Bach that marital fights will continue to be about the same basic subjects. Either they are Incompatible-Image fights ("Why aren't you the way I imagine you to be?" the answer to which is, "Because I am not imaginary"); or they are Equal-Involvement fights ("I care more about [you] [this marriage] [the children] [the dog] [appearances] [spiritual values] [. . . fill in the blank . . .] than you do").

Worst of all is having to face the fact that you can program yourself blue and still the fights are never going to stop. Sure, sure, "nonfighting is *extremely* unhealthy," but no matter how many times the Peter Lorre voice says it, it is difficult to get used to the idea that you are going to tumble into your grave still locked in mortal combat. Furthermore, although you and your beloved assuredly will develop your very own, unique "fight style"—one is tempted to say "erosion pattern"—as the years pass, you will go through the same five general stages of intimacy as everybody else. At each stage, you will have the same kinds of fights. Though not a thing can be done to avoid it, brave readers may wish to know what they are in for.

THE COURTSHIP STAGE. In this preliminary period, both partners "sit on eggs." They indulge in "date talk," which is to say they talk about nothing at all. Sentences all end in question marks because each one is afraid to commit himself or reveal his true feelings for fear he might thereby lose the other. In the jargon of psychology, "the relationship is characterized by extreme fluidity."

THE HONEYMOON. This second period, Bach says, is "psychologically exhausting because the danger of the whole house of cards collapsing is so great." When such a collapse comes, it is violent. She literally walks out; he literally hits her; or both; or even—for that matter —vice versa. In Bach's clinical experience, this *Götterdämmerung* occurs on an average of five months and nine days after the wedding.

As the dust begins to settle, the newlyweds feel stunned, then stuck. "Boy, she sure fooled me!" he rages. "All my dreams are shattered," she sobs. Secretly they both also feel great shame. But soon comes the first big rapprochement, or to use the German term which Bach favors, the *Versöhnung* of the relationship, in which each partner in effect tells the other, "Thank you for the fight. It was terrible while it lasted, but we needed it to clear the air."

In handling this crucial fight, newlyweds make three common mistakes: they refuse to take the fight seriously, they immediately set about fanning the flames again, or worst of all, they *apologize.* Whichever way they choose, nothing is really settled and intimacy is not increased. The best solution is for both sides to grit their teeth and fight it through. In such straits a sense of humor is invaluable.

THE CHILDREN. Offspring are at the center of the Stage Three fights, which can go on for years. The main theme usually involves the equitable distribution of affection within the family; often these battles overlap and intertwine with Stage Four.

THE SEVEN-YEAR ITCH. "This phenomenon is caused by fatigue," says Bach. "The internal satisfactions of the nest are no longer enough. The best solution is for the parents to get back into the main stream of life—hide the children, resume social contacts with old friends, take a trip. Anything that will get you out of the nest for a while."

Finally the children grow up. Now, depending on whether or not the couple has achieved true intimacy or just substituted a phony, zombie-like apathy "for the children's sake," comes the Fifth Stage. It can take two forms.

FREEDOM—OR—THE VOID. The choice is either the most stress-free period of the individual's entire life or a time of hideous rude awakening. Bach is presently treating a Stage Five couple who did not have a single fight for two decades. Why are they consulting a psychotherapist now? Because on the day their only son enrolled at Harvard, literally as they stood on the steps of the Harvard Union watching their boy walk inside, the husband turned to his wife and said, "Well, that's that. So long." Turning on his heel, he then walked down the steps and kept right on going. The woman was dumbfounded. Her husband had said, "Yes, dear" for twenty years; she had no idea he was just filling his gunnysack and biding his time.

But if the preceding stages have gone well, Stage Five will be a period which Bach calls "the golden years of glorious fighting. The couple shows a growing tendency to form a unit against the world, eventually a gradual disengagement from the world, but not from each other."

With his two daughters now in high school and his son in college, Bach himself is experiencing an intense desire to sink his teeth into his own golden years. One of the things he has always looked forward to having in this period is a large dog. He has already begun poring over canine catalogues, comparing the merits of Irish wolfhounds to mastiffs to Great Danes, and so on. Peggy Bach, whose own vision of the golden years does not include hair-strewn furniture and muddy carpets, is not enthusiastic. Lately the incompatible Fido image in the Bach household has touched off some impressive Yablonskys.

Life—May 17, 1963

9

Diary: 1976

When the piece on the Fight Doctor was published, it reeked of commercial promise, and book offers poured in. The year was 1963, and
American marriages were beginning to break up in epic numbers. The Togetherness generation of the fifties was coming apart at the seams, in part
at least because people didn't know how to fight properly. The phenomenon was nationwide, and in parts of Southern California, where I lived,
the divorce rate had by then reached 125 per cent, which means, I think,
that the average citizen had been divorced one-and-one-quarter times.

George Bach and I decided to write the book in collaboration. We
called it The Intimate Enemy. The title was George's. George was great
on titles—it was he who thought up "The Feminine Eye," when Life
said the title of its new column should contain a hint of the author's
gender—but he was timid about trying to write a popular book. Though
he had lived in California for a quarter-century, his mind still worked
in German. I didn't know much about fighting, but my mind worked
well in English, and we struggled together on The Intimate Enemy for
a couple of years. Though ultimately we both found collaboration intolerable—perhaps we didn't fight enough—the experience turned out to
be therapeutic and liberating for each of us. George got over his long-
standing writer's block, and wrote The Intimate Enemy by himself. I
got over my longtime fear of marital fighting, went through some exceedingly painful struggles—nobody but nobody believed in marriage more
than I did—and eventually got a divorce.

So, farewell marriage, R.I.P. A few years later, McCall's beckoned,
and I said farewell to California. When I arrived to take up my new
duties, I came upon a scene of Carthaginian ruin. I discovered I was the
seventh editor to enter that revolving door in a decade, and that the man

who was expected to help me learn the ropes was ex-editor number six. One could scarcely blame him therefore for his signal lack of enthusiasm for this pedagogical assignment. Finally, the most crucial member of the staff—our art director—had just been fired. So all I had to do was learn how to run a magazine, try to rally staff morale, find a new art director, and submit myself to a barrage of publicity about being McCall's *first woman editor. (I hadn't know about that, either.) The publicity buildup was important because my major function at* McCall's, *though I didn't understand it then, was cosmetic; I was intended to serve as a human Band-Aid over a very messy wound. So when the management told me they also expected me to continue writing "The Feminine Eye"—on the side, as it were—I balked. "Just do one column," they said, "to announce your own first issue." This seemed a reasonable request, and besides, there was no way out. I figured either I had to do it, or* McCall's *first woman editor would have to ask how they'd like me to stick a broom up my ass and sweep the floor, so I took the coward's way out and wrote the column. It might have been okay if it had appeared only in* McCall's, *but a few days before we hit the newsstands, our ad boys surprised me again. Without telling me, they had placed the column as a full-page* McCall's *ad on the back page of* The New York Times. *In the* Times, *they abandoned "The Feminine Eye," and the new headline they used was even more excruciatingly coy than the copy itself seemed. "Crochets and glees . . ."* CRIMANENTLY! *I wanted to die, and twenty months later I finally did.*

10

Here I Am.
Hello.
This Is Me.

It is difficult to walk out onstage and introduce yourself. One would prefer a modest flourish of trumpets blown by somebody else. But that is not the way it works in the editing business. In the editing business you have to take a deep breath, walk out there onto the pages of your own magazine, and say: Here I am. Hello. This is me.

Some of you may already know me. For nearly five years, I have been standing on another stage, over at *Life* magazine, writing a column called "The Feminine Eye." We chose that name because at the time it seemed important for readers to know that the writer whose opinions, crotchets, and glees would appear on that page was a woman. Since my mother had neglected to make the matter of my gender immediately obvious—a writer herself, she knew that in naming children, as in the other important choices in life, subtleties of sound and of sentiment come first—the editors of *Life* undertook to rectify Mother's irresponsible vagueness.

It occurs to me now, as I stand here performing my self-introduction, that I owe still another debt of gratitude to *Life*'s editors. Gentlemen, dear friends, ex-colleagues, I thank you all. Without your authoritative establishment of my gender, in print, I might never have come to *McCall's*.

Being a woman has everything to do with my presence here. It is both what pushed me and what pulled me out onto this particular stage, and this page, now. It is why I wanted to come, and surely why I was invited.

For the good fortune of being female, the geneticists tell me, I may thank my father. Thank you, Father. Personally, I have always liked being a woman. But as a lifetime journalist, I lived and worked always in a man's world. I liked that, too. Then came the miraculous advent of "The Feminine Eye," and this returned me to the world of women. It taught me to enjoy the companionship of women, and to appreciate them, study them, and try so hard to express what women themselves really feel, and not what men say we do.

Myself, I have never enjoyed being a woman quite so much as I do right now. Partly I suppose that is due to my own age, to the advent of—awful word—maturity. Forty is so much more fun than twenty. (Thirty is unspeakable.) But mostly I think it is due to *our* age, to the age that we all share, 1970.

I am quite sure that being a woman now, particularly an American woman, is more interesting, challenging, exciting, and rewarding—and more complicated—than it has ever been before. As for being a woman editor, which means talking, and listening, to so vast and varied an audience of other women—well, it's awesome of course, but I like that, too.

That is really why I am here today. Once I was offered this job, I couldn't find good enough reasons to turn it down. I could have said no, but I didn't want to. I wanted to find ways of saying yes. Yes to

McCall's. Yes to women. Yes to the idea that women are important. Yes to the idea that women are thinking, feeling beings different from men, but not less than men, and in many ways today, more interesting than men. Men are much the same as they were a generation or two ago, but women are changing very fast, in ways we cannot yet quite see. Certainly child rearing and the housewifely arts do not interest us one bit less, but the world outside the home interests us more. Women know more, they feel more, they experience more, and they think more than at any other time in history.

I studied anthropology in college, and I have always wondered if there are any innate differences between men and women, beyond those you can see in the mirror or, for that matter, on any movie screen. The one difference I feel sure about is that women are by nature conservative, or rather, conservators. Women like to make things, to make environments; they are natural nest-builders. I think this is why women are so deeply involved in the things that can save this country: conservation, education, politics, the arts. And somehow today I feel that women are more liberated in their minds than men, more idealistic, and often crazily brave.

In many ways, say a thousand or so, I'd rather not appear onstage at all. Ever. My natural habitat is the wings, sitting on a stool, watching the show. Now that I *am* in the editing business, running a magazine instead of buzzing around the world like a female Green Hornet, I can think of a thousand more reasons to remain backstage, as an editor should. Then, in a year or so, if you like what we're doing—because it will take a year at least to do it; magazines are big, slow-moving beasts like whales and elephants, but beautiful and wise and responsive like whales and elephants, too—then, in a year, if you like the show, I might be persuaded to step out for a modest bow.

But a magazine is a very personal thing to both reader and editor. It should seem less like an object, more like a friend. So I would like to hear from you as we go along. And from time to time you are likely to hear from me. But for now I want only to say, Hello, here I am, this is me. And Merry Christmas of course, and heartfelt wishes for peace in the New Year.

McCall's—December 1969

11

Diary: 1976

Twenty months and several days after this tone poem to womanhood was published, McCall's *fired me, or more accurately, they offered my job to someone else without bothering to tell me. It was not a* Godfather *offer. She could have refused it, but she didn't, which taught me something about the difference between Godfathers and Godmothers. But that is for another book.*

For a long while after this happened, I thought I had died. Me: R.I.P. It turned out that what had died was some illusions not worth hanging onto. Farewell, delayed adolescence. The McCall's *experience had made a woman out of me.*

Instead of a requiem this time, I wrote—eventually—a state-by-state guidebook to women's legal rights, a subject of which I was by that time acutely, even painfully, aware, having been married (twice) in New York, divorced in California, and later moved back to New York, with all the attendant problems of custody, credit, property, and so on, not to mention my professionally sleazy but contractually solid and complex relations with The McCall Corporation. The notion to survey the state-by-state variations in women's legal rights seemed obvious enough to me at the time, but it turned out to be a project nobody had ever attempted before, possibly because lawyers—the only people qualified to undertake the task—had more sense than to tackle it. But now it was early 1971, feminism looked like a good bet to base a book on, even a book of statistical research, and so the Dreyfus Fund came up with the necessary seed money to put a battery of law students to work in the law libraries. My own contribution to the book was to conceive the idea, to divide the law into the nine areas that interest women most, and then to rewrite the legal information collected by our researchers in these nine areas into reasonable, comprehensible English. It seemed to me that the occasions in her life when a woman might need or want to know the law were when she reached legal age, when she got married, when she had children, or adopted a child, when she wanted an abortion, when she wanted a divorce or annulment, when she was raped, when she was widowed, when she went to work, and when she committed a crime. These topics became the book's chapter-headings. It came as a shock to realize that, of the nine ways a woman might encounter the law, I had experienced seven. Widowhood and prosecution for a major crime are life-experiences that still lie ahead.

By the middle of the twentieth century, American society, and particularly the role(s) of women in that society, had begun changing with frightening speed. The widespread geographical movement of people to suburbia, and away from city or farm, plus the breakup of the extended-family pattern of living into smaller, more mobile "nuclear family" units, was devastating to established ways of raising children. Whole groups of people, particularly a child's cousins and older relatives, disappeared from his view. The disappearance so impoverished his spirit that Margaret Mead suggested putting grandmothers in trailers and towing them around the country from grandchild to grandchild so the kids growing up grandmotherless in nuclear suburbia could at least see what one looked like. When my legal rights book was finally finished, I dedicated it to my own dearly remembered grandmothers, and put mini-portraits of each one into the book's introduction.

12

Requiem for Grandmothers

I was named after my great-grandmother, or, rather, two of them. Each one was named Shana; each was a peasant woman and knew her place: obey her husband, bear children, keep house, keep quiet.

My two grandmothers also shared the same name: Fanny. Both Fannys were baby girls when they left the old country, but in the new land each Fanny still knew her place. Each dutifully became the near child-bride of an older man, kept house, bore children, et cetera. If you had asked either Fanny what she believed her legal rights were, she wouldn't have known what you were talking about. A woman didn't have rights, she had duties; she was expected—and she *expected herself* —to be dutiful daughter, dutiful wife and mother.

A critical difference between the Shanas and the Fannys was that the Fannys could read and write. They read the same things, the Bible and the newspaper, and wrote the same things, letters and lists. Their letters were full of gossip, foreboding, sorrow, and loss. The lists on the other hand were sunbursts of organized optimism: favorite delicacies, winning numbers, happy birthdays, hat and glove sizes of children and grandchildren.

I remember one Fanny small and one stout, one with blue-gray eyes and one with amazing violet, and both smelling wonderfully of baby powder—or could that perhaps have been *me?* Anyway, in my childish memory, my grandmothers are very clear. The Fanny in Chicago is at her kitchen table, chopping herring and singing to her canary; the Hollywood Fanny has just announced an expedition to Grauman's Chinese Theater. "Look up!" she directs us, ages four and seven, tapping the newspaper neatly folded back to the movie page. "Look up!" She is so proud that already we can read and write, and even tell

time from the wonderful upside-down crystal ball watch suspended on
the shelf of her bosom by a black silken cord.

The son and daughter of the two Fannys—that is, my own mother
and father—became professional writers, one a composer, the other a
critic. My sister, Laurel Bentley, is a special kind of technical writer,
and *her* eleven-year-old daughter, Soft-Hearted Hannah, named in wry
salute to one of my father's songs, writes and publishes her own
monthly magazine, *Kid's Lib.* My daughter Kathy is a poet and math-
ematician. What a tribe of scribblers!

From *Shana Alexander's State-by-State Guide
to Women's Legal Rights*, 1975

13

Diary: 1976

*"Spectrum," on CBS radio, and sometimes TV, for which the following
two pieces were written, is intended to be just that: a balanced cross
section of opinion on topics of the day. I have always suspected that it
also was conceived by the network's news department at least in part to
refute Spiro Agnew's charges that newsrooms are hotbeds of liberalism.
For me, the show was a delightful opportunity to let off short puffs of
very personal steam. More importantly, "Spectrum" gave me a whole
new voice. On it I was not only a talking woman. I was a woman who
talked out loud. The show gave me confidence in my own voice. Show
business began to seem appealing, not terrifying. I felt warmed instead
of chilled by the spotlight. Inside the middle-aged introvert, a happy little
extrovert had begun signaling wildly for attention. And getting it, too.*

14

The King Is Dead

The obituaries are rolling. The cortege is gathering. The blackbirds are crying: the Duke of Windsor has died.

Not for him the ancient words: "The King Is Dead; Long Live the King." For this Windsor is truly dead and gone. For him a more modest ceremony is planned. Not a statement of guns, but a stammer. He gave up much. The last thing he gave up was his funeral. Had he been King, all the bells of England would have been breaking their sides today.

Dead and gone, too, is the special kind of romance which endured so long in the slender, brittle figures of him and his American Dutchess. The royal couple, in love and in exile—condemned to live out both beyond any normal boundaries—seem not so much dead as extinct. As rare as the whooping crane, as preposterous as the dodo bird, the breed is finished now, wiped out, over.

It is impossible to imagine their frail clockwork likes again. No loving couple of this age—no amorous politician, nor pulsating rock star, however glittering—can ever again incarnate such prim and tidy fantasies of high romance. I myself was about ten years old, and heard his famous words of abdication literally at my mother's knee, both of us sniffling, beside the family Philco: ". . . without the help, and support, of the woman I love." It was probably the first honest-to-God English voice I'd ever heard, let alone a royal one, and like the rest of America, I was profoundly stirred by his halting affirmation of "the woman I love."

Looking back, it seems to me that the whole situation of royalty condemned—for love—to perpetual exile was a ten-year-old's conception of romance; destined to remain always a ten-year-old's disembodied love story, while the bodies themselves aged gently, imperceptibly, finely, until the twin figures became covered with a near-invisible network of cracks, like old porcelain.

Why was it, really, that he was discarded like a set of old plates? The secret history of the abdication is yet to be written—perhaps because, English-style, it was never even spoken aloud.

In any event, on this side of the water, the entire affair can only make sense as romance. As history, it was outrageous; medieval in its cruelty; and ultimately, to Americans, a story not so much unacceptable as it is beyond all human comprehension.

CBS "Spectrum"—June 1, 1972

15

Fashions in Funerals

A man in the remote jungles of New Guinea not long ago murdered another man with an ax. Tribal justice ensued. First the murderer was shot and killed with an arrow, and then seven other members of the tribe cut him up and ate him.

When word of the feast reached civilization, the authorities concluded that on this occasion justice had literally been served, and perhaps a bit too swiftly, so they hauled the seven cannibals into court, where a wise Australian judge dismissed all the charges, and acquitted the seven men. "The funerary customs of the people of Papua and New Guinea," he explained, "have been, and in many cases remain, bizarre in the extreme."

What, I wonder, would the judge have to say about the new, high-rise mausoleum now under construction in Nashville, Tennessee? When completed, this model of modern funerary design will be twenty stories high, fully air-conditioned, and capable of holding 65,000 bodies. A second slightly less deluxe tower on an adjoining site will have facilities to entomb 63,500 more. Nashville's enterprising mortician-entrepreneur points out that his high-rise mortuary will be self-contained on only 14 acres, whereas it would require 129 acres to contain all these caskets in the, uh, conventional manner.

Well, not exactly caskets. In the new-style funeral, you will be laid out—after embalming, of course—on something called a "repose," described as "a bedlike structure," complete with white sheets, pillow, and blanket. When the ceremonies are ended, bed, pillow, sheet, and blanket are all whisked away; a fiberglass lid snaps down over what remains; and—zap—it's into the wall, stacked seven-high, with a neat bronze marker attached to the face of the crypt.

The forward-looking undertaker who thought all this up is already respected, in the trade, for bringing to Nashville the one-stop funeral.

But the most important advantage of the high-rise mausoleum is that by putting everything-but-everything under one roof you cut down on the high cost of dying. Maybe so, maybe so. But I can't help thinking it would be even cheaper to die in New Guinea, where the funerary customs are certainly no less bizarre, and a lot more practical.

CBS "Spectrum"—August 18, 1971

16

Diary: 1976

Occasionally an interviewer has an uncanny experience of intense recognition, as if one were meeting an old friend for the first time; as if the subject were not a stranger but oneself somehow reflected back in the mirror of an entirely other persona. These encounters are mystical, somewhat frightening, indescribable moments of heightened emotion. It may be that one arrives at the interview in an already-heightened emotional state which one then projects onto the unsuspecting subject. I don't know. Like love at first sight, the thing cannot be explained rationally. I can recall having had the experience perhaps half a dozen times in thirty years, and the only thing the encounters seem to have in common is that each time I have lost my notebook. And I never lose notebooks. It happened to me once in a Negro Baptist church in Selma, Alabama; once when I met a city—Rome; once when I met the actress, Liv Ullmann. The last time it happened, the person I "met" was invisible: Patty Hearst. A few weeks after she was kidnapped, I thought I recognized in the vacuum created by her disappearance, and in the whole cyclone of action and emotion that bizarre event stirred up, a mirror or metaphor for America in the mid-seventies. At any rate, here is Liv, followed by a couple of glimpses of Patty which were sketches for a larger work now in progress.

17

Beyond the Doll's House: Liv Ullmann

"Sometimes it is less hard to wake up feeling lonely when you are alone than wake up feeling lonely when you are with someone."

The words struck me as so true that the next time I woke up feeling lonely I took off impulsively after their author, the Norwegian actress Liv Ullmann, who turned out to be in Philadelphia rehearsing for her first American stage appearance, as Nora in Ibsen's *A Doll's House.* On the train down, I knew I was on my way to making the old Easter Bunny mistake all over again, the Easter Bunny being any great actress, writer, statesman, first baseman—anybody one admires from afar. The mistake is to get too close. Addled by one's own adulation, one is drawn inexorably nearer, moth to flame, until it becomes impossible not to see that the Bunny is only a cardboard rabbit. My last Easter Bunny had been a Great Writer in London, insanely admired until found to be merely mortal. Miss Ullmann, on the other hand, turned out to be transcendentally mortal, and so luminously herself—yet in certain ways so much like myself—that I babbled away our hour talking about me, not her.

One occupational hazard of being a professional interviewer is that you tend to fill up, up to *here* at times, with the emotional rainfall of other people's feelings. Lacking a dependable bartender, priest, or spouse on whom to spill it out again, you are in trouble, and possibly I was in that kind of trouble the day I met Liv. Our conversation felt halting and awkward, and I still cannot tell you very much about her. But she could, if she cared, tell you a great deal about me.

Liv was troubled that day, too. In addition to the normal anxieties of any theatrical tryout, she was, and is, made uncomfortable by her unique and lonely position in the theatrical firmament. For Miss Ull-mann is not just the best movie actress around these days, she is almost the only one. Streisand, Fonda, et al. are character actresses beside her, angular and mod. She is also the only stage actress, or actor, around just now who could sell out every seat in advance for a six-week run. One paradox of Liv is that she is an entirely contemporary woman who satisfies everybody's nostalgic craving for an old-fashioned girl. Her quality is warm, clean, clear, friendly, and blooming. There is nobody else like her. Women and men flock equally around her. Homosexuals write to say that the progression of *Scenes From a Marriage* describes their relationships. Everybody wants to enlist behind her banner. She is a modern Maid of Orleans who cannot quite hear her own voices.

Meaning something special to everybody, she is not sure what she means to herself. She is full of doubts, guilts, and tremblings, certain only of one thing: the importance of truth, openness, and vulnerability, of living in the moment. Like other great natural actors, she continually suspects that everybody else is acting—not acting onstage, but faking it in real life. Of Nora and her husband in Ibsen's 1879 play she says, "Both are guilty. Both are vulnerable. Both are victims. But they don't know *where* they are hurting the other, because they're never asking: who *is* the other one? Really they're speaking to someone who doesn't exist. Somebody whom they have made up."

Dear Abby, have you ever heard a better description of modern marriage?

What happened to Nora after she walked out the door? "I don't think it's important. Whether she became a whore or a politician or whatever, it makes no difference. Because the important step was going out. When you do such a thing, you never go back the same, not even if you go back the next day."

Well, then, how far have women come since Nora's day? "In some ways I think they have gone a step back. Because in those days I think to try to get your freedom was such a big step that when you reached for it, it was something *you* had to do. Today we sit down and wait for it. We are very spoiled."

Liv does not like people who sit down. Liv is very stern, open but naive, childlike but full of folk wisdom. Onstage she is as appealing and together as a bunch of violets. Her performance is all virtuosity, control, disciplined art. So one is not prepared for the disarming, wide-eyed creature one meets back at the hotel. Milkmaid-pretty, and milkmaid-sturdy, too, she is a country girl who believes in discipline, hard work, self-reliance, and self-denial.

Although she was once married to a psychiatrist, she does not much believe in his science. "I think we *need* our troubles, and we are the better for them," she says. "The important thing is not to arrive, but to be on your way."

Troubles Liv Ullmann has surely had. When she was six, her father died walking into an airplane propeller. When she was twenty-five, she met Ingmar Bergman, the great Swedish director, who was forty-six. To her "he was God." Liv became his biggest star, his mistress, and eventually the mother of his child. In puritanical Norway, the scandal was great, and eventually Liv, yes Liv, had to offer an explanation on national television. Some time after, Bergman married another woman. Now their daughter is eight, and Liv and Bergman remain professional colleagues. Although *Scenes From a Marriage* is in no sense autobiographical, aspects of it reflect stages in their own long relationship. "We have sort of found an understanding which we never speak about any more," Liv laughs. "Because that might ruin it. And I think we both have the same needs. This way he can use me. And I can use him *because* he is using me, and that makes me able to do what I want to do. . . ." Surely nobody understands the endlessly circling, Ping-Pong nature of human relationships better than Liv Ullmann.

A perhaps inevitable side effect of women's liberation is that true female heroines have vanished from the American scene. Patty Hearst and Bella Abzug are not much to cling to. Hardly a cardboard rabbit, Miss Ullmann seems to have arrived just in time to reincarnate everybody's faith in womanhood.

In the play, when Nora's husband says, "No one would sacrifice honor for the sake of love," and Nora replies, "Millions of women have," Liv's audience buzzes like a million angry bees.

A Doll's House is ninety-six years old. What does "honor" mean now? Liv thinks that for many men and women today, "your profession is your honor." During rehearsals, she had asked her co-star (Sam Waterston) if he would give *his* profession away to follow some woman to an island, if necessary. He told Liv he couldn't do that. "Then I asked myself, could I follow a man? And I said yes, I could: many women could. Because we have some fantasy, or maybe real feeling, that love *is* more important."

"And do you think that is because we put too low a value on what we do?"

Blue eyes blazed in a milk-white face. "No. I think we have a high value on what we *are*."

Newsweek—February 17, 1975

18

The Girl in the Box: Patricia Hearst

Every few days the headlines scream NEW HEARST CLUE!, the latest being a green notebook. I found my own best clue to the puzzle in my hotel-room drawer, courtesy of the Gideons, the day I arrived in San Francisco. It was right there in Genesis: the story of how a vengeful God punished his people for their arrogance by making them unable to understand each other.

What first grabbed my ear in the Patty Hearst story was the sharp realization that each figure in the drama was speaking an entirely different language, and nobody seemed able to understand what anybody else was saying. Patty talked revolution, Daddy talked moderation, Mommy talked religion. The SLA said, "I am that nigger . . ." Steven Weed said, "I think Patty still loves me." The Attorney General said Patty was a common criminal. And after weeks of holding back, the FBI finally seemed to be saying—to one another, if not aloud— "Go get her, dead or alive."

Not only was everyone speaking his own tongue. Everyone was being held prisoner by someone else: Patty by the SLA, the SLA by the media on whom it depends for the oxygen of publicity; the media by the SLA which brilliantly manipulates the press for its own propaganda purposes; the FBI by the feelings of the Hearsts; and—most touching of all—the Hearsts by their feelings for their willful, flipped-out, or coerced daughter.

From the beginning, the public agonies of the senior Hearsts, masked and zombie-like in grief, have been heartbreaking to watch. Night after night, they appear at regular intervals like Dresden clock figures in the doorway of the mansion whose orchid-banked steps look more like a thirties stage set than a platform for a bizarre family tragedy.

All the actors in the drama—police, press, left-wing advisers, government officials, and the Hearsts—seem to be prisoners of their own backgrounds, captives of their own viewpoints. Rigid-eyed, blinkered, they stare straight ahead, unable to see events from any angle other than their own, like a carved procession on an ancient tomb.

Watching at our TV sets, we in the national audience have become captives of the spectacle, too. The situation at the moment reminds me of the old-time illusionist's trick in which the magician constructs before our eyes a sturdy, star-spangled box, and motions his saucy little assistant to hop inside. Bang goes the lid, and the conjurer thrusts a dozen or two flashing silver swords one by one every which way through the box.

Patty Hearst is the girl in the box, and the intersecting swords are all the divisions that for a decade have been ripping our world apart: youth against age, black against white, left against right, rich against poor. Political terror, economic anarchy, and sexual revolution are in the box, too. Or should that read sexual anarchy, economic terror, and political revolution? After a while, you can link up the words like the swords in any random pattern and it scarcely matters. The point is that whatever is inside the box—world, girl, or American way of life— appears certain to be sliced to bits.

Just now the magician has thrown a cloth over the box; he would divert us with a display of snake charming. A trill of fancy flutework, and a seven-headed cobra rises out of its basket across the stage.

They are well-named, this Symbionese Liberation Army. Undeniably an *army*, deadly and brainless as its cobra symbol; *liberated* from every civilized restraint; and *symbiotic* as all get-out. Symbiosis means the mutual interdependence of two unlike organisms. Shark and pilot fish are frequently offered examples. Interdependent within the SLA is a weirdo mix of ex-cons, rip-off artists, Vietnam veterans, and white radical women. John Bryan, a gifted San Francisco writer, calls it "the most fantastic goulash imaginable of politics and psychology, old and New Left rhetoric, Afro-American nationalism, Bezerkeley future-vision and current time-warp, Sixties Movement frustration and hopes for regeneration, oodles of sophomoric romanticism—the most stoned-out South Campus doper's hallucinatory mix of Marxism, mythology, street shuck and jive. . . ."

But the SLA is more. At its core is the mutual tension-attraction between educated young women with class and sexual guilts still to be shed, and lives still to be lived, and stir-wise escaped convicts with nothing to lose.

When women struggle to liberate themselves, what is liberated first is sometimes female rage. When this flood, so long repressed, reverses and turns out, the torrent is deep and deadly. It rushes through San Francisco and Berkeley today.

Enraged at the world, awash in free-floating empathy for the down-trodden, such people step out the door each day with an empty leash, looking for underdogs. In the cruel, teeming California jails, they found them by the hundreds, even thousands. What matter that the violent psychopath Donald DeFreeze was no Cleaver or George Jackson? The so-long-empty leash had been filled at last.

Perhaps when she was kidnapped Patty already carried such a leash —I myself once did—or perhaps she found one in the SLA. It may be that female rage mixed with long-caged black male aggression just make an explosive cocktail. In the enforced closeness of a colony of self-styled outlaw "revolutionaries," hiding out in the middle of a big city, dependent for their lives on total mutual loyalty, that cocktail must produce a fantastic emotional "high." It is not difficult for me to imagine that, captive in and embraced by this truly symbiotic human stew, Patty Hearst may have thought she felt a greater human warmth and closeness than she had ever known.

But to see the SLA as political revolutionaries is a fool's illusion. They are a tiny terrorist band, a marauding wolf pack who, by capturing the media, have become squatters in our imaginations, black-clad figures of nightmare encamped in the back of all our minds. Could these gun-toting Barbie dolls be *our* children, we wonder. You bet. If this could happen to a family of upper-class Waltons like the Hearsts, it could happen anywhere. Every family today has its own Patty Hearst

—girl or boy—dropped out, tripped out, or thrown out, but gone and missed nonetheless.

Until the final cloth is whisked away, the Hearst case will doubtless continue to mean all things to all men, and women. Its final meaning, unlike Rosebud in *Citizen Kane,* may turn out to be nothing at all. Gertrude Stein once said of Oakland, "There's no *there* there," and the same in its own way may be true now. Perhaps one can say only that while the story lives, Patty and the SLA live. When it ends, and no matter which way it ends, the illusion will die, too, and some small parts of ourselves as well.

After that—I am sure—historians, novelists, playwrights, and other amateur archeologists like myself will sift the ashes of the event, and the dry, shuffling sounds of old newspapers and scratchy replayings of the tapes will testify to our efforts to understand the languages of our times.

Newsweek—April 29, 1974

19

Diary: 1976

The Newsweek *piece about Patty Hearst produced an unprecedented outpouring of fan mail. Letters arrived from such distant spirits as John Wayne, writing from Hollywood, and Dr. Timothy Leary, writing from prison. (Leary's first letter came from Vacaville, seedbed of the SLA. Later, he was transferred to the same federal prison to which Patty was sentenced by Judge Carter on the first day of Holy Week, 1976. Mutatis mutandis.) The piece also produced a determination in me to expand and amplify these themes into the book on which I am now at work. Its title, at least for now, is* American Pie, *and an excerpt from an early draft of it appeared in* Life's *special 1975–1976 year-end issue, under the title, "Images Of Patty." It is the last-written piece in the present volume.*

20

Two Letters

Dear Miss Alexander:

I have never been quite sure why I subscribed to *Newsweek*. After reading your article "The Girl in the Box," I have the answer. The article is logic couched in excellent English.

Sincerely,

John Wayne

Dear Shana Alexander . . .

This is a strong signal of congratulations to you for your April 29th essay on "The Girl in the Box."

For two months I've been watching and listening to everyone's pronouncements on the Great Scandal with exactly the perspective and with the same reaction you present in your column.

Scanning the media these days one is left with the uneasy feeling that some sort of neurological pollution has occurred—which prevents everyone from speaking simple common sense or revealing the obvious. It is a great pleasure to read your essays. You seem to be the only journalist able to look at events with detachment, to listen to all the points of view and to describe the interaction of insanities with a patient and saving humor. It's a good time to be a woman.

It is nice to report that there are some signs of intelligent life on the planet.

The fact that I agree with you is no big thing, of course. Except that part of my education has recently placed me in positions very similar to those you describe in "The Girl in the Box." Including being kidnaped-arrested, brain-washed (?) and put on parole by Eldridge in Algeria. Escaping from same. Etc.

It's illuminating to be in contact with a star. Shine on.

(signed) Timothy Leary

21

Images of Patty

Once I looked directly into a beating human heart. The man was undergoing open-heart surgery, and I was above him in the surgical amphitheater, taking notes. In over a quarter-century, I have strained to see into hundreds of hearts, and I remember many images. Judy Garland backstage pumping up her ego by shouting obscenities in rhythm with the overture . . . "Clang, clang, clang!" . . . before sailing out onstage to face her own music. A rabbi intoning the Kaddish from the pulpit of a Negro Baptist church in Alabama while Dr. Martin Luther King joined hands with a Greek prelate and a Quaker woman and a Catholic priest to sing "We Shall Overcome." One afternoon in a Vietnam jungle an Army doctor yanked me through the green tent-flap of a field hospital. Six very large and hard-muscled young men, three black, three white, lay unconscious and naked save for gauze, blood, and a medical jungle of plastic tube. These images were real.

The paradox of reality is that no image is as compelling as the one which exists only in the mind's eye. The paradox of Patricia Hearst is that no one noticed her before she was kidnapped. She was made visible by her disappearance. When she was dragged off half-naked and screaming, she started a media hurricane. She was the stillness at its center, and into its vortex were drawn all our fears and fantasies. She was not in herself interesting. Her power was in her absence. She was the thumb in America's eye.

The abduction of Patricia Hearst pushed America's every emotional button, touched every sore point. *Hernap*, FBI teletype code for the case, somehow managed to defile all our sacred symbols at once: family, property, purity, and flag. It raked up the fears of parent and child, of rich and poor, of men and women, blacks and whites, haves and have-nots, young and old. To look at length and in depth into the Hearst kidnapping could be a way to look into the beating heart of America itself.

Patty Hearst seemed to be the classic tabloid heroine: a kidnapped heiress—young, helpless, innocent. And she starred in the quintessential tabloid melodrama: bizarre, violent, and capable of arousing America's deepest racial and sexual dreads. That the central mom and pop were grief-stricken millionaires did not put the usual distance between the rich and the rest of us; it just made the story better. Randolph and Catherine Hearst became our newest reflection of the American family. Bewildered and sad, appearing night after night on TV, their zombie faces masked in grief, the Hearsts offered the nation an image as stoic as Grant Wood's gaunt couple in "American Gothic." In this suffering pair, and later in the faces of the other bereaved SLA parents, we saw with our own eyes that money buys grief as well as happiness.

But Patty herself broke the classic tabloid rules, ripped up her grandfather's old Hearst formula, and hyped the big story higher still. A swift twist of the kaleidoscope, and instead of an abducted maiden, a gun-toting girl guerilla appeared in the fractured lens.

More swift shocks followed the bank heist. There was the Los Angeles shoot-out and holocaust, finally the long underground flight in the wilderness. Months passed. Through it all we knew next to nothing about the real Patty. We had nothing to go on except the barest sprinkling of biographical facts, a few photographic images, and our own imaginations. Three photographs were repeated over and over. The first image smiles: a conventional debutante, white-throated, dreamily anticipates life. The second image—the bank film—moves: jerkily, as in an 1890's movie, a slim black-haired girl in a pea jacket skitters sideways across the bank floor, gripping an automatic rifle. The third image burns: before the SLA's crimson banner—a seven-headed cobra rampant on a field of blood—stands Tania, girl guerilla, armed for combat. These three pictures became as if tattooed on the inside of everybody's eyelids. Soon America could see Patty Hearst with its eyes closed.

The story of Patricia Hearst recalled the oldest figures of myth: the beautiful maiden, the Sleeping Beauty, the sorrowful king and queen, the magic spell, the coiling dragon, the black goat-god, the wicked sorcerer, the heroic outlaw, the stolen child. No matter that Patty's mythological beast was a seven-headed cobra, no matter that her sorcerer may have brainwashed her. As Tania, she became the newest symbol of rebellious youth. She stood for all of today's uncommitted and overprotected young, the generation deprived of nothing except denial. Longing for action, empty of values, unseasoned by human experience, such people often become passionate injustice-collectors, the sort of zealots who charge out the front door each morning with an empty leash, looking for underdogs.

Untainted by reality, Patty's image could have lasted forever. But suddenly, after nineteen months and eighteen days came the stunning news: Patricia Hearst captured alive and unharmed. The nation's invisible icon had become real. It was time to open one's eyes.

On September 19, the day after she was caught, Patty appeared in court to ask for bail. She appeared in court again in November, when the judge ruled she was competent to stand trial. She will be in court again January 26, when trial begins. Until that day, Patty will remain as invisible to the public as the lawyers for both sides, and the family, can possibly manage. The public may be eager to get to know the real girl, but attorneys preparing a delicate and difficult defense are quite naturally determined to shield her from public scrutiny until the controlled drama of the trial begins. Patty's own true wishes and feelings are unknown, and likely to remain so for some time. We must still judge by appearance, but at least it is the corporeal Patty we now see in tantalizing glimpses.

At the September bail hearing, three new and different images of Patty were added to the old collection. There was also the new astonishment of scale. As an invisible girl, Patty/Tania had loomed larger than life. The gun in Tania's hands further increased her stature, so that it was a shock to discover that the real person is doll-size, slim and barely five feet tall. I saw her first from the back, facing the judge, one tiny hand hooked in her jeans. Standing before the high bench, she looked slouching and tough, a transvestite Dead End Kid in lilac tee shirt and dyed red hair. The only way I could see her at all in the packed courtroom was to rise on tiptoe for a quick peek. Other spectators did the same, and throughout these tense proceedings the surface of our dense human throng rose and fell like a pot of bubbling oatmeal. The second peek revealed Patty in profile seated at the defense table. From the side, she looked like an entirely different girl. She was dainty, porcelain pink, and matronly-soft. Newspaper photographs taken through the police car window outside the courthouse had shown us still another girl. That one was a lantern-jawed, leering, loony-looking creature with mouth open, fist raised. So who is Patty/Tania? Who is this skinny girl who looks plump? This kid who looks old? This debutante stoned-out doper in dirty rubber sandals, chewing gum, grinning idiotically at the cameras, clenched fist held high? Patty's reappearance did not answer these questions. It only raised more. Would Judge Carter let her out on bail? No, he would not. "I don't have a tough view on bail, but in this case we have a person who has announced to the world her intention to have a revolution against our system. I presume she means it." Pregnant pause. Judge looks over the top of his spectacles. "She said it loud and clear . . . and she said it punctuated by gunfire."

Would the public buy her first lawyers' incredibly lurid story of how Patty was drugged, tortured, brainwashed? No, they would not. A jury might not buy it either. Instead Randolph Hearst bought his daughter a new lawyer. Enter F. Lee Bailey, gravely shaking his great, brachycephalic bison's head. The casting was perfect. Bailey is the boldest, the Douglas Fairbanks of defenders. Beyond skill and swashbuckle, Bailey brings commitment, passion, himself.

By the time I returned to San Francisco for the sanity ruling six and a half weeks after the arrest, a lot had happened in the world. Sara Jane Moore tried to shoot the President, Hirohito visited America, Ali beat Frazier, New York City's troubles grew worse, Andrei Sahkarov won the Nobel Peace Prize, George Wallace toured Europe, Generalissimo Franco lay on his deathbed, the eighth Democrat announced his candidacy for President, Lebanon erupted into full-scale civil war, the President fired his CIA chief and reshuffled his high command, Rockefeller made his own move on the political chessboard, the United Nations voted that Zionism equals racism, one-third million Moroccans began walking into the Sahara Desert, a New Jersey judge ruled that an anguished family could not unplug their vegetabilized daughter, and civil war broke out in Angola.

All this time, Patty Hearst had languished in the San Mateo County Jail, crocheting, chain-smoking, talking to her lawyers, and having either long and cordial or curt and painful visits with her family, depending on whose papers you read. Details of her jail existence were exceedingly sparse. Security was tight. Patty had talked to no members of the press except, of course, those members of the press to whom she is related by blood. Their reactions are not known. Her normally gregarious father has ceased giving interviews. Her mother has labeled all the press "ghouls," an opinion not at this point difficult to understand.

Patty has seen a few old friends, but not her one-time fiancé, Steve Weed. By mutual agreement, that difficult confrontation will be delayed until the trial in order to spare the defendant any unnecessary emotional stress. All her visitors except the lawyers are separated from Patty by inch-thick bulletproof glass, and converse with her by telephone. "If she wanted to feel the warmth of a human cheek, she could not," Bailey observes with a choke in his voice. Nonetheless, he believes that alone at last in her tiny cell "Patty at this point is happier than she has been in a long time."

Lawyers' visits are conducted face-to-face, and knee-to-knee, in a small, airless room which co-counsel Al Johnson calls "the iron telephone booth." Johnson is Bailey's sidekick, a soulful ex-Marine with choirboy's eyes and con man's heart. Aside from inmates and guards, Patty's measure of the world *is* Al Johnson. He visits her daily, and has spent literally hundreds of hours in the iron phone booth establishing the delicate rapport and trust which must exist before trial begins. Johnson says Patty fills her days eating, reading (mostly feminist works), sleeping, washing and setting her hair. She is also knitting him a ski mask. That she can joke about the ski mask is taken by her lawyers as a sign of returning mental health. Johnson's language these days is sprinkled with psychiatric jargon. "When I first met her," he says, "she was just a cipher. Just sitting there. Very apprehensive, with an affect as flat as the Charles River. Not interested in the trouble she was in, the trial she was facing, the people who were vying for her attention. We think she is now transitioning rather nicely."

Patty has also spent hundreds of hours with the court-appointed psychiatrists, often when the questioning got too tough running out of the room in tears. The doctors' reports are under court seal; only a few details have leaked out. The prisoner was forcibly kidnapped, spent her first nine weeks in close confinement, and was subjected to crude but effective brainwashing techniques. She was kept in a small closet, was permitted only a pail for hygienic purposes, and sometimes not even that. She was told over and over: "We'll kill you. As soon as you serve your purpose, you will die. We are right and the world is wrong." In short, she was isolated, humiliated, and terrorized. Her lawyers believe that every one of her taped messages, including her decision to "stay and fight," her denunciation of "the pig Hearsts," her confessed bank robbery, her denial that she was brainwashed, and the tender eulogies for the comrades who died in Los Angeles, was written out in advance. She was always reading from a script prepared by the SLA.

The defense intends to demonstrate that Patty's participation in the Hibernia Bank robbery was no more her own doing than the prepared script. They will maintain that the "evidence" of the bank film proves this. They will discount the eyewitness reports of bystanders, and the tape-recorded boasting afterwards.

From the moment he came on the case, Bailey has maintained his client was so traumatized by the brutal circumstances of her captivity that she was not only unable to stand trial, she was unable to cooperate with her lawyers in the preparation of her own defense. "I've got to have something more than a piece of meat to defend," he told the judge in November.

"Is it amnesia, or a reluctance to talk, or what?" I asked.

"I think it's a reluctance which is subconscious, meaning not deliberate," Bailey replied. "It's like a girl trying to tell over and over again how she was raped. By her father when she was nine. You'd call that amnesia, because she may not want to talk about it, and her lawyer says: you must. But it's just a terribly painful thing to do."

One of Bailey's thorniest problems will be to separate Patty in the jury's mind, and possibly in her own mind, from her former comrades Bill and Emily Harris. The Harrises now await trial in Los Angeles on a variety of charges including kidnapping and armed robbery. Patricia Hearst is a codefendant. Bailey hopes that these and other charges against Patty will be dropped if he can convince a San Francisco jury that his client was so thoroughly brainwashed while she was with the SLA that they were able to persuade her to rob banks.

It is difficult to imagine a plausible future for Patty, no matter what the jury decides. She cannot go home again, nor return to the life she had before she was kidnapped. According to Bailey, she has no wish to be a revolutionary. Lawyers on both sides have suggested numerous alternatives: going underground, changing her name and life-style, altering her face by plastic surgery, or living in the Caribbean as a "protected" government witness, in return for cooperating with the authorities against the Harrises and others. None of these choices seems plausible for the twenty-one-year-old heiress; or even if she must go to jail for some years first, for a thirty-one-year-old heiress.

Says Bailey, "I can only give you two futures, examples of two people I've seen go through this kind of very high-intensity, nationwide, controversial experience. Captain Ernie Medina got back into society. Dr. Sam Sheppard wound up in a grave."

Public opinion on Patty has soured. Death threats pour in. The sheriff beefs up security. He wants no "Jack Ruby incident" in his well-tended jail. Says Bailey, "People don't accept that Patty is a very serious and pathetic victim of a very violent gang."

Bailey's job is to create that climate of acceptance, to make the Dresden-pink Patty image prevail over the loony Tania image, and over the defiant Dead End Kid image in the public mind. Patty's fate will depend on which one of these images the jury ultimately accepts as the real Patty. Though the Dresden-pink victim image is obviously more desirable, Bailey is not especially bothered by the stoned-out loony picture. "If I'm gonna defend her on brainwashing, I don't need to have her looking sane."

Although a certain segment of the public still perceives Patty as a willful adventuress of no deep political conviction who has caused a great many people including her parents untold pain and suffering, Bailey has been waging a strong campaign in the press and on TV talk shows to gain public sympathy. He feels he is slowly gaining ground. "I think people are finally settling down on this, and asking themselves the only question I want them to ask: could this girl be my daughter?"

Put this way, it is difficult for any honest parent *not* to answer in the affirmative. Furthermore, Bailey's planned brainwashing defense has the assistance of history. Americans believe in brainwashing. Its mysterious power was invoked to explain the behavior of our POW's in two wars, Korea and Vietnam. But as a defense, it has been used only in military courts-martial, never in a criminal case. Thus Patty's trials will offer new testing ground for the intersection, or possibly the collision, of psychiatry and law.

Hernap has already resulted in the deaths of at least eight people, and several innocent bystanders have been killed or wounded. Many,

many friends, lovers, and families of all these people have seen their own lives destroyed. Patty/Tania may have been destroyed most of all. The most fascinating question of the upcoming trial is not how Patty was brainwashed, terrorized, or otherwise converted into becoming Tania, no matter how titillating that story is certain to be. The big question is when, and how, did Tania die? For the jury and public to buy Bailey's answer, for them not to perceive Patty as a betrayer of her one-time SLA comrades and protectors, will require Bailey to orchestrate the death of Tania with the delicacy and skill Verdi lavished on the death of Camille.

The public's last glimpse of Patty was on November 4, back in Judge Carter's courtroom. Two hundred press queued up in the corridor, waited two hours, got searched, rushed for seats. I was lucky and got one in the second row. Even that close, I had to crane my neck to see around the phalanx of burly federal marshals, impossibly broad-shouldered in their cowboy suits. Suddenly the suits part, cleave, and she's there again. Tiny, jailhouse sallow. A small, pale girl. I'd forgotten how sallow, how small. A copper coin's profile, Roman nose, red-gold hair gone dark at the roots now, and a matronly-brown pants suit with pink, figured blouse. Sartorially, these lawyers may be overdoing the victim-image. Lawyer Bailey and U.S. Attorney Browning sit at the heads of their respective tables and teams. Patty looks composed, alert, attentive to her counsel. But she does not look around.

Directly behind her in a straight line, not moving, sit her parents, sisters, a cousin, all of them rigid, formal, and familiar to us as Egyptian figures painted on a tomb. Dad wears the patient, horn-rimmed glasses, Mom the cotton-candy hair. Bailey wears powder-blue stripes that nicely bring out the color of his eyes, which are narrow. Addressing the court, he manages to point out that the psychiatric reports are voluminous. One of them "documents the whole story more fully than some briefs I have seen submitted before the Supreme Court. It describes the defendant as literally a prisoner of war for twenty months."

To Bailey, this is the telling point. Myself, I'm not so sure. The judge doesn't use the word voluminous; he says *verbose*. The prosecutor points out that "the law says a defendant needs a 'reasonable degree' of rational understanding. It doesn't say she needs a 'maximum' degree of competence. Nowhere in these reports can we find conclusions that she's *incompetent.* . . ."

As might have been expected, not one of the four psychiatrists entirely agrees with another. The judge says he will ponder, and issue a written opinion in a few days. When he does, the opinion is eleven pages long, and forty Xeroxed copies, not stapled, are delivered to the greedy press as if the stenographer were feeding sea gulls.

The judge's finding of competency is a disappointment to the defense. They decide to appeal. "Is the defense trying to delay trial?" the prosecutor is asked by newsmen.

"In my experience, most criminal defendants are not anxious to go to trial."

As we left the courtroom, the public got its last glimpse of the little girl who for so long wasn't there, and who may not be altogether there now. Henceforth, it will be too dangerous as well as cruel to put her on public show. The papers said that Patty did not acknowledge her family that day in court. But they missed seeing the acknowledgment. As she rose to leave, Patty half-turned toward her mother and mouthed a silent "hello," the smallest, barest, grimmest possible greeting. I was sitting behind Catherine Hearst, and the daughter's look chilled my blood. But appearances deceive no less than photographs. Later her lawyers said Patty had been carefully instructed *not* to smile.

Perhaps they felt the loony newspaper grin image should not be reinforced. Or perhaps they felt a smile might look too "normal." On such obscure and gossamer points-of-image will this case continue to turn.

In any event, the mother's Gibson Girl profile acknowledged the silent "hello" with the faintest compression of lips, the tiniest imaginable lift of chin, which made me ache for Patty's mother in a way I never had before. And when the Hearst family filed out of court through a rear, private exit, the father stood for a long moment framed in the brightly-lit doorway, looking back in. He appeared rueful and sad, reluctant to depart even this bleak suggestion that maybe someday with all the money and time and anguish paid, everything with this family would be all right again.

Life, Year-End 1975

SECTION 3

Thumbsucking–The Feminine Eye on Watergate

1

Diary: 1976

My three-year span at Newsweek *encompassed the era of Watergate, and while the drama was unfolding I, like many other Americans, was unable to tear myself away from the TV set. The biggest political story of my lifetime was on that tube; I had to watch. Thus it was that I became guilty of a practice known around newspapers and city rooms as "thumbsucking." Thumbsucking means ruminating without reporting; thumbsuckers are people who loll around and think, rather than rush around on their feet and report.*

I got the message in a roundabout way; a hint was conveyed to me through a third-party mutual friend that Newsweek's *owner, Katherine Graham, was less than dazzled by my Watergate commentaries. As my private relationship with Ms. Graham goes way back before my employment at* Newsweek, *and had always been characterized by the most absolute, straight-from-the-shoulder directness I had ever encountered from another professional, I was distressed now more by the obliqueness of her message than by its content. I telephoned Kay at once and asked her to tell me precisely what she didn't like, and please cut out the boarding school niceties. The point, I heard myself saying firmly, was that I wanted the straight, unbuttered truth, wanted to hear it directly from her, my old straight-shooter friend, and not second- or thirdhand. So she told me, right then on the phone, and again at greater length at lunch. Sheer personal opinion, she said, unbolstered by on-the-spot reporting, unseasoned by any special professional expertise in the subject matter, devoid of the warm blood or cold blood evoked by actual contact between writer and subject, no longer works. Even Walter Lippmann couldn't get by with it today.*

"Thumbsucking, Shana, is not what's needed."

To my horror, I was devastated, demolished by her remarks. "Hit me in the face with a flounder," I had begged, but when it happened, I dissolved. I couldn't write another word for weeks, months, could only loll there in front of the TV set feeling guilty and helpless, a hopeless Watergate junkie, and now a mute one as well.

Looking back now, I think that generally speaking Katherine Graham was right: thumbsucking by columnists is not what's needed. (Most going columnists are not what's needed either. What's needed are good ones. I can name six.) But Watergate was not an ordinary news event. It was so unusual, in fact, that rules of good journalism needed to be broken to accommodate it. Watergate demanded an intense, personal reaction. I think these eight pieces, taken together, make a nice, unbroken song-cycle even today, a Lieder *recital in contrast to the journalistic grand opera then thundering out of Washington. My own favorite among the eight, and the first to call down ire, is "Love Song to Martha Mitchell." Along the Potomac, it may have seemed like thumbsucking, but to me it was a successful attempt at combining two opposed styles, tongue-in-cheek and straight, at writing with forked tongue. The piece also called down a response from the Fifth Avenue apartment where Martha Mitchell was holding herself incommunicado. The message arrived while I was out to lunch. When I returned, a note from my secretary lay on my desk.*

"Mrs. Mitchell phoned to say she liked the column. Says to tell you she wanted to tell you so herself, but she never speaks to the press."

This particular column also contains my proudest non sequitur: *the paragraph about* defensive *espionage. When Osborn Elliott, Newsweek's elegant and devoted editor, saw the* non sequitur *paragraph that April Saturday afternoon, he gently pointed out that it didn't at all "track."*

"I know it doesn't, Oz," I said, "but I think I've suddenly figured out what the Watergate burglars were really after, and I need a place to be first to say it in print."

So we left it in, and I believe I was *first, as well as right. In his definitive book,* Nightmare: The Underside of the Nixon Years, *published three years later, J. Anthony Lukas comes to the same conclusion.*

2

Watergate Overture: Love Song to Martha Mitchell

Pop, pop, pop, pop. Mitchell, Dean, Haldeman, Stans. One by one, the ducks fall down. Watergate has no heroes. But it does have a heroine: Martha Mitchell.

Martha Mitchell, where are you? *How* are you? I wish I could call *you* up tonight. If ever a heroine was unsung, it is you; yet you are the only one among them who has behaved honestly in this whole hugger-mugger affair. "A dirty business" you called it from the very beginning. Through jeers, threats, and exile, your story, and your outrage, has not varied a jot. Your gold pompadour is the single unmoving light in the entire Watergate constellation of orbiting alibis, doom-bearing comets, and showers of Republican falling stars.

It turns out that you were the only one of them who was exactly and no less than what you seemed. When the President wanted you, you served him. You were the only spice to his dull, drab company. Did he need Happy Headlines? You supplied them! You dared to do something that the icebound ships—Haldeman, Ehrlichman—could not even conceive. You throbbed. That must be why your man loves you so. You are *alive*.

How could they not know what kind of woman they were dealing with? How could they miss the independent spirit under the gold pompadour? Even your name, Martha Mitchell, is so American, a covered-wagon, frontier name, the female echo of a Founding Father's name, evoking Barbara Frietchie most of all:

> "Shoot, if you must, this sprayed gold head
> But spare John Mitchell's name," she said.

Once as a young reporter I accompanied two policemen to the scene of a family fight. We found the wife on the floor, black-eyed and bloody, but when the cops tried to take the man into custody, she leapt to her feet shouting, "Keep your hands off my husband!" That's you, Martha Mitchell.

You are not interested in pushing your husband in the normal way of the executive wife, not interested in pushing him up success's ladder, up to the two-car, three-TV set, swimming pool, country club, heart-attack way of life. You are interested in commitment, and yours is utter. When you can't give it, that's when your life falls apart.

For the first year or two in Washington, you were like a rodeo girl riding a bucking horse. You were the star of the show, and how you loved queening it, milking it for all it was worth. Of course, you had the liberty of the clown, but you had more: you told it like it was, you called 'em as you saw 'em. That's what made us laugh.

Then they put you out, ostracized you to the Watergate, needled your derriere, even locked you in "for your protection." The gray, icebound ships saw you as an embarrassment to their probity and sobriety, but failed to see that they themselves had much to be embarrassed about, beginning with their own cold-bloodedness. Finally, they banished you. Or did you leave town in disgust? "Choose between me and them" is the ultimatum John Mitchell told us then that you had given him. Was this really *your* proposition, I wonder, or just his version of it? In any case, it would appear now that he tried to have it both ways. You could have told him that never works.

What I like best about you is that you tell the truth. Maybe not the whole truth, but certainly nothing but the truth as you see it. If there is something on your mind, you say it. You are incapable of dissembling. If you like a drink once in a while, well, so do I. Anyway, it's mostly the sober people who tell lies. Drinkers can hardly wait to tell you the truth, as every bartender knows.

"A dirty business," as you've said. But it also strikes me as such a silly business. Why did they do it? They already knew more about the Democrats than the Democrats knew about themselves. And they were already just about certain to win the election. So why take the risk? Watergate up to now is a plot with no plot.

Want to hear my theory? I don't think the primary objective of the raiders was to dig up dirt on the Democrats at all. I think they were making a very careful check to see exactly how much dirt, if any, the Democrats might have on them. Watergate, in short, was defensive and not offensive espionage. The concept of defensive espionage is wholly consistent with the President's well-advertised admiration for vigorous, aggressive play, for always carrying the fight into the enemy's territory.

Anyway, Martha, another thing I like about you is your mistrust of the written word. The spoken word is safer in these Alice in Wonderland times. So don't give them a written deposition on Watergate. Don't put anything in writing. Insist they put you on the stand. You want the right to explain yourself at long last. One can scarcely blame you for that.

Your husband appears oddly ambiguous on this point. "She'd be delighted to testify," he says, but "God help the committee if she does."

I'm not sure what he means by this—in fact, I am having a lot more difficulty understanding his behavior than I am yours. But it occurs to me that if it turns out under oath that you did indeed know about the "dirty business" from the very beginning, it will be even harder to believe that the President himself knew nothing.

Loyalty is the supreme virtue of Nixon politicians, their bottom line. When somebody says, "I'd walk over my grandmother for Richard Nixon," that's fine. But when someone says, "I'd walk over Richard Nixon for my husband," that is danger. It takes the kind of guts they fear. It accounts both for your vulnerability and for your threat to them. It is the final reason why I like you so very much.

You were not born, they sneer, but sprang full-grown from the pen of Al Capp. Wrong! You are in the best tradition of American womanhood, defending your country, your flag . . . but most of all, defending your man. You are folk art, an American primitive. I doubt you know or can even conceive any other way to respond to a man than with utter loyalty, an 007 kind of love. Only when love and loyalty die, will your kind of woman go find another man.

It appears to me just now that yours may be the only loyalty of Watergate.

Newsweek—April 30, 1973

3

Nixon's High Command: The Crazy Gang

Now while we wait for the indictments to come down, everybody has his own theory about Watergate, and I have one too, gentler than some. I think they were all crazy. Let me explain.

From the instant the burglars were caught red-handed and rubber-gloved in the offices of the Democratic National Committee, there has been only one good period for the Watergate bad guys. That was the few weeks between the end of the trial and the fatal moment when McCord's letter to Judge Sirica opened the whole mess up again. In this brief time, the hush money was in the pipeline between White House and jailhouse, and everybody who could make trouble had been either paid off or buttoned up. The top Nixonmen were free to turn their full attention to the proper affairs of state.

So, down with permissiveness, pornography, drugs, and welfare! Up with law and order! On with hard work! And what was the White House working on so hard during this brief era of domestic tranquillity? A new, get-tough crime program, that's what: a package designed to attack crime "without pity," to bring back the death penalty, to override "soft-headed judges," and oddly, to abolish insanity as a defense against prosecution. Ironically, the bad guys thereby knocked out the one defense that could surely save their hides.

The insanity defense states that a person cannot be found guilty of a crime unless he knows the difference between right and wrong, unless he is capable of understanding the consequences of his acts. What has appalled many of us from the beginning about Watergate, even more than its criminal aspects, are the moral aspects. Crooks in government are nothing new, though we may never before have had so many of them. What is new is the impression of widespread moral bankruptcy at the highest levels. It is enough to give nightmares to anyone who believes in constitutional government.

As nightmare, Watergate is easy to explain—they were all mad. Drunk with power, cockeyed with arrogance, unseasoned by political experience, untempered by much human feeling, and unencumbered by any political ideals beyond the ideal of remaining in office, the top Nixonmen were susceptible to the contagious, pernicious lunacy of power. Such a madness could not afflict men with experience in public life, men who comprehend at least the *political* consequences of their acts, men alert to the public, and sensitive to other politicians; men who know that the politician is always part leader, part follower. But one by one the seasoned professionals—Rogers, Finch, Klein, Laird, Harlow—had been pushed aside. The new men knew only the power game, and the image biz.

What does one make of a man who writes, as Ehrlichman did in his letter of resignation, "I have always felt that the appearance of honesty and integrity is every bit as important . . . as the fact of one's honesty and integrity"?

The new Nixonmen didn't even know the difference between disagreement and disloyalty. Although they held the substantial jobs of the Administration, they themselves were insubstantial, because they had no moral weight. The machine they managed was powerful, hurtling over millions of heads, but inside it men like Mitchell, Colson, Dean, Stans, Haldeman, and Ehrlichman were floating, suspended, weightless. They knew the law; if they were breaking it, they certainly knew that. Yet in some loony way they seem not to have fully understood the difference between right and wrong. They did not really appreciate that the inevitable consequences of their acts would be to scuttle the ship of state.

The other morning on TV, Governor Ronald Reagan, the West Coast solon, explained that the perpetrators of Watergate were "stupid and foolish, but not criminal."

"Illegal," he then suggested, would be a better word than "criminal." At that point, something in me snapped (we are all a bit loony these days) and I heard myself shouting back at the TV screen. "Stupid . . . foolish . . . illegal . . . criminal . . . What in God's name did all those people think they were doing!

"Those Cubans in rubber gloves," I yelled. "Maybe they thought they were fighting Communism! But what about all the sleek lawyers, the men who know the law like the trout knows his pool? What did they think *they* were up to?"

I began to draw up a list.
- The Cubans thought they were fighting Communism.
- Liddy and Hunt thought that they were attending to plumbing, fixing leaks.
- Dean thought he was holding the truth at bay, but found out he was holding the bag.
- Ex-Navy Captain L. Patrick Gray thought he had no need to know. So he served his flag by burning the bag.
- Ehrlichman thought to nail Ellsberg on moral grounds, but the man with the moral hang-ups was Ehrlichman.
- Haldeman thought he could package the Presidency.
- Mitchell thought he had "deniability."
- Ziegler thought he could declare the record "inoperative."
- Kalmbach thought that he could sell indulgences.
- Vesco thought he could buy his way out by buying his way in.
- Stans, with his nose for gold, thought he could sell hope on a *caveat emptor* basis.
- Kleindienst thought he could speak the unspeakable word: impeachment.

It was in fact Kleindienst's insufferably crude and arrogant flaunting of this word before the Senate committee which triggered the latest wave of disclosures. And Mr. Nixon? Despite the appalling banality and self-pity of his latest speech, we still don't know what he really thought. But as James Reston points out, it is wise with Mr. Nixon not to pay attention to what he says but to what he does.

As for the unspeakable word, I, like almost every other American, dislike uttering it. I, like all but the vulture-hearted, want to believe that Mr. Nixon walked the water unwet in the sea of corruption of his Administration. I, too, want to believe him ignorant, more ignorant than myself.

This week, for the first time since the scandal broke, I have come to believe that this national ignorance will pass. I have begun to feel confident that with the continuing help of the vigorous free press, an honest judiciary, and the attentive concern of an aroused public, the ship of state will right itself. The convoy of separate investigations now forming up like escort vessels around a damaged craft will enable her to ride out the storm.

The good news this week is that, after so many months in the doldrums, the ship has begun to desert the rats.

Newsweek—May 14, 1973

4

The Seven (New)
Deadly Sins

Perjury, conspiracy, obstruction of justice, burglary, forgery, destruction of evidence—these are the names of some of their crimes. But they are not the names of their sins. We are still arguing about those.

The shock waves set off by Watergate run so deep that, eleven months later, with a dozen separate investigations under way, we are still trying to define what the essential evil is. We still can't agree on which of all the many illegal, distasteful, immoral, unethical, and criminal acts known collectively as "Watergate" was the original sin, father to all the rest.

Not that we lack for suggestions. Americans have always been sin-struck, and Watergate has done much to revitalize the punishing, puritan strain in our national character. Modern-day moralists read the sin of Watergate in as many ways as the six blind men once read the elephant. Some say the money was the root of all evil. It was all those safes and suitcases and pockets full of $100 bills, uncounted and unaccounted for, that made the corruption inevitable. Others tell us that the essential crime involved ends and means, espionage means to achieve political ends—a confusion that was fatal to the electoral process.

All in all, we are hearing a lot about *process*. Senator Ervin opened his hearings by identifying the overriding crime as "interference with the electoral, political, and judicial process." And former Senator Eugene McCarthy, who as both politician and Catholic scholar has made the study of temptation a lifetime work, tells his students that "the ultimate temptation in this case was the lure of controlling the process." Control-of-the-process became first the *program* of the Administration, and then its *policy*, so that finally Ehrlichman or Dean or

Haldeman or Mitchell could say, "If the President wants it, I will do it," and believe he had made a moral judgment.

Dr. Daniel Ellsberg puts the blame on *secrecy*. Secrecy inevitably corrupts, Ellsberg points out, whether in Vietnam or Watergate or the National Security Council, because it confers on those who know the secret a false sense of power, and a dangerous illusion of moral superiority.

John Gardner and many others blame *power*. "Unbridled Presidential power . . . accumulated over the last four decades" led inevitably to its misuse, he has written.

While there is much truth to this, I incline more to George Bernard Shaw's theory that "Power does not corrupt men; fools, however, if they get into a position of power, corrupt power."

Certainly too much power, and too much money, were aspects of the evil. So too was the creeping toleration of lawlessness engendered by a decade of Vietnam. So was the fatal combination of too much permissiveness—oh, irony!—with too little character. Obsessive secrecy was also part of it, as was corruption of the process. All these evils are in part to blame, and probably we shall have to wait many years for time's bony finger to point out the worst worm in the apple.

But one thing is already clear. That worm will represent a sin both Original, and original. Run down the list of the seven deadly sins, the good old vices of mankind, and it is startling how little they relate to the present crisis.

Avarice? Hardly. Unlike Teapot Dome, nobody this time seems to have been in the swindle primarily to line his own pockets.

Envy? These men worked together as model bureaucrats. There was a minimum of infighting, for people operating at such high levels of power.

Gluttony? They all eat moderately and drink sparingly, if at all. The favorite Oval Office lunch is ketchup on cottage cheese.

Lust? Inoperative.

Sloth? They got to the office at 7 o'clock in the morning, and left by moonlight, lugging home full briefcases. Between times, they jogged and played squash.

Wrath? Up and down the courthouse steps we watch them come and go, hounded everywhere by rushing newsmen. But has anyone ever seen happier, more carefree smiles? The girls in the Miss Universe contest look positively peevish by comparison.

Pride, then, the overweening sin? No, not even pride. Nixon's men did not want to become God. They were happy just to be like Him.

Perhaps what we need is a new set of seven deadly sins, special ones for our times. Playing with this temptation, I have come up with Numbness, Dumbness, Beaverism, Euphemism, Riggery, Laundery, and Trickery. Admittedly this leaves out marginal sins like Forgery (false evidence) and Shreddery (real evidence). But my game plan is to reduce this thing to its essential evils.

Numbness, then, is total insensitivity to the rights and wishes of the electorate, and to the intentions of the Founding Fathers.

Dumbness is thinking they could get away with it. (It is fashionable, I know, to assert that they almost *did*, but the details so far offered make the break-in look a lot like a scene from a Three Stooges comedy.)

Of *Beaverism* it might be observed that the real work of a beaver is to create a very big tangle, complex enough to hold everything back; in fact, a watergate.

As for *Euphemism*, consider the use of "winding down the war" for "winding up the bombers"; of "ideological plugola" for "truth"; and of "I accept the responsibility" for "I dodge the blame."

Riggery goes to the heart of the matter. Riggery of the political and judicial and governmental process reigns over these new seven deadly sins, as pride does over the old.

Laundery is not only the cleaning up of dirty money. It is also the ad man's special vice. It is what washes whiter than white.

And *Trickery* is the name of the game, the Watergate bottom line. Reading the newspapers and watching the hearings on TV, one becomes mesmerized after a while by the seemingly endless parade of dirty tricks: trickery—lies, trickery—thieves, trickery—cover-up.

Trickery.

Dickery.

Dock.

Newsweek—May 28, 1973

5

Watergate Metamorphosis: Nixon into Nixxon

The Watergate scandal expands like my favorite shiver movie, *The Blob*. Hypnotized, we watch The Thing grow, new figures and new institutions daily engulfed in its watery jelly. Like The Blob, Watergate appears to be a living organism, but one that lacks an identifiable, beating heart, or even a central organizing principle. All we can say with certainty is that The Thing changes continually, and it grows.

What to do? There are three schools of thought. Some politicians want to grab machetes and pitchforks and stab it quick, before it grows any bigger, though any science-fiction fan could tell them *that* never works. Others want to inchworm slowly all around The Thing until they figure out what's going on inside. A third faction, mostly lawyers, favors throwing a black cloth of indictment over The Blob and hauling the whole mess into court for a "fair trial."

But there is only one way to get rid of The Blob, and that is to destroy it with fresh air. The immeasurable value of the televised hearings is that they inform the public, and reestablish the people's right to know what goes on in their government. The hearings are educational TV of the highest order, *Sesame Street* for grown-ups. Of course there must also be fair trials. Of course the accused must be presumed innocent unless proved otherwise. But justice, the blind goddess, always protects the mighty at least as well as the meek, and there is no reason to fear she will fail them now. Not only is The Blob in a continuing state of flux and growth, the actors in the Watergate drama constantly assume new forms.

Possibly the man who has changed most, and most often, is Daniel Ellsberg. His dramatic transmutations from hawk into dove, from thief into martyr, from traitor into patriot, from professional spyman into secrecy's archfoe can best be viewed in terms of allegory. Like the hero of *The Pilgrim's Progress,* Dr. Ellsberg has journeyed from the City of Destruction through the Slough of Despond and the Valley of Humiliation, and then up through the Delectable Mountains of vindication to the guaranteed safety of the Celestial City of the Fourth Amendment.

Even lesser characters in this drama change with startling speed. Lawyer Fensterwald was just that, a competent defense attorney, until lawyer Alch testified that Fensterwald had told him, "We're going after the President of the United States." What a windmill! Fensterwald metamorphosed into Don Quixote, dreaming his impossible dream, recruiting James McCord as his improbable Sancho Panza.

McCord has appeared in several guises, as befits his profession. With his letter to Judge Sirica, the convicted burglar was reborn as a courtroom hero, or anyway antihero. Wireman became Batman, and Loyal Jack Caulfield was this Batman's Robin.

Consider the metamorphosis of baby-faced Ron Ziegler. Not too long ago, Ziegler at White House news briefings was the Dutch boy at the dike, single-handedly, even single-fingeredly, holding back the deluge. Poor Ziegler. Suddenly all around him has changed, both outside and inside the closed door he so faithfully guards. Now the brave Dutch boy looks more like the central character in a Polish or (as they say around the White House) a Polish-American joke.

Ziegler in German means "brickmaker," and it now looks as if this Ziegler, in his vain struggle to wall off the Oval Office, has merely bricked himself in.

Enlightenment on Watergate will surely not come from playing the name game. But having read that Abplanalp means "from flat mountain," I have hauled out the German dictionary to discover that *Halde* is an archaic term for "slope, declivity, slag-heap, or dump," whereas *ehrlich* connotes "honest, honorable, open, reliable, true-hearted."

Kissinger is a man from the town of Kissen; but *Kissen* also means "cushion, pillow, or padding," and certainly the President's foreign-policy adviser brought the cushioning presence of intellectual respectability, even culture, into the stony atmosphere of the throne room. Of all the recent deflations, Dr. Kissinger's is to me most sorrowful. In wire-tapping members of his own staff, he appears to have sunk from statesman to mere electrician at the throne of power. His subsequent claim that he did it for their own good, to protect their innocence, suggests a most sinister minister.

The master quick-change artist of American politics over a quarter-century has been Richard Nixon. As the President struggles now with the seventh and by far the gravest of the crisis which have enriched his career, it is useful to look back over his famous Six, and to remember that it is always possible to see a Nixon crisis two ways. His eagles, like the Hapsburgs', have two heads.

In his first, the Hiss case, did we see a ruthless persecutor of Comsymps, or a fearless prosecutor of traitors? Was the Checkers speech an open confession, or a brilliant political "save"? Did President Eisenhower's heart attack show us anything other than the public piety of the Number Two dog? What lay under the spattered egg in Caracas —the staunch visage of courage, or the sneer of North American might and power? And the figure in the kitchen with Khrushchev, was he a tough diplomatic counterpuncher, or part of a public-relations setup, like Betty Furness at her refrigerator? And sixthly, at the close of the 1960 campaign, was the Republican candidate a man tempered by the furnace of defeat into stronger steel, or merely a sore loser?

Just now our chameleon in chief is invisible, doubtless off in the wings shedding another skin, molting again. What new form will he assume this time? His problem is to scrap a stained, ambiguous, used-up image and to substitute a shiny new one. "New" is the operative word. The change of image must be drastic, total. There must be no link whatever between the Before and the After, not even the invisible genetic link of caterpillar to moth.

What he must achieve now is an overnight miracle. The closest parallel I can think of is not biological but technological, even etymological—the President must pull off the same instant miracle the Standard Oil Company of New Jersey did when it so mysteriously, brilliantly metamorphosed into Exxon.

Standard Oil's new form is not only catchy, clean-cut, and red-white-and-blue. Best of all, it has no connection whatever with its former self.

It will be a neat trick: Nixon into Nixxon.

Newsweek—June 11, 1973

6

The Need (Not) to Know

Visiting the ornate Senate Caucus Room where the Watergate hearings are taking place is like walking onto a stage set. Up so close, the visitor is distracted by unsuspected scuff marks on furnishings and people. The only unbattered object the day I was there was the man in the witness chair, Robert Mardian, former chief of internal security for the Justice Department. Across the expanse of rumpled green baize, our old friends Doc, Happy, Grumpy, Sleepy, Bashful, Sneezy, and Dopey faced a man of Teflon, cold and perfectly smooth. It has been Mr. Mardian's profession to deal in secrets, and he certainly gave none away to the Committee on that day. But he did supply a clue to what Watergate is largely about.

In intelligence circles, only persons with a demonstrable "need to know" are told what is going on; no one gets a bigger crumb of the secret than is necessary. But the man at the top has an overriding need to know everything. Under Richard Nixon, the White House was run on these same spook principles, even unto the bugs in the walls.

Watching Senator Ervin's exuberant performance, I thought how different this man is from Mr. Nixon. Nixon bends forward in secret, listening to his tapes. Ervin leans back in public, waving the Constitution and crying out the first principles of the Republic. Democracy is based on knowing. No one rules us; we rule ourselves. Therefore we *must* know.

That evening, I met Henry Kissinger, a sorrowful and bitter figure now forced to watch his own historical monument dissolving in Watergate's acid rain. "The American people don't yet realize how gravely wounded the country is," he said. "This is Dunkirk."

Dr. Kissinger believes we will never get to the bottom of Watergate.

Bob Haldeman may know 95 per cent of it, he told me, and Ehrlichman perhaps 70 per cent. But no individual knows the entire story, not even the President.

I wonder what final message he does take from his very private tapes, the tapes made necessary by this Commander in Chief's special need to know? In fairness, the notion of an overriding need to know has been freely invoked on all sides. The government's need to know what is going on in some people's heads in the name of "national security" is the basis of the wiretap law that Senator Ervin sponsored in 1968. Daniel Ellsberg released the Pentagon Papers because he felt the public has a need to know what the government does in its name. The CIA shrinks agree. Their famed "psychiatric profile" concludes that Ellsberg acted from patriotic motives.

Watergate introduced a counternecessity into White House calculations and that is the need (not) to know; the elevation of calculated ignorance to a state of grace; the pursuit of deniablity as the one passport to survival. Compulsive ignorance is as contagious as compulsive secrecy, and the know-nothing plague was already epidemic in the land. It helps explain our long toleration of the Indochina war. It contributes to the hostility people feel toward the media. It fuels astrology freaks and crunchy granola nuts, and it has cropped up again in the secret bombing of Cambodia, a vast and dirty business that Dr. Kissinger, Mr. Laird, and the former Secretary of the Air Force have all denied knowing the full truth about.

This aggressive need (not) to know is the wrong note that sounds throughout the Watergate testimony. When Treasurer Hugh Sloan, Jr., gets worried about the *purpose* of the huge amounts of cash he has been ordered to hand out, Maurice Stans admonishes him, "I do not want to know, and you do not want to know."

When Sloan tries to tell Ehrlichman, *he* doesn't want to know either. He tells him to get a lawyer. Sloan's trouble is not with the law but with ethics. He has some. In this zoo, he is odd man out.

Donald Segretti assures a potential recruit for his spy apparatus: "Nixon knows that something is being done. It's a typical deal: don't-tell-me-anything-and-I-won't-know." Liddy tells McCord things look good for the break-in providing the Attorney General can be assured "deniability." Pretty Sally Harmony, that secretary of sublime discretion, needs (not) to know the meaning of the coded gabble she is transcribing from tapes. Charles Colson, the man who originally recruited Hunt, refuses for five months after the break-in even to answer his old pals' phone calls. "I wanted to be able to say I don't know the first goddam thing about it," he later confesses, "because I thought that was the best way to protect the President."

Of them all, Kalmbach is most pathetic. He fears his motives in sending to the burglars a quarter million dollars in secret cash may be misunderstood by the grand jury. On Ehrlichman's self-bugged phone, he confides that he intends to maintain that he didn't know he was doing anything improper. But he is worried; in his mind's eye, his double knit suits are already turning to convict's stripes.

> KALMBACH: Are they still going to say, well, Herb, you should have known?
> EHRLICHMAN: I don't know how you could. You didn't make any inquiries.
> KALMBACH: Never. And the only inquiries I made, John, was to you after I talked to John Dean.
> EHRLICHMAN: And you found that I didn't know just a whole helluva lot.

Later Kalmbach is asked how he felt when he found out that he had been paying hush money, and had committed an improper, illegal act. He says it felt like being kicked in the stomach. That's what *knowing* can do to a person.

Way back in June 1972, when former acting FBI Director L. Patrick Gray, III, told his boss, "Mr. President . . . people on your staff are trying to mortally wound you by using the CIA and the FBI . . ." Mr. Nixon allegedly replied, "Pat, you just continue to conduct your aggressive and thorough investigation," and thereby began asserting his own Presidential right (not) to know.

In case anybody missed the point, he makes it three times more: in August, he assures us that no one presently in the White House is involved. Next he says, "There has been an effort to conceal the facts —both from the public—from you—and from me." Still later he says, "I took no part in—nor was I aware of" the cover-up.

Mr. Nixon's need to know nothing seems to be violently at war with his need to know everything. Secretly, he bugs himself. But even bugging is not enough. He needs to know which corporations have "problems with the government" and might therefore be disposed to make large campaign contributions. He needs to know who his public "enemies" are, so that after the election they can be "taken care of." He confides to Mardian in San Clemente that the Pentagon Papers leak means that "his very ability to govern was threatened; the peace of the world was threatened." So he needs to know things that even the FBI and the CIA won't dig for, and he sets up his own secret spy force. It is not hard to imagine a man so at war with himself sitting alone, late at night, playing his tapes and asking himself: "What did I know?"

Newsweek—August 6, 1973

7

Perfect Secretaries: Sally and Rose

Washington has no heroes left. Not only has the spreading scandal destroyed our national leadership—*all* of it, not just the man at the top —but familiarity has rubbed the stardust from the shoulders of the men who did the job, the various lawyers, prosecutors, investigators, and members of the Senate committee. Judge Sirica and possibly lawyer Cox are exceptions, but their enduring shine is the luster of the law itself.

I'm not complaining. It's necessary to toss out old heroes from time to time, spring cleaning of the mind. But we have hit a unique dead spot in the national cardiogram; the pulse is nearly flat. A few weak blips of admiration do appear on the scope, but they are not heroes. They are heroines, and minor ones at that: Rose Mary Woods, Sally Harmony, and all the others who helped their bosses Get Things Done. Strictly speaking, these heroines are not all secretaries, not even all female. We feel the same stirrings of sympathy for Odle the office manager, Sloan the accountant, and even for the four "Cuban-Americans" whose quick slapstick turn in blue gloves was curtain raiser to the drama.

But the virtues of these low-level aides were quintessential secretarial virtues: loyalty, discretion, and good organization. Without such support, an executive wobbles like a broken three-legged stool. Too often, a fourth secretarial ideal—ready likability—is sacrificed to the imperatives of the other three. But this was surely not so in the case of Sally Harmony. The secretary to G. Gordon Liddy was immediately likable from the moment she stepped on-camera last spring in her pleasant smile, pretty fluffy hairdo, and nice office-chic polka-dot frock. Miss Harmony! Even her name must have been reassuring to the frazzled executive. As for the cardinal virtues of loyalty, discretion, and order, the girl was a paragon. With perfect composure, she testified how she had spent days transcribing tapes of gabble, garble, and gobbledygook between personages named Sedan Chair One and Sedan Chair Two, onto special "Gemstone" stationery, without ever wondering what the hell was going on.

Miss Harmony had a wonderful way of expressing herself. "To me, 'clandestine' does not mean illegal; but I can keep a secret" is one of Sally's more memorable secretarial quotes, which I find scribbled in one of my old notebooks.

As for *her* old notebooks, they don't exist. Miss Harmony is such a model of orderliness and discretion that, she also swore, after she had shredded every scrap of office paper on which Liddy's handwriting appeared, she even fed her own notebooks into the shredding machine —so selfless an act as to constitute secretarial infanticide.

I had been wondering what became of Sally after her first appearance on page one. Did she ever get that promised trip to Florida, the one they said she had earned with her overtime exertions at the shredder? In November, I was pleased to notice that Sally was the only member of the old CREEP office staff who didn't show up for their gruesome-sounding election-night anniversary party. "Good old Sally," I thought. I knew that girl had taste. But what *had* become of her? Was she too dancing alone somewhere, like Rose Mary Woods, who had been glimpsed one warm summer night doing a poolside tango solo at San Clemente? Had Sally, like poor, forsaken Rose Mary, been forced to hire and huddle with legal counsel of her own?

Then suddenly this week Sally was back on page one. Asserting the public's "right to know," Federal Judge Charles R. Richey, God bless him, ordered made public a sealed deposition Miss Harmony had given last May regarding Howard Hughes's campaign contributions. That

Sally "reappeared" in stenographic, deposition form seemed a nice touch.

Sally testified that before the new campaign-gift law went into effect, a Hughes man brought her a bunch of signed checks. They were made out to the President's reelection committee, but the amounts were left blank. Sally's job was to type in the numbers. Needless to say, she could remember every detail of this except how much money was involved.

When my daughter was little, she used to talk about her memory and her "forgettery." Sally's forgettery was a beaut.

Her reappearance reminded me of another beautifully named Washington secretary, Mildred Paperman, secretary to Sherman Adams' friend Bernard Goldfine, during the Eisenhower years. Miss Paperman even went to jail for her boss. Later, when she was out but Goldfine was still serving time, the ever-loyal Mildred used to smuggle the boss's letters in and out of the clink.

As loyalty is the supreme virtue in the Nixon regime, it is not surprising that the only heroic figures turn out to be the secretaries. Secretarial loyalty is not the exclusive property of any Administration or party. But if any President put a premium on the secretarial virtues, it is Mr. Nixon. He has always sought some kind of filter between himself and reality. That filter may be bulletproof glass or rose-colored glass as the occasion demands; it may be isolation gained by geographical distance (the tropical and mountain retreats) or the electronically achieved distance from others seemingly offered by the tapes; it may be a phalanx of perfect secretaries led by the redoubtable Miss Woods, each with telephone hold-button and glib excuses at the ready.

I have already written of the President's seeming compulsion not to know details of what is going on in his own Administration, and then deliberately to place that need in opposition to the public's right to know as guaranteed by the Constitution. This strange information phobia turned up again last week in the official White House explanations of the ITT case and the milk deal, in which Mr. Nixon asserted that he was "unaware of any commitment by ITT to make a contribution to the expenses of the Republican National Convention."

In any case, I am glad that the so-called "Operation Candor" is over; its two so-called "white papers" turned out to be an embarrassing shade of tattletale gray. Not for the first time, a Nixon position has turned out to mean the opposite of what it appears to say: "full disclosure" means cover-up, "war on drugs" means war on drug victims, and "peace with honor" turns out to be not much honor and no peace.

Defending his record last March or April, the President asked rhetorically "who is to blame?" and then in slow, magisterial cadence replied, I accept "responsibility," which is not quite the same. But it now appears that once again the reverse is the case, that Mr. Nixon will accept the blame for Watergate if he has to, but still refuses responsibility.

In that other ugly utterance when he said, "I'm not a crook," he might more precisely have said "I'm not *even* a crook." For it now appears that the entire basis of his present defense is that, like Sally, he did not understand anything that was going on.

Newsweek—January 21, 1974

8

Big Graffiti:
The Nixon Tapes

Now the President is fishtailing, lashing from side to side in a vain effort to elude his pursuers. What will history make of the extraordinary litter of paper he has strewn in his wake? On inspection, these voluminous White House tape transcripts turn out to be amoral, scarcely coherent, and not even exculpatory. In fact, they are Mr. Nixon's ruin. Though issued as defense, the 1,254 pages give only offense. Their release has both shocked the world and clubbed their maker to his knees. Why did he do it? What was he trying to say?

The Oval Office dialogues have now been publicly labeled "disgusting" (Senator Hugh Scott); "a terrible indictment . . . awful" (Lieutenant General James Gavin, Retired); "a distasteful brew of suspicion, distrust, and cynicism unworthy of any public official" (William G. Milliken, Republican governor of Michigan); "squalor . . . and sleaziness" (historian Arthur Schlesinger, Jr.); "sliminess . . . horror" (historian C. Vann Woodward); and "ugly, corrupt, amoral, and unprincipled" (president of the New York Bar Association).

As I read through this awful indictment, published in full in *The*

New Yorker, another explanation for the tapes suddenly suggested itself to me: perhaps they are a kind of oral *graffiti.* Big graffiti, to be sure; bigger even than all the throbbing innards of the New York subway, bulkier than all the scratchings in the rubble of Rome. But graffiti nonetheless, I was pretty sure, by every accepted definition of that term.

To be certain, I telephoned an art historian friend. "What's graffiti?" I demanded, not saying why I wanted to know.

"First, it's plural," she replied, academic cool icing her voice. "From the Italian word for writing: *graffito.* And it is any inscription scrawled on a wall."

"Plural . . . scrawl. That fits!" I yelled, demanding more.

"Graffiti are important in two ways: they are invaluable to historians, and also invaluable to the individual's own psyche. I remember Claes Oldenburg saying when he first came to New York that he found the place so alien that making graffiti seemed to be his only way to control his environment. It's an assertion of one's own existence."

Another interesting thing about wall-writing, I learned, is that it's all alike, whether you come upon it in prehistoric caves or on modern lavatory walls. It is always completely unprofessional, the result of some spontaneous need to project an image of one's immediate feelings. That is why so many graffiti are explicitly sexual. At least they used to be. Last time I took the subway, I rode in a car spray-painted with a host of angels. Today's graffitists may have cleaner minds than some of our politicians.

Certainly, the transcripts are not explicit, either sexually or in any other way. Could they be the first abstract graffiti in history?

The original impulse to make the tapes was entirely different and should not be confused with the suicidal impulse to release them. Yet each in its way can be seen as a kind of graffitic urge. Though the tapes might originally have been intended partly as a potential tax deduction, I think they also suggest a pathetic effort to create instant history, to achieve at least the appearance of some consistent political philosophy, if not the reality. Then, when things began to reel—or unreel—and fall apart, what once had been seen as instant history was now perceived as instant alibi.

"Ask not what your country can do for you. Ask rather what you can do for yourself" had once been his battle cry. *In extremis,* he tried to practice what he had preached. On his TV show, gesturing toward his stack of green notebooks embossed with the Presidential seal, he had tried to sell his version of history like TV sells headache pills: give the product impressive packaging, don't mention the side effects, and bank on the fact that nobody will read the fine print.

But he was wrong, and "wrong" in his own peculiar sense of that word. One value of actually reading the transcripts is that they provide a clue—an imperfect Rosetta stone—to the mystery language of Nixonese. The transcripts establish that the President's famous six-word assertion of March 21 to John Dean ("it is wrong that's for sure") has but one meaning, not two. The transcripts reveal that the President and his men speak an entirely amoral language. Thus "wrong" means "it won't work." "Wrong" cannot mean "immoral" because, in Nixonese, there is no such word.

Some longtime Nixon watchers had believed that, once he actually got into the White House, the Presidency would improve the man. Another ordinary Vice President, Harry Truman, was thought to have transcended himself and been lifted to new heights of character and command simply by the act of moving into the top job. But this time even old friends were let down. This time the crucible of power did not reforge the man. It merely melted down the office.

More than any other man who held that office, this President wanted an imperial reign. But he lacked all the trappings of empire. No landed estates, only a piece of the action in a Florida land deal. No palace, only a realtor's dream-house on the bluffs of California, named for Saint Clement. "He is venerated as a martyr, but there is no good evidence that he was one," says my desk-top hagiology. Nixon did not even have a royal hunting lodge, only an abandoned Army camp in the lonely Maryland mountains; no royal scepter and mace, only the little flag lapel pin; no crown jewels, only the calculated diamond flatteries of Faisal. He had no Scheherazade to distract him, only Bebe the Silent; no court jester, only Martha Mitchell to throw stones at; no palace guard, only chocolate soldiers; no defenders of the faith, only Dean, Mitchell and . . . Bork? He did not even have good spies, only surgical-gloved bumblers and over-the-hill CIA hacks.

How could he possibly hope to succeed? He was as ill equipped for his impossible dream as Don Quixote. Worse. The Foolish Knight had at least an ideal of honor to dream of. His only ideal was reelection. So when things began to fall apart, when he was up against the wall and there was nothing else left to do, he finally did something human: he wrote on it.

Newsweek—May 27, 1974

9

Watergate Finale:
Good Guys and Bad Guys

The rich plankton of pop heroes and pop villains on which we Americans are accustomed to feed, the daily media soup of sports figures, ax murderers, politicians, and rock singers, the ever-running river of celebs, heavies, and oddballs that we use to spice up our own relatively humdrum lives has of late become a very watery gruel. Where have all the good guys and bad guys gone? Why does everyone out there look so gray?

Particularly in this uneasy time of waiting and watching to see how events in Washington will work themselves out at last, who will win and who will lose how much—and at what cost to the nation and to ourselves?—one longs for the simple days of only last summer when headlines were thronged with heroes and villains and it was still a simple matter to tell which was which.

What tipped me off to the change was a phrase in an old White House memo by Chuck Colson, the penitent Presidential axman, who comes about as close to being an honest-to-God villain as one can expect today. When Colson first saw Daniel Ellsberg on the eve of his indictment for the Pentagon Papers, he wrote a secret memo to Haldeman proclaiming Ellsberg "a natural villain."

"To the extent he could be painted evil," Colson noted, Ellsberg was the perfect figure to "arouse the heartland," to stir up the silent majority (which didn't give much of a damn about purloined documents, but could readily be whipped into hating the press for printing them), and to boost the boss. Colson saw in Ellsberg the potential of another Alger Hiss. Indeed, it was to make this dream of old glory a new reality that the White House "plumbers" were born.

Natural villains are hard to come by, what with all the shrinks and social-scientist types threatening to understand everybody into the ground, so one can imagine Colson's delight at discovering a perfect specimen on the White House doorstep: disloyal soldier, ungrateful child (to his spiritual father, Henry Kissinger), and thief of state secrets, all wrapped up in one loathsome, pointy-headed, un-American package. While I agree Ellsberg is the demagogue's delight, I would call him a natural scapegoat, not a natural villain.

My own idea of a natural villain is Colson. In my view, his evil lay in his perfect, unquestioning servitude not to a man, nor even to an idea. His loyalty seems to have been to loyalty itself, a deity I find as unworthy and undependable as, say, a polygraph machine. But that is my own prejudice, and it takes all kinds of disloyalists, I am sure, to make the world go round.

A "natural villain" used to be the man you loved to hate. Last summer, when Watergate was unraveling on TV like a combination detective serial and courtroom drama, public enthusiasm for the chase ran high, and Senator Ervin reigned with good-humored waggles of eyebrow and pious tag lines of scripture while, on the other side of the table, the screen fairly crackled with miscreants high and low, fools, knaves, and scoundrels of every shape and degree.

Now it is not that simple. The punishments have begun, and the game just isn't fun any more. Jail seems to be a vain and inadequate response to these crimes. Restitution to the people of what was taken from them seems necessary.

Another problem with the Watergate heavies was bad style, or perhaps lack of style. They are too much like ourselves; villain tends to dissolve into victim before our eyes.

Something curious seems to be happening to our good old American archetypes. Good guys and bad guys alike seem to belong on the endangered-species list. It is as hard to find heroes as villains today. We know too much. Hero worship has always required a certain distance between subject and observer, a necessary blank space in which the halo may shine.

We don't have to give up heroes and villains. What we need is new, updated definitions that suit these roiling, uneasy times. People in white hats, or black hats, are happily out-of-date. What is wanted is not cartoon good guys or bad guys, but people with subtle minds. Today the courage to go hatless is itself heroic.

I can identify a few other newly heroic qualities. In a nation of celebrity worshipers, amid followers of the cult of personality, individual modesty becomes a heroic quality. I find heroism in the acceptance of anonymity, in the studied resistance to the normal American tropism toward the limelight.

Consistency is another heroic quality in this age of future shock. Difficult as it is to adapt to a world of continuous change, it is even more difficult to maintain a consistent posture toward the few things that do not change. Indeed, the ability to remain oneself when the winds of change are howling about one's head may be heroism incarnate.

Equally heroic is the flexibility to change when necessary; to dare to be inconsistent; to admit error; and to grow.

Most difficult is the willingness to be complicated. I reserve my greatest admiration for those who continue to struggle to embrace the whole impossible tangle of snakes that is our society; those who fight to identify and strengthen human connections, and defeat polarizing forces that strain to drive us apart.

Finally, laughter remains heroic, and no gesture is more gallant than the courage to spit in the eye.

As for new villains, the one devil everyone can agree upon is the media. Some criticize its lack of accuracy, others its lack of objectivity, others its tendency to stifle debate and substitute dogma, but these dangers have all proved manageable by a free and responsible press. More worrisome is the media's unique vulnerability to capture by streakers, hijackers, the SLA, or anyone else who may jump up in front of the lens. New protections must be devised. What most needs guarding today is not the freedom of the press, but its unique exploitability by media freaks.

Television's ubiquitous eye can do evil in another, subtle way—it gives the illusion of being a candid camera, but wherever it pokes and glides, it alters reality by the fact of its presence. It can be dangerous, even wicked to pretend otherwise. The Loud family was victimized by this illusion.

When it was agreed that the deliberations of the House Judiciary Committee on Watergate guilt and responsibility would be covered by live television, the danger of such distortion was very real. TV, by its mere presence, might trivialize the proceedings, much as happened with the Senate committee hearings last summer. But this did not happen. By the end of the week, the parade of thirty-eight speakers, each striving in his or her own way to do honor to himself, the system, and history, had done much to restore one's faith in this nation's moral tone. There was nothing heroic about these thirty-eight people save their common humanity. That turned out to be more than enough.

Newsweek—August 5, 1974

SECTION 4

At the Sexual Delicatessen

1

Diary: 1976

Here are some comments about the sexual alarums and excursions of our times, plus two long profiles of two people who led the sexual revolution: Marlon Brando and Helen Gurley Brown. Marlon embodies sex in our time, in a much more serious way than Marilyn Monroe. Poor Marilyn was mostly a movie studio confection . . . and victim.

2

Marlon Brando

"Acting is only slipping and sliding," Marlon Brando said. The noble, astonishing head slid suddenly east to west like a Hindu temple dancer's. "Just slipping and sliding," the oddly light, gentle voice repeated, and now the head glided back across wide, still shoulders. "Everyone is really acting all the time."

He said this in Rome, seven years ago, and I have been debating the matter with him off and on ever since. I am beginning to feel like Penelope waiting for Ulysses to come home; this interview is my tapestry. I weave, fate unweaves; or lawyers do, or Brando himself, who despises and forbids all interviews, though not sometimes until after he has granted them. Our original meeting was arranged, with difficulty, by mutual friends. Now we are friends, and our debate has acquired momentum and rhythm of its own.

"Are you an ectomorph?" Brando may suddenly ask. "What kind of underwear do you wear?" "Did you know you have a twitch under your left eye?" I don't mind this grilling. It is part of the pattern in the tapestry. We have become yoked together, two oarsmen rowing in opposite directions in the same boat. Actor and writer, extrovert and introvert, Aries and Libra, yang and yin and you-name-it—could any two creatures be more unlike than Marlon and me? We do not understand each other at all.

I cannot conceive what it is like to be an actor. To me, it is agony to stand up in front of an audience. A spotlight feels like a stake through the heart. But Brando says everybody acts all the time. "You can't *live* and not act. If you expressed everything you thought, nobody could live with you. Say your daughter comes in wearing the ugliest dress you've ever seen—spangles here, and a big brown butterfly in the armpit. She made it in school, and she says, 'Mom, isn't it gorgeous?' Well, you can't say, 'Jesus, sweetheart, it really is horrible.' You can't do it! You've *got* to pretend."

"But Marlon," I say, "most people have trouble not in disguising their feelings but in expressing them."

He gives me the patient-guru look. "The biggest gap is not expressing what you feel but knowing what you feel. Most people don't know."

Most people know what they feel about Marlon Brando. They think he is the greatest natural-born actor alive, and they have been saying so for a quarter of a century. I think so, too, but don't say it; not to him. Brando hates to hear those words. He has learned that people rarely make a declaration of love without expecting a response. They wait to hear what he intends to do about it. When they discover he doesn't intend doing anything, they become angry, hurt, or betrayed. Success in this country has its own rules, and Brando seems to flout them all.

Our rules state that if you can, you must. Painters must paint, athletes must play, politicians must run, actors must act. There can be no equivocation. Gifts must be developed. Capacity may not be kissed off. Genius must be cultivated. Art must be served. In the aristocracy of ability, as of blood, noblesse oblige. Otherwise, life implies darkly, if talent is ignored, if the gardens are not cultivated and the paper is left blank, then everything may fall apart. Brando's heresy is that he refuses to worship at the altar of himself.

Twenty-five years ago, he impacted into the world of acting like a meteor, blazing. "Blazing" may not be quite the word for Stanley Kowalski, picking his nose and scratching his behind in *A Streetcar Named Desire*. But certainly it was a potent new style, not just in acting but in high-voltage sex, and suddenly the Errol Flynn and Clark Gable types became less interesting, and the exciting new actors were Montgomery Clift, and Paul Newman, and all the other new mutations of the cool Brando style. Today we have another group of low-key naturalistic actors: Dustin Hoffman, Jack Nicholson, Al Pacino. So at forty-seven, Brando finds himself not only Godfather but in a sense grandfather to a third generation of actors. Yet he is more: there is mystery at the center of this man, an enigma that lifts him out of the chocolate box which contains every other movie star.

Do not imagine Brando is himself unbemused by the mystery, or without a moral position on the matter. He has a moral position on everything, from Bangladesh (for) to panty girdles (against). Indeed, the attachment of moral valences to every idea, value, thing on the face of the earth may be the most predictable aspect of his fizzing, foaming mind. Caught in this constant tension, this alternating current between serving his talent and trying to ignore it, to respect it, and to exist independent of it, Brando vibrates his life away.

This vibration makes Brando far more interesting offscreen than most actors. He is also charming, fun, various, tantalizing, exasperating, tender, rude, intelligent, intuitive, kind, puppyish, catlike, leonine, slothful, and I suppose, anything else he feels like being. He is the actor. A couple of weeks ago, I went to see him in Paris, to talk to him about *The Godfather*, and finish off our interview. Or did he send for me? With Brando, I have learned, nothing is fully clear. He is as comfortable in ambiguity as a sailor in a hammock.

In the soft winter twilight of the hotel suite, the figure lolling in the inevitable Japanese robe looked more handsome than ever—the head dazzling, small, perfect; a broken, noble nose; eyes that suggest bruises or smudges in a Mayan mask, until they crinkle in laughter. His longish hair is whitening and tied back with child's ponytail elastic, leaving a becoming nimbus of wisps around the face, a sort of burning, Japanese chic. Brando glows.

I congratulate him on persuading a certain tycoon to invest in one of Marlon's many save-the-world projects, this one to extract protein from seawater. "Wasn't hard," he says. "All I had to do was rub his hump with yak butter, and suck on his earlobe a little." He grins. The dart has been perfectly placed.

On the floor by his bare feet is a copy of the *Whole Earth Catalog*. In it, he tells me, he has at last found a statement of purpose that matches his own. This purpose, and *The Godfather*, are to be the only official topics of conversation. To Brando, any public discussion of his private life, even the merest mention, is impermissible. This is why he forbids interviews. "Navel-picking" is his stock term for interviews with famous people. Interviews about one's personal life are characterized as "Navel-picking, AND SMOKING IT!"

"For reasons that are not completely known to me consciously, I cannot reconcile myself to sitting and blabbering to you for public benefit, and money." This strikes me as a strange remark for an actor to make, and I say so. It is why later I realize to what degree Marlon is my opposite number: to him, interviews are fake; acting is real.

"This reminds me of those discussions you see on television where people sit in front of the camera and give the impression they're having an intimate conversation," he persists. "But it's all designed for an effect that has hardly anything to do with the two people. It has to do with fourteen million people watching, and ratings, and money, and other considerations that are very carefully hidden and disguised and painted over."

Very politely, but nonetheless aghast, he is asking me: *How can you do what you do?*

I try again to explain. "If I were writing about pollution, or politics, you'd say okay. What distresses you, Marlon, is that I'm writing about another person. And it's you."

"Look," he says, hoping once more to make me understand. "If I were a dentist, I wouldn't be here. If I were a lumberjack, I wouldn't be here. If I were a scuba diver who went down with a welding torch to fix bridges, I wouldn't be here. But because of this nutty thing they call the American success story, *I'm willing to be a product!* I have my peaked cap on, and my pushcart, and I'm out hawking my tomatoes . . . aauugghh . . . it's navel-picking, and it's odious."

For the record, then: Marlon Brando has had a mother, a father, several siblings, and several children by several wives. He owns an archipelago of uninhabited islands near Tahiti where he spends as much time as he possibly can, camping out with the children in a Swiss Family Robinson idyll, a boyhood dream made real. I remember a producer remarking once that "the only trouble with Marlon is that his frontal lobe isn't quite up to his lower brain." The producer was wrong. What is unusual about Brando's brain is that frontal lobe and lower brain are not linked by the poor, shriveled, meandering goat path with which most of us must make do when we wish to visit our subconscious or commune with long-buried emotions. Brando's goat path is an eight-lane highway. Brando's boyhood was middle-western, middle-class, and outwardly unremarkable. But since this boyhood is the deep well out of which Stanley Kowalski and Fletcher Christian and Zapata and Napoleon and Mark Antony and Major Penderton and now Vito Corleone, the Godfather, have all been drawn, perhaps he is wise not to let anyone look into waters so rich, dark, and deep.

Brando seems able to dip into the well at will and reel in whatever characterization he seeks. He has been gifted with an instant retrieval mechanism, an extraordinary ability to fantasize, and a kind of perfect pitch. But it gets harder every time. "It's like sustaining a twenty-five-year love affair," he says. "There are no new tricks. You just have to keep finding new ways to do it, to keep it fresh." And there are other problems.

"You have to upset yourself. Unless you do, you cannot act. And there comes a time in one's life when you don't want do it any more. You know a scene is coming where you'll have to cry and scream and all those things, and it's always bothering you, always eating away at you . . . and you can't just walk through it . . . it would be really disrespectful not to try to do your best."

There are certain aspects of Brando's profession which he does enjoy. "Human behavior has always fascinated me," he admits. "Actors *have* to observe. They have to know how much spit you've got in your mouth, and where the weight of your elbows is. I could sit all day in the Optimo Cigar Store telephone booth on Forty-second Street and just watch the people pass by.

"But I've always tried to run acting down, tried to be very tough about it, and I don't know why. . . . It's a perfectly reasonable way to make your living. You're not stealing money, and you're entertaining people. Everybody has had the experience of feeling miserable, of feeling: Christ, the world is coming to an end. And you go watch John Wayne ride across the prairie, and see the grass blowing and the clouds, and he grabs the girl and they ride off into the sunset. You went in there feeling awful, and you come out feeling good. *He* made you feel good. That's not bad, that's not a bad thing to do in life at all. . . ."

What the actor does, I suggest, is to give blood to the fantasies of the audience. "That's right!" he exclaims, captivated by the phrase. "That's the great hustler's policy, one that I follow. If you want something from an audience, you give blood to their fantasies. It's the *ultimate* hustle."

Brando doesn't go to see his own movies. He feels he can learn nothing from watching himself, and might even do himself injury. "You don't learn to be effective from film, but from life. Actors who watch themselves tend to become mannered. The less you think about how effective you are, the more effective you are. If you *try*, what finally shows is the effort. Of course, this isn't true with Kabuki theater, or Laurence Olivier, who . . . choreographs, and who orchestrates. But that is a different form."

He says he refuses even to watch daily rushes. It's forty-five minutes he would rather spend doing something else. I say flatly that I don't believe him, don't believe he never examines his work and considers how he could make it better. After all, I think nothing of rewriting a page five times.

"Look," he says, speaking in the elliptical, Zen-master style he favors when forced to talk about something he doesn't want to, like making a movie, and maybe questioning his own performance. "Look. If I'm riding a horse, and it's supposed to get me to Duluth in sixty-eight days from Sonora, Mexico, and the horse goes lame—I'm not gonna kick the horse in the ass. Or hate the horse. It's paid for a lot of groceries." While waiting for another horse, Marlon "would prepare myself and lay about. But when it comes time to get up and get hit with the pig bladders again—Christ! I honestly don't care."

"What are the pig bladders?"

"Well, the pig bladders are . . . failure."

There will be no pig bladders for *The Godfather*. The picture is as full of life as a Brueghel painting, and full of death as a slaughterhouse. Any actor can die, actor-like, of gunshot or garrote or knife; and in *The Godfather*, dozens do. Amid this wall-to-wall blood, one is stunned by the great power of the actor who can move us by falling dead of natural causes in a vegetable garden, as Brando does.

At the beginning of his final scene, the Godfather is a frail old man, romping with his little grandson. But as the fatal seizure grips him, some of the old mafioso's bull-like size and weight magically return, and a shaggy old Minotaur crashes to earth among the tomato plants. It is not a trick of camera or makeup. Brando has been his own, and only, special-effects man. By dying the way we all expect to die—unexpectedly—he teaches the difference between death as titillation and death as terror.

Brando *has* seen *The Godfather,* but only because he had to redub the sound track to banish the Brando mumble. I ask him what he thought. "I'm glad Bob Evans gave me the part," he says, "because I felt the picture made a useful commentary on corporate thinking in this country. I mean, if Cosa Nostra had been black, or socialist, Corleone would have been dead or in jail. But because the Mafia patterned itself so closely on the corporate model, and dealt in a hard-nosed way with money, and with politics, it prospered. The Mafia is so . . . American! To me, a key aspect of the story is that whenever they wanted to kill somebody, it was always a matter of policy. Before pulling the trigger, they told him: 'Just business. Nothing personal.' When I read that, McNamara, Johnson, and Rusk flashed before my eyes."

Brando would like to retreat to his island for good. "Being in Tahiti gives me a sense of the one-to-one ratio of things," he says. "You have the coconut in the tree, the fish in the water, and if you want something to eat, you somehow have to get it." This, he explains, is where the *Whole Earth Catalog* comes in, and he reads aloud: " 'We are as gods, and might as well get good at it. . . . A realm of intimate personal power is developing—power of the individual to conduct his own education, find his own inspiration, shape his own environment.' " Following this credo, Marlon wants to establish a research station on his island to find ways to tap solar energy and wind energy, and to extract nutrients from seawater. He is in a hurry because "the three factors that concern us all are pollution, overpopulation, and aggression—and they're interlocked. If we don't solve all three problems, we can't really look to the future. Some people say it's already too late, and we're just knitting and tatting and playing Monopoly to kill time before we and the planet die. But even though you're going down in a plane, and the wing is off, you pull your seat belt tight, and say, 'Maybe I'll just make it.' "

Thinking back now over the seven years, I remember all the voices. Actors, moguls, women, yearning directors and writers, gossips, fans, strangers on boats and planes, and audiences around the world who have felt his mystery—all these people talking, talking about Brando. He lolls at the still center of this turning babble, unanswering his telephones, enraging all the talkers who can't get through to him. But what is he *doing* in there? He is doing whatever it is that he at that moment wants to do: sleeping, lifting weights, making lists, dreaming about his island, stirring his fire, fiddling with his telescope, speculating about Buddhist philosophy, tropical sex practices, bioaquanautics, Indians, Eskimos, the ten deadliest animals in the world, famine relief, the social life of apes, poisons of the Amazon, Japanese erotica, Black Panthers. . . .

To whoever happens to cut through to this unreachable place, Marlon will give time, money, ear, and heart without stint, and he will talk freely about all these matters, or anything else, providing it is not for publication. In fact, the one and only thing he finds difficult to talk about, even in private conversation, is acting. That is why this marathon interview has gone on for seven years. I have come to realize at last that perhaps an actor like Brando who unspools everything out of himself *dares* not discuss acting much. To do so might risk giving oneself away, mouthful by mouthful, until no one is left, no *persona* inside his skin. But he has been understandably reluctant all along, or too courteous perhaps, to say flat out that it appears to him that what I have been suggesting is that he unweave *his* tapestry so that, from its raveled threads, I may weave mine.

Life—March 1, 1973

3

Diary: 1976

The Brando piece took me seven years to write, was enormous fun, and cost Life *two round trips from Hollywood to Rome, plus side trips to Tahiti, Paris, and other garden spots. My Brando expense account surely helped in its small way to put* Life *out of business. But the wear and tear on everybody around* Life *was pretty great in those days, as the following note by editor Ralph Graves takes pains, blood-spattered pains, to explain.*

4

Editor's Note

This week's article on Marlon Brando by Shana Alexander is something of a landmark. Although she has written over 100 articles and columns for us, this is her first *Life* piece in almost three years. She left our staff in 1969 to become editor of *McCall's,* and she has also been busy with radio and TV appearances, speeches, the women's political movement, and a collection in book form of her *Life* writings. It is wonderful to have her in the magazine again. But the Brando piece is another kind of landmark: it represents Shana's all-time record between the moment of assignment and the moment of publication. That is saying something.

Shana has written well about more or less everything, but she has done a number of articles on show business personalities, beginning with Lassie in 1957 and including Judy Garland, Tony Curtis, Burt Lancaster, and Barbra Streisand. Shana's system, if it can be called that, is to agonize for some time before actually tackling her subject. First meetings are painful, and they are followed by a sustained period of doubt about whether the story should be done at all. Additional meetings lend her hope, and eventually she reaches a position of confidence with her subject. At this stage, she becomes determined to know absolutely everything and that also takes a fair amount of time. Finally, steeped in knowledge and crowded notebooks, she has to face the ultimate hurdle of writing.

When she undertook her column called "The Feminine Eye," she was living in California, but her pieces had to close in New York. This led to a situation best summed up as "stress." The deadline was every other Wednesday, so it was not possible for her to go through her customary months of agonizing. Still, she did the best she could with the time at her disposal. Her copy would start coming in by teletype, often late and incomplete. Splendid opening paragraphs might be followed by erratic and even desperate ones. As Shana's editor, I would get on the phone to her in Los Angeles and point out the shortcomings. A tense, little voice replied that she knew all that and was even, at this very moment, engaged in repair work if I would only get off the phone. Indeed, in the exquisite fullness of time, the well-wrought repairs would come over the teletype. After another, slightly less tense phone call to clarify minor matters, we would say good night, each silently thanking God that "The Feminine Eye" had closed again.

Despite all difficulties, the column was remarkably successful. I used to think how much easier it would all be if Shana were in New York instead of Los Angeles, but this was delusion. Once she came East to do a column on the Liston-Clay fight, and it was one of our worst closings ever. In her terminal anguish over writing, Shana accidentally stabbed her own arm with a ball-point pen, with the result that her column arrived on my desk with real blood on it. Even telephone and teletype were better than that.

As for the Brando piece, Shana got the assignment seven years ago.

RALPH GRAVES, Managing Editor
Life Magazine

5

Diary: 1976

I am a very slow writer. One day I remember my editor bringing me all the way in to New York from California and then taking me out to a very grand lunch only to point out gently, over the brandy, that in the past year I had only contributed three pieces to Life. *I was shocked. Shocked that anybody had been* counting. *Certainly I hadn't. I may have been somewhat chagrined as well, because I remember completing my next assignment in less than a week. Helen Gurley Brown was the easiest* next assignment in less than a week. *Helen Gurley Brown was the easiest person I ever tried to write about. I understood her and her message so perfectly, all I had to do was type it out. Later I was astonished when my editors cabled back: Boy, you really nailed her!, the implication being that I was making fun of Helen* and *her book. I was of course doing no such thing, and the editors' misperception was a measure of how much they didn't understand women. Either one of us.*

After the piece was published, Helen and her husband and I became and have remained good friends. The same thing happened with Brando. I mention this because in my line of work the phenomenon is rare. Always anticipate enmity, rage, scorn, and injured feelings from your subject; you will seldom be disappointed. Years after I wrote about him, Burt Lancaster was still going around telling people how disappointed I'd been that he didn't take me to bed. Fancy! The people who were good friends of mine used to ask me: how come? A tough question, perhaps the female equivalent of: when did you stop beating your wife?

The piece on Helen ends with ". . . boy meets book!" A switch on the usual formula: boy meets girl. In real life, Helen went on and met Destiny, as the brilliant editor of Cosmopolitan. *Boy—who in my story was Helen's then-new husband, David Brown—went on to meet shark, in* Jaws, *and to make himself $20,000,000 or so as coproducer of the most successful movie of all time.*

Helen made Cosmopolitan *the most successful women's magazine of all time. Her secret was simple: she knew exactly what women wanted to hear about, and was willing to work like hell to tell them. I was not surprised to learn from Steve Weed that* Cosmo *had been Patty Hearst's favorite magazine. Her affection had nothing to do with the fact that her daddy owns it. One way to understand Patty's character, and her seemingly facile conversion to the heady life-style of the SLA, is to say that Patty was the kind of very young girl who would read all of Helen's nutty ad copy about "That Cosmopolitan Girl!" and—unfortunately—would really believe it.*

6

Helen Gurley Brown

Once upon a time, in an improbable place called Hollywood, an advertising copywriter said to her new husband, "David, darling, I'm so unhappy at the office. I wish I could quit and write a book. But what could I write about?"

"Helen, dear," answered her husband of five months, "you must write about *what you know.*"

It is conceivable that Helen knew a bit more than David bargained for. What she knew, in her own words, was "what it's *really* like to be single. For seventeen years I actually had been quite a swinger, and a solid citizen, too." The book Helen Gurley Brown, now forty, wrote was *Sex and the Single Girl,* a manifesto in favor of female single blessedness which is supposed to do for the unmarried American female what Charles Atlas did for the ninety-seven-pound weakling.

"Theoretically a 'nice' single woman has no sex life. What nonsense!" Helen proclaimed in Chapter One. "She has a better sex life than most of her married friends." The moment her memoir was published, it leaped onto the best-seller lists. Some 137,000 copies have been sold at $4.95. It has been translated into ten languages and is still selling a brisk 2,500 hardcover copies a week at home. A paperback edition will be published this fall for the benefit of additional thousands of working girls who presumably are tired of being protected by heaven.

In retrospect, it is not surprising that Helen's book has sold so well: there are twenty-three million unmarried women in the U.S., one third of the adult female population. What is surprising is that the movie studios immediately began jockeying for film rights. Not only does Helen's thesis violate the fundamental Hollywood dogma that all love must sooner or later be licit, but the entire book is innocent of any semblance of plot. There are only bits and pieces of Helen's personal story, fragmented like walnuts and sparsely scattered through a gummy chocolate fudge of grooming hints, advice to the lovelorn, jokes, snippets of psychological insight, decorating suggestions, exercise regimes, stock market tips, and recipes. There is even some bold talk about sex, but no orgies.

Yet within two months of the book's publication, Warner Brothers had not only closed a deal to make a movie, but a deal with a price tag of $200,000—the highest sum Hollywood has ever paid for a nonfiction book—or, more accurately, a nonfiction nonbook.

To those who have actually read *S.A.T.S.G.*, the $200,000 figure is downright incredible. Helen, the most indefatigably cheerful female since Ma Perkins, conjures images of a liberated single girl, complete with Capri pants, a sophisticated little apartment, and a delicious absence of guilt feelings. Nothing gets Helen down. If the reader doesn't know any men, Helen has oodles of hints on how to begin:

"Live-bait barges hire girl clerks. . . . Fuller Brush men are usually darlings. . . . Outsiders are permitted to attend Alcoholics Anonymous meetings. . . ." If the Fuller Brush man turns out to have a wife and kiddies back in Cucamonga, Helen does not panic. "During and after an affair, a single woman suffers emotional stress," she admits, but asks, "Do you think a married woman can bring [an affair] off more blissfully free of strain?"

And if that sounds like unpromising box office, consider this: the big climax of Helen's second longest chapter is an amour-arousing recipe for herb bread which ends with the ringing words, "You will now have greenish-looking butter. With a knife, spread it between the slices of bread. Really sop it on." How can anybody make a movie out of *that?*

According to a studio spokesman, what Warner's bought was not the book but simply its title. Current Hollywood economic theory holds that the safest bet is to put one's money into a "pretested property" that has a "presold audience," and a best-selling title is considered the safest guarantee of all. By the same theory, to be sure, a truly super-colossal epic might be fashioned from Irma S. Rombauer's *The Joy of Cooking.* (Mountains of Aspic in *breathtaking* Technicolor! Savage Timbales *seared* in *white hot flame!*) Still, *Sex and the Single Girl* is a pretty fine movie title, as indeed any title should be which assays out at $40,000 per word.

To devise some plot to hang onto its five-word, solid-gold handle, Warner's appointed a tyro producer named Saul David, who had originally distinguished himself as an idea man in the paperback book business. He was also an old and good friend of Helen and David Brown. In fact, Helen had shown a draft of her first chapter to Saul David while he was still in the book business. "Great stuff, kid!" he had exclaimed. "Finish it and I promise I can unload it for you."

Little did he know that fate would ultimately load the book back onto his own frail shoulders. The retribution has been almost Greek. *S.A.T.S.G.* became Saul David's very first assignment as a movie producer—and he has admitted it may well be his last. For seven months, he has spent night and day trying to wrest a workable screenplay from Helen's jottings. More than plot and characters were needed. Warner's also wanted him to find a point of view which would remain faithful to the blithe spirit of the book ("During the past seventeen years I believe I was The Girl of at least twelve eminently successful men") and yet make a reasonably acceptable movie. *Quelle* nightmare! as Helen would say.

About all the hapless Saul has had to go on are a few tantalizing hints of Helen's own Cinderella story. She describes her movie-producer husband as a "brainy, charming and sexy" man once "sought after by many a Hollywood starlet." There are lyric descriptions of the marital estate she has won: "Two Mercedes-Benzes, 100 acres of virgin forest near San Francisco, a Mediterranean house overlooking the Pacific, a full-time maid and a good life." Yet not long ago, Helen confesses, she was a "mouse-poor secretary . . . not bosomy or brilliant . . . with the world's worst case of acne," who washed her hair in Woolite and lived in a room furnished with orange crates.

Faced with such material, Saul has already gone through three screenwriters, a deskful of Alka-Seltzer and some bloodcurdling sessions with the Front Office. He has tried a story in which the girl sinned but suffered, and another in which she didn't and didn't. He tried deploying six girls in a Dostoevskian anthology of suffering. He even tried a Texas yarn, pitting the suave head of a posh department store (Cary Grant?) against a rough-hewn fertilizer tycoon (John Wayne?). Nothing has worked.

But while Saul and his writers have been writhing in creative agony, back at the Mediterranean house overlooking the Pacific all has been, in Helen's words, "Success City." David Brown has abandoned his own career as a movie producer to concentrate on managing his wife's burgeoning empire. One of his most brilliant managerial decisions was to insist on a contract with Warner's relieving Helen of any responsibility for converting her book into a usable screenplay. Thanks to David's foresight, Helen has been free to bask in the glow of rising success and the fringe benefits of best-sellerdom.

She bought a slew of new clothes and began lecturing to women's clubs on such subjects as "Doing What Comes Unnaturally." She wrote an LP record, "Lessons in Love," and narrated it herself. Side one, addressed to females, advises secretaries to "love your boss with all your heart. There may be days when you are the only person who does." On the flip side, Helen switches to a more low-cut voice and tells her male students, "Never, never cheat on your girl with anybody— except your wife." The jacket of this disk is prominently stamped, "For home use only. Not to be played on the air." It is selling nicely.

The fan mail at Helen's seaside villa is waist deep, almost all of it favorable. Many correspondents tell Helen they have read her book at one sitting, read it many times, memorized whole pages. They use it as a personal rulebook, and give it away wholesale at Christmas. The letters come from women of all ages, occupations, and parts of the U.S. "Girls just seem to crawl out of the woodwork to find me," Helen says. On the evidence of Helen's mail, *S.A.T.S.G.* is also attracting a growing number of male aficionados—for obvious reasons. Nor is all of the mail from anonymous "little people." Both Harry Golden and Suzy Parker, says the author, have written fan letters. Joan Crawford, in Helen's irresistible phrase, "went ape." Linda Christian was moved to ask for an autographed copy.

Undoubtedly Helen has achieved a state of bliss in proportion to the fame, money, and comforts her book has brought. "It's me, me, me! That's what's so heady about it," she crows. But criticism of her magnum opus drives her correspondingly wild, especially if the critic suggests that the tremendous success of *S.A.T.S.G.* is due more to its title than to its content.

Helen's title was thought up by husband David, and when she first heard it, she hated it. "It sounded to me like just another Kinsey report," she says now. "Anyhow, I can think up lots of sexy titles. But if the books are garbage, nobody will read them." Then, casting the peculiar, fixed, hooded glance which she calls "The Sexy Look" and recommends in the chapter devoted to flirting, she adds, "I simply cannot tell you how *sincere* this silly little book of mine is."

She need not try. Helen's passionate sincerity on matters of man-trapping, date-baiting, and so on throbs out of every page. Accordingly, she was deeply hurt when her hometown paper, the Los Angeles *Times*, published a scathing review by book critic Robert L. Kirsch. After branding *S.A.T.S.G.* "as tasteless a book as I have read," Kirsch warmed up with phrases like "her purpose is manipulation. I detect a thorough contempt for men, who are the marionettes of this manipulation." He eventually worked himself up into a perfect lather of loathing: "She rushes breathlessly from punchy paragraph to compressed exposure, a creature of the advertising age, endorsing the phoniness and hard-soft subliminal sell which substitutes for individuality, candor, sincerity. What she describes as sex is not sex at all but a kind of utility. Perhaps futility would be a better word."

But Helen's revenge has been neat and sweet. Somebody at the *Times* apparently figured that any woman who could provoke such an outburst from its normally phlegmatic book critic probably could also sell a lot of newspapers. Result: beginning April 15, Helen's thrice-weekly newspaper column, "Woman Alone," will start appearing in the *Times* as well as other newspapers coast to coast. If the column goes as well as the syndicate expects, it may ultimately earn Helen $100,000 a year and bring her total earnings from *S.A.T.S.G.* to perhaps half a million dollars by the end of this year.

Since Helen's own story has been a Hollywood fairy tale come true, a wrap-'em-up happy ending for all hands seems both necessary and inevitable. Last week, the fairy tale began to take final shape. Helen was halfway through the manuscript of her second book. It will be called, not at all over her dead body, *Sex and the Office*. With Helen's career nicely programmed to go into its second orbit, the Browns planted a for sale sign in front of their Mediterranean-style house overlooking the Pacific. They are now packing to move to New York City where, on the same day that Helen's first syndicated column is scheduled to appear in the nation's newspapers, husband David will assume his new duties as an editorial executive of the New American Library.

And what of their friend Saul David, the movie producer? At the moment, he thinks he may have solved even his enormous problem. "I finally realized that the *book* is our star!" he now exclaims triumphantly. "When the picture opens, *Sex and the Single Girl* is already a best-seller. We see this guy, a book critic, pounding away at his typewriter, really steamed. He thinks it's garbage. Then we see Helen, smoke streaming from her nostrils as she reads his review. . . . It's a whole new concept—boy meets book! I don't see how it can miss."

Life—March 1, 1963

7

At the Sexual Delicatessen

Bare breasts, get dressed! Bottomless go-goers, begone! Four-letter words, shut up! I am sick of you all. The same goes for all you sensuous women and glib obscenity lawyers and leering TV hosts and naked cellists and unshockable sex therapists; all you heaving, straining novelists, obscene rock stars, art-book porn boys, and swinging psychiatrists; you purveyors of X-rated cartoons and nude-encounter manuals and organ delicatessen by mail. Not that it's all bad, you understand . . . just that I'm sick of it.

We are on a sexual binge in this country. Never mind that this binge follows a long sexual famine that in its denials of sensuality may have been even more injurious to life, liberty, and the pursuit of happiness. It is possible to have too much of even a very good thing. One consequence of this binge is that while people now get into bed more readily and a lot more naturally than they once did, what happens there often seems less important. People used to be wary of making love. Now they're wary of feeling it. I'm not sure that's much of an improvement.

In his newest movie, Marlon Brando calls the binge the pursuit of hap-penis, a pretty good ad lib. One reason Brando is America's greatest actor is because he has always been uniquely able to embody Americans' fantasies. Once more his instincts are right, his pun dead-on.

Both the highest and lowest expressions of our erotomania are concurrently visible on movie screens. The highest is Brando's own film, *Last Tango in Paris*. Dazzling, intensely erotic, often brutal, sometimes funny, very beautiful, it investigates to the outermost, unbearable limits what Lesley Blanch called the wilder shores of love, although in *Tango* it is men, not women, who mount and lead the expedition.

Is *Tango* pornographic? To some, no doubt. It is also suffused with mystery, and has moments of gaiety and wit that mere porn dare not risk. Laughter is too apt to extinguish the sexual candle. *Tango* is the encounter of a great director and a great actor who dare to unmask, to work as naked in self as in body. Most of all, perhaps, *Tango* is sex perceived as epic warfare.

In the thrusting-pen school of cinema criticism, it is fashionable now to insist that sex *is* violence. Certainly many recent hit movies—*A Clockwork Orange, Straw Dogs*—make one wonder whether sex is fully erotic without it. It is, of course. Gentle sex is even preferable, as most women and a lot of men will testify.

In any case, feeling as I do about *Tango*, I deemed it a journalistic obligation to also have a look at the porno-chic all-time hit, *Deep Throat*. Besides, I was curious and, I thought, inoculated against sexual shock. Wrong. *Throat* is hideous. It is also witless and endless. But mostly to me it was just plain ugly. I left after half an hour and I don't know how many of the famed eleven acts of oral sex I sat and watched. But the connecting up of giant genitalia in glaring light appropriate to a surgical amphitheater proved too tough for me to take. Truman Capote is right: "You see it at your own peril." And that peril is disgust, and the deadening of feeling. After only a few moments at *Throat,* one's lifelong opposition to any form of sexual censorship becomes difficult to defend.

It seems necessary to add—such are the uncertainties of a modern woman—that pornography is not new to me, nor do I claim immunity to its sometimes sleazy charms. Pornography is sex fiction, and like its respectable brother, science fiction, it comes in all grades of quality. But unless you are used to it, today's pop porn makes you upchuck your popcorn. If you are used to it, you get bored. The real weakness of all porn, it seems to me, is its necessary repetition. Since the body is finite, with only seven or eight immutable orifices, the pornographer must continually invent new sauces for old meats.

If *Tango* and *Throat* have anything in common, it is that both are products of male sexual imagination. They describe predicaments women are unlikely to dream up. Come to think of it, there *is* no separate tradition of pornography for women. There is just porn, and the same stuff is expected to turn on either sex. Not only expected to; it does, or it used to in the dear postcard days before fem-lib reared its Medusa head. How sad that so often nowadays the "emancipation" of the female turns both sexes to sexual stone.

Is all erotica male fantasy then, in which women merely collude? Certainly the only strictly female-minded porn I have encountered is the kind designed for lesbians. Ellen Willis, a young and thoughtful writer and one of the very few persons I have read who makes any sense on the subject of female sexuality, says that the only place she has seen an attempt to convey women's special sexual feelings is in gay films made by men. A confusing business.

My spirits lift to learn that the British have now banned the movie version of *Oh! Calcutta!* A few weeks back, they forbade the TV airing of some Andy Warhol homosexual home movies. Nothing, I suspect, is lost to art, even to pornographic art, by the suppression of these two works. The only loss is at the box office, which is fine with me. The newfound, big-business status of pornography particularly offends. It is worth noting that our climate of permissiveness has allowed what we used to call dirty movies and magazines to become a $550 million business, and the federal government claims to be investigating how much of the financing of hard-core porn comes from the Mafia.

But to be sick of sex is not enough these days, though there are moments when I wish it were. Something very complicated is going on here. Casual couplings and multiple organ-encounters may signify a society that has achieved sexual liberation, but I doubt they do much for the corresponding achievement of feeling. Indeed, it seems to work just the opposite. The price of shallow sex may be a corresponding loss of capacity for deep love.

When casual sex gets easy—and so many gritty grapplings on today's pages and screens are not only easy but flippant—serious sex kind of dries up. The fear of love grows as the hunger for it becomes unappeasable. The slow growth of feeling between two people used to be what drew bodies together, along with minds. One result of the new permissiveness is that the first tremor of genuine emotion is apt to send people scurrying for cover—in opposite directions.

Mind and body are not to be taken lightly. Their connection is intimate and mysterious, and better mapped by poets than pornographers. For all the floodlit, hairy close-ups, the spasm may be in the flesh, but the feeling is in the mind. So that in the last analysis (which I sincerely hope this is), I would agree with Raquel Welch. Asked by a TV interviewer to identify her most erogenous zone, Raquel pointed silently to her forehead.

Newsweek—February 5, 1973

8

Hanging Out in Sexual Space

The only Washington figure left with genuine job security may be Mrs. Grundy, that mythical guardian of public morality. When the Supreme Court ruled again a couple of weeks ago that obscenity is a matter best left to "contemporary community standards," Mrs. Grundy was assured her place in the driver's seat for an indefinite term.

The trouble, as always, was in the language. Who today even knows what a "community" is—town, village, city, state, peer group, or state of mind—let alone what its standards are?

I find the situation arbitrary but not particularly distressing. Freedom for porn is not important on any scale of priorities; freedom *from* it was becoming a national necessity. If some citizens of Georgia cannot see *Carnal Knowledge*—one of the test cases along the way—it is no great loss to carnality, to knowledge, or to art. But if expensively produced Hollywood movies can be turned off at the whim of any small-town, small-time Mrs. Grundy, the potential loss at the box office could be catastrophic. Enter Mr. Jack Valenti, president of the Motion Picture Association of America, breathing hard.

Valenti's engaging personality is inside out: he is emotional on the surface, prudent at the core. Thus he is best remembered, unfairly, as the man who said he slept a little better each night because his boss Lyndon Johnson was in the White House. Presumably he is sleeping even better as movie czar, now that the MPAA has just rewarded him with a fat, new five-year contract for successfully steering the movie industry through heavy weather since 1966.

In the old pre-Valenti days, Edward Anhalt wrote a picture, called *The Sniper*, about a fellow who got his kicks from shooting women. The official movie censor said shooting women was perversion, and "perversion" was expressly forbidden by the motion-picture code. Anhalt argued that shooting women was not perversion; shooting *men* was perversion. He got his seal.

It was partly to avoid this sort of inanity that Valenti five years ago installed the modern movie-rating system which labels films G, PG, R, or X, so that moviegoers, especially parents, will have some idea what to expect for their money. Public recognition of the new rating system had risen to a record high of 87 per cent and acceptance to 66 per cent when the Supreme Court brought Mrs. Grundy back into the act.

The Court's decision to turn the definition and prohibition of obscenity back to local authorities "left us hanging out in sexual space," Valenti told me. "We're now in a legal never-never land, where there are no rules of evidence, no guide lines of any kind." Amid these swirling mists, Valenti sees his own mission clearly. He is the self-appointed spokesman and champion of "the real world," a world whose standards are changing with "avalanching, frightening" speed. As he quite rightly points out, blue-movie artists and hard-core porn merchants did not create this world. If anything, it was the other way around. *Deep Throat* and Andy Warhol are creatures of our times. Every world creates its own art, just as it creates its own pornography.

As befits a declared realist, Valenti's rating system deals only with what it sees. "We don't presume to judge quality, so we don't care how sleazy the stuff is," he said. "We don't make moral judgments, we don't care if the good guy loses or the bad guy wins. We just rate what's on the screen, in four categories: sex, language, violence, theme.

"We look for what's excessive in each one. But what *is* too much sex? People say we rate by inch of pubic hair. Sure, we try to keep breasts out of PG, but that's because parents get uptight about it.

"What's excessive language? You may hear 'horseshit,' or 'piss on you' in PG, but beyond that, it goes into R.

"What is too much violence? Is it John Wayne landing at Iwo Jima with four hundred machine guns, or is it one man slowly taking another apart with whips? We're rating for parents, rating on what Mr. and

Mrs. America get uptight about. Excessive sex they mind. Too much violence they don't."

And that is the trouble. If there are no laws making the depiction of violence a crime, there should be. In Valenti's—and our—"real world," violence is the only pornography left.

The President's Commission on Obscenity and Pornography has been able to find "no evidence to date that exposure to explicit sexual materials plays a significant role in the causation of delinquent or criminal behavior among youth or adults." The same cannot be said of violence. Constant exposure of children to explicit violence in movies and TV certainly has a damaging, dulling, blunting effect on their sensibilities. People know this instinctively. That is why two-thirds of Americans say they are sure there is too much violence on TV.

If the movie producers were really interested in protecting children from bad influences, and not in protecting themselves from bad publicity, or bad box office, I think they would leave the sex alone, but take the violence out. Children can handle sexual material, even if their parents can't. Children understand that sex is a part of life, and not a secret part any more.

What I hate to see, and myself walk out of, is the aimless, brainless violence, especially sexual violence, of pictures like A Clockwork Orange and Straw Dogs. What shocks me is the sudden ugly prevalence of movie rape scenes—twenty in recent months. As a sexual turn-on, the rape scene in the seventies has replaced the obligatory bubble bath of the 1930's. I agree with critic Aljean Harmetz that "the attack between the thighs is only an extension of the bullet between the eyes."

You cannot legislate morality, as everybody knows. Perhaps the absurdity is greatest not in trying to legislate or regulate morality, but in trying to calibrate it. When Californians voted recently to restore the death penalty, Governor Reagan suggested that the state secretary of health and welfare try to find a more "humane" way to kill people. The secretary has since been searching for some method midway between crucifixion (too cruel) and a death pill slipped without warning into the food (insufficient deterrent).

I find this attempt to calibrate execution both absurd and obscene. I find Deep Throat also an odd mix of absurd and obscene. It is the absurd element in all porn which makes it seem silly to suppress it. Why repress fantasy? Can you suppress fantasy? Doesn't that create wilder fantasy?

In any event, we can and must suppress the brutality which another age will recognize as the one common hallmark of all our commercial entertainment. Kids' TV cartoons, pro football, the nightly news, all TV drama, and all movies now reek with sadism and gratuitous gore. Even Mrs. Grundy knows that a people that has become anesthetized to violence is in far more serious trouble than a society merely over-sexed.

Newsweek—November 12, 1973

9

Out of the Closet:
Masters and Johnson

I used to have the same trouble with Masters and Johnson's sex books that their patients had with their sex lives: when I dove between the covers, nothing happened. At least not what I was hoping for.

What I hoped for in *Human Sexual Response* and again in *Human Sexual Inadequacy* was a real *book;* ideas as well as data and clinical jargon. The jargon overload, I have since learned, was deliberate. All those polysyllables were an attempt to keep the general public at arm's length until the medical profession had had a first look at the potentially explosive subject matter, the first descriptions ever of the detailed physiology of sex. But the strategy didn't work because the professionals wouldn't pay attention, and the public wouldn't wait. The sexual revolution against puritan restraints had begun before Masters and Johnson came along in the mid-sixties with the basic research to support it. While other doctors and psychiatrists scoffed, the public clamored for honest information. As a result, the two books became the most-bought, least-read best-sellers in publishing history, and the authors were driven into a kind of professional shell shock from which they are only now emerging.

The occasion for their coming out is the publication of a third

Masters and Johnson book, *The Pleasure Bond,* which is very good indeed. Among its points are that promiscuity is tiresome, that vulnerability is sexy, that the important thing is commitment and that if pleasure isn't mutual, it isn't much fun. In short, the new book is full of the kind of things people used to talk about before the sexual revolution and its attendant avalanche of push-button sex manuals. Pornographic hard- and software and circuit-riding sex therapists temporarily knocked a lot of us off our pins. While the avalanche was at its height, the pulsating world of women's magazines probably could not have survived without receiving regular transfusions of original Masters and Johnson material, carefully decanted, it seemed, in secret sex labs somewhere in the Midwest and, suitably diluted for home consumption, shipped in lead phials to panting editors in New York. I know because I used to be such an editor myself, and in those days Masters and Johnson were more elusive than J. D. Salinger, harder to talk to than Trappist monks. So I was surprised when the once-aloof pair began turning up recently all over the tube on the talk-show circuit. Gone were the white coats, the carefully neutral faces. In their place sat a happily married middle-aged couple, just plain Bill and Gini, the Ma and Pa Kettle of gynecology. What had happened? Why had they decided to come out, to be normal human beings at last? Surely there was more here than a desire to plug a book.

I found them holding yet another press conference in their New York hotel suite, serene and smiling in the face of dirty coffee cups, flashing cameras, abrasive questions. He is somewhat stiff and remote, "not a people person," as he says, but she has a throaty voice and splendid smile. It is impossible not to like them. Their own estimate of their accomplishment is modest. "We don't try to change attitudes, just behavior," says Mrs. Johnson. Nonetheless she thinks their work has contributed "some comfort factor" to younger people. "You remember that old visceral clutch, almost painful, when you had to say certain words aloud?" I said I certainly did.

"Well, that's gone, and we think we've got across the idea that sexuality is honorable," says Dr. Masters. But their greatest pride is that they have learned how to treat sexual dysfunction, a condition they say afflicts 50 per cent of everybody at least some of the time. Its cause is fear of failure and of rejection.

Masters and Johnson have had to learn the hard way that professional rejection can be just as painful. When their early work, published in medical journals only, drew sniggers and scorn from their colleagues, "It traumatized them," says *Redbook* editor Robert Levin, coauthor of *The Pleasure Bond.* How could their fellow scientists see them as "white-coated monsters"? Hoping to dissolve this image before their second book came out, they embarked on a cross-country lecture tour of medical schools. "We wanted to disabuse other doctors of the concept we were some sort of freak," says Masters. But it didn't work. Although the scientific validity of their research has never been questioned or opposed, they remain "freaks" in many quarters. They have drawn the most fire for allegedly taking a "mechanistic" view of sex. "Of course we know you can't take out a person's sexuality and put it in a box and study it," says Johnson.

Masters and Johnson (who have been colleagues twenty years and husband and wife since 1971) also worry about what their notoriety did to their four teenage children from previous marriages. "We realize now that the kids took an awful beating from their friends," they say, though they don't admit the pain they feel at the beating they took themselves.

Overall, one senses that even today pride in their extraordinary achievements is still clouded by their sense of professional isolation. "I would have been so happy *not* to have been a pioneer," Dr. Masters says. "It's been a quarter-century since Kinsey, and nobody has tried to replicate *his* work, let alone ours. We have almost no followers, no young people. We're still entirely alone."

The skies were darkening over Central Park outside their window, and as I left their suite I remembered how, as children, we had giggled when a prankster shot out the letters E-S in the red ESSEX HOUSE sign atop the hotel. How far have most people really come since then in seeing sex as "something honorable"? No way of telling. What can be known for sure is that having truly pioneered, having ventured to the very brink of human knowledge, having looked at the forbidden mystery of life and challenged the sexual mystique that this country both worships and dreads, Masters and Johnson became shamans willy-nilly, modern-day witch doctors, white coats or no. So they are permanently apart and different, no matter how many chatty press conferences and talk shows they endure, no matter how "normal" they now try to be. If they have earned a place in history, they have also paid its price— a certain unbridgeable apartness from ourselves.

Newsweek—February 2, 1975

SECTION 5
Kids' Country

1

Diary: 1976

I've been writing about kids for years. The biggest kid I ever met was Tony Curtis. He was also my favorite movie star—he loved it so! I interviewed Tony for five months nonstop, because so long as I kept asking questions and he kept talking, I didn't have to start writing . . . and I'd encountered my first severe writer's block. My first Life *article, on Judy Garland, had been such a smash success, it got me the job as* Life's *first woman staff writer, and first staff writer permitted to live outside of New York City, at a safe 3,000-mile remove from our needle-eyed editors. I was scared to death about piece Number Two: Tony. Tony was scared, too, because so long as he kept talking, he didn't have to face the fact (unknown then to me) that his analyst had dumped him, his marriage was breaking up, and his studio had suspended him for contract-breach.*

Well, no. The biggest kid I ever wrote about was Packy, an elephant whose birth weight was 225 pounds. Packy's mother is an Oregon elephant called Belle, and her pregnancy lasted twenty-one months. I attended most of it. Belle's baby was the first zoo elephant ever born in the United States, so far as I am aware, and I am something of an expert on elephant maternity—having seen so much of it, and at such close range.

The story of "The Elephant's Child" was my all-time favorite assignment. It still is. I was a new mother myself at the time I wrote it, and quite deliriously happy. The book with which I hope to occupy my own old age is a history of the elephant in America, which began when an elephant sailed upriver with Henry Hudson. I've kept in touch over the

years with the two men responsible for this giant blessed event, veterinar-
ian Dr. Matthew Maberry and animal importer Morgan Berry, owner of
the mighty Thonglaw. (Belle and Packy were owned by the Portland
Zoo. Until last year, Thonglaw was a boarder there.) The 1975 letter to
me from Berry describes his tragic demise.

Thonglaw was not the only male elephant to come to a horrible end
in a way that touched me personally. In the same year that Thonglaw
first became a father, a couple of medical researchers in Oklahoma City,
also interested in the mystery of elephant sexuality, injected another
fourteen-year-old male, also obtained from Morgan Berry, with LSD.
They believed the drug might be chemically similar to the not-well-
understood elephant hormone which causes mature males periodically
to go on musth. *Within moments, the unfortunate creature was stagger-*
ing uncontrollably; in little more than an hour, he was dead. Fourteen
years later, I came across a detailed report of this experiment in a thick
pile of scientific papers, research credentials, submitted to a court in San
Francisco, prior to the trial of Patty Hearst. The writer was Dr. Louis
Jolyon West, authority on brainwashing and Patty's chief defense psy-
chiatrist.

"Operation Baby Lift: A Sentimental Binge," a piece on the mass
importation to this country of thousands of Vietnamese babies at war's
end, is almost the last thing I wrote for Newsweek, *and the one of which*
I am most proud. It may not be the last word on this tricky subject, but
I think it is the best.

2

The Elephant's Child

Despite what you may have read, O Best Beloved, the Elephant's Child
is born with his trunk fully developed and firmly attached. It is pink-
tipped and hairy and, when the Child is hungry, it makes a noise like

a leaky balloon. But your ignorance, Best Beloved, is most understandable: until this spring, a baby elephant had not been seen in these parts for almost half a century, not even by other elephants.

Today there are 301 elephants in the United States. Three hundred of them were born in the wilds, plucked from their native jungles at a tender age, and caught their first glimpse of America through the stout bars of a shipping crate. But the 301st elephant first saw the light of day on Saturday, April 14, 1962, over the transom of the maternity ward in the city zoo in Portland, Oregon. There, at 5:58 A.M., after lying-in for twelve weeks in an accouchement fit for a czarina, a ten-year-old Siamese elephant named Belle sounded one final blast through her trunk and then quietly gave birth to her first calf. He was the color of boiled veal and hairy all over from wrinkled rump to tip of his eight-inch trunk.

The nativity of elephant Number 301 was big zoo news any way you looked at it. Elephants are the largest beasts on earth, the most popular menagerie attractions in the world, and one of the most difficult animals to breed in captivity. Since the first U.S. elephant arrived in New York aboard a ship in 1796, only six baby elephants had been bred and born in North America. Four were the progeny of Alice and Snyder, a pair of uncommonly devoted circus elephants who flourished here in the years just before and during World War I. Each of Alice's unfortunate offspring endured a hideously traumatic birth, and each died suddenly in infancy. Alice bore her fourth and final calf in 1918; thereafter, for a number of reasons, America's elephant birthrate stood at zero for forty-four years.

When Belle's 225-pound son finally appeared, he looked like a fatigued anteater. His three-ton mother looked exhausted herself. But by far the most bone-weary of all was Dr. Matthew Maberry, the zoo veterinarian. Since January 18, Dr. Maberry had attended Belle's confinement. When at last it ended, Belle, the zoo men, and the population of Portland barely had time to shout hooray and exchange cigars before many postnatal problems arose. The zoo's problem: what to name the baby. In a citywide contest, Packy finally won out over Belle Boy, Ding Dong, and inevitably, Nogero (Oregon spelled backwards). Belle's first problem was to teach Packy the facts of elephant house life: beware of the moat, don't fall into the bathing pool, don't —for heaven's sake—get near the bars. Packy had only one major problem: his eight-inch nose. He seemed to have no idea what his trunk was there for. Over and over again the puzzled infant lowered his head to try to taste an apple or a slice of bread lying on the floor, and over and over again that long dangling thing got in the way. But today, despite the early confusion, Packy is in every way a happy, healthy elephant's child.

Portland first heard the news of the impending event on January 10. A front page item in the daily *Oregonian* announced that Belle was eighteen months pregnant and some 1,000 pounds overweight. It also revealed that three other female elephants at the zoo were probably pregnant, too! When Portland realized that its pink-painted elephant house was in fact a vast maternity ward, a carnival mood swept the city. One radio station began broadcasting hourly "Belle Bulletins"; another launched a "Name the Baby" contest. Toy departments boosted their stocks of stuffed elephants. Schoolchildren were assigned to draw pictures of what they imagined the baby would look like. Newspapers blossomed with headlines like ELEPHANTICIPATING! and ELEPHANTRICIANS ALERT! The zoo was deluged with gifts ranging from gold-plated diaper pins to a hand-knit baby elephant. A florist created a gigantic papier-mâché bootie and filled it with 300 roses.

Meanwhile, back at the elephant house, Belle appeared to be bearing her great burden well. Viewed head-on, she bulged amidships as if she had just swallowed a half dozen watermelons. But in profile, her swollen condition was not especially notable. A thousand extra pounds on 6,000 pounds of well-fed elephant is not as eye-catching as one might suppose. Attended by her three ponderous ladies in waiting, Belle strolled heavily around her quarters, nibbling hay and gazing back benignly at the throngs of visitors staring through the large glass windows of the 20-by-80-foot indoor elephant enclosure. Alert visitors could see her great gray flanks twitch whenever her unborn child administered a small, elephantine kick.

Seven feet inside and parallel to the windows was a row of four-inch steel pipes filled with concrete. The narrow alleyway between the bars and the glass was soon jammed with reporters and movie equipment. Overhead, a row of floodlights was being installed so that the momentous nativity which, at the time, seemed so imminent, could be recorded on color film in the interests of science. When the monstrous florist's bootie arrived, the 300 long-stem roses were pushed through the bars into the maternity ward. The expectant mother and her companions slowly ate them all, fastidiously discarding each blossom and munching dreamily on the thorny stem.

Belle is an exceedingly sweet-tempered elephant. She was hand-raised from the age of two months to one year in the Seattle basement of her owner, Morgan Berry, professional importer of wild animals, and she was treated much like one of the Berry children. Until she was eight months old and 400 pounds, she particularly enjoyed motoring through Seattle traffic in the back seat of the Berrys' convertible, her trunk wrapped lovingly around the driver's neck. When she was one year old and 660 pounds, Belle moved to a more capacious home in Seattle's Woodland Park Zoo.

At present, Berry owns two other elephants besides Belle: seven-year-old Pet, whom Belle once regarded as her adopted daughter, and a fourteen-year-old bull called Thonglaw. All three work in the Seattle zoo in summer, and board at the Portland zoo each winter. The Portland zoo also has two year-round female elephants of its own, Rosy, twelve, and Tuy Hoa, eight. All in all, the Portland-Seattle relationship is a cozy arrangement for the zoos, and even more so for the elephants. Elephants are notoriously slow to mate—even in the jungle a prolonged courtship must take place before a female will accept the bull's advances—but the high-spirited Thonglaw is a formidable pachyderm Don Juan. Rosy expects her own calf this summer, Tuy Hoa in the fall, and though it still is a bit early to confirm the condition of little Pet, chances are she will give birth in early winter.

Until last year, Thonglaw and his devoted harem shared the same spacious quarters in Portland. But early in January, the normally manageable bull had to be hauled out and locked up alone in an isolation cell. Otherwise Belle's human attendants would not have had a chance to get anywhere near her. The expectant father had suddenly turned into a homicidal maniac. He would charge any man who approached him, even Berry, with intent to kill.

Reflecting her gentle upbringing, Belle continued to be the very model of lady-like elephant deportment. Although she was certainly aware by mid-January that there was much unusual activity both inside her and out, she appeared not to notice. Sometimes her disposition seemed a trifle edgy; this the zoo men understood perfectly. It may be assumed that Belle had not the slightest idea what was happening to her. She had never seen another elephant in her own ballooning condition, nor even seen a newborn elephant. Neither, in fact, had any of the zoo men, and they were growing a trifle edgy themselves.

Perched uneasily on bales of hay in the back room of the elephant house, the six men most directly involved in the coming accouchement gathered to plan their strategy. Their unusual predicament was comparable to the fabled six blind men of India: each knew something about an elephant but none knew the whole story.

The team was headed by veterinarian Matt Maberry, a man of unusual fortitude, stamina, and—as he would reveal in the coming weeks—great personal courage. He also had had broad obstetrical experience; he has delivered lions, tigers, buffaloes, and bears, and he has performed Caesarean sections on cattle and horses. But an elephant is not only much larger, she is differently constructed in certain significant respects than any other animal on earth. And Dr. Maberry had never delivered an elephant.

The veterinarian's two consulting physicians were Dr. Howard Tatum, professor of obstetrics at the University of Oregon Medical School, and Dr. James Metcalfe, associate cardiologist at the Medical School and president of the Oregon Heart Association. Though expert in their own fields, the two doctors knew nothing about elephants.

Owner Morgan Berry knew a lot about elephants but nothing about obstetrics. Zoo Director Jack Marks knew a lot about how to run a successful zoo (the Portland Zoological Gardens is one of the most modern, complete small zoos in the west) and it was no accident that the only pregnant elephants in North America were residents of his establishment. The sixth man, Head Keeper Alvin Tucker, had eight years' experience watching, feeding, and cleaning up after the largest animals on earth.

Each man on the team had his specific assignment. Dr. Maberry would supervise the expectant mother's general health, make examinations, keep records, and preside over the delivery. His equipment included surgical instruments, a resuscitator, respirator, 110-volt electric prods to prevent the mother from trampling the newborn baby, floodlights, and a borrowed set of shipping-room scales.

Dr. Maberry was prepared, but not prepared for, well, anything. In the event of difficulty, he might have to perform a Caesarean, and he wondered how much anesthetic it would take to knock out an elephant, and how he would administer it. "Getting a mask on her might be a problem," he mused. He had an oxygen tent, but that wasn't big enough. He thought a pup tent would be about right, if he could make it airtight.

What about transfusions? Even in an emergency, whole blood would be out of the question. There was no information available on elephant blood types. But he did have gallons of plasma substitute on hand. He also had a stethoscope on which he could pick up the fetal heartbeat loud and clear, and a rectal cattle thermometer lashed like a Neanderthal's spearhead to one end of a wooden yardstick. An elephant's normal body temperature is about 98° F, and Maberry had been warned to watch for a sudden drop of up to three degrees which would signal that birth was only twelve to twenty-four hours off. During the final months, Maberry took Belle's temperature at least twice a day.

Dr. Tatum, the obstetrics professor, was especially eager to get his hands on, or more accurately, to get his arms around an elephant placenta. He wanted to take a biopsy of this eighty-pound organ, and make tissue cultures to grow in his laboratory for further study.

Dr. Metcalfe had a specially rigged electrocardiograph contraption with four feet of additional wire. He also had paraphernalia for making blood tests. He calculated that Belle contained enough blood to fill a fifty-five gallon oil drum, and that to supply her tremendous mass of tissue with energy and rid it of waste products, her heart had to pump 320 pounds of blood a minute. "The metabolic problems of an elephant are positively fantastic," he remarked with relish.

Owner Morgan Berry knew valuable details of the patient's history, including the vital fact that she had been bred to Thonglaw on July 19, 1960, had not come into season since, and hence in January was almost certainly eighteen months pregnant. Berry offered the opinion that Belle's maternal instincts would kindle naturally when her baby was born. By way of confirming that judgment, he cited the fact that when two-month-old Pet first moved into the Seattle zoo, Belle had served as her foster mother and dry nurse. Not all the other observers shared Berry's confidence. They recalled that more than forty years earlier, Alice, the devoted mate of Snyder, had attempted to trample each of her four calves to death the instant she laid eyes on them. Since nursing was clearly out of the question at Alice's savage breast, her offspring had been fed various concoctions of condensed cow's milk. Autopsies later disclosed that the baby elephants died not from the severe maternal maulings administered by Alice, but from an inability to digest their baby food. For this reason, if Belle could not or would not nurse her infant, Berry planned to feed it a specially prepared formula based on powdered milk, which presumably is free of the lethal protein that dispatched Alice's progeny.

Zoo Director Marks arranged extra security guards and barricades to handle the crowds, dealt with eager VIPs from the Zoological Society and the Parks Commission, and policed the clamoring Oregon press. Belle was even assigned her own news photographer.

Keeper Tucker doled out mountains of hay and elephant delicacies. Belle's daily diet included one and a half bales of best timothy hay, three gallons of oats, six pounds of bread, fifty pounds of carrots, half a box of apples, twenty-five pounds of bananas, a quarter-box of oranges, and ten pounds of freshly dug dirt. Like other expectant mothers, Belle developed special cravings. Her favorite tidbits during the last weeks of her pregnancy were discarded cartons from photographic film and containers of black coffee donated by reporters.

Without some specialized knowledge of Order *Proboscidea*, it is difficult for the general, peanut-throwing public to grasp the extent of the problems that shortly confronted Belle's six attendants. An elephant is the strongest animal on earth and certainly not scared of mice. But it is easily startled by unexpected noises, bright lights, and strangers. Its sense of smell is so acute that it can be spooked even by a sudden whiff of Arpege. An elephant is a wild animal; it can be trained, but never tamed. Though it rarely uses its full strength, it is fully aware of its potential. It does sometimes kill, but not by accident. It is a vegetarian and does not eat people, ever. But because its digestion is only about 40 per cent efficient, it must eat *something* almost constantly. Its trunk is a miraculous organ—a French anatomist once dissected 20,000 individual muscles in an elephant's trunk, and quit only after estimating he still had that many more to go. It has a striking force of many tons, yet the delicacy to pick up a grape or stealthily untie a man's shoelaces. An elephant's life span is about the same as man's —three score years and ten—and its memory is dreadful. Elephants forget things all the time.

Information on the reproductive habits of Order *Proboscidea* is especially hard to come by. In *Patterns of Mammalian Reproduction*, a standard reference book of 437 pages by Professor S. A. Asdell of Cornell University, only one and a half pages are devoted to elephants. The gestation period is reported to vary from 500 to 720 days, based on twenty-five recorded cases. Furthermore, the book expresses considerable doubt about the animal's age of puberty. It has been variously recorded as age nine to fifteen in the male and eight to sixteen in the female. Thonglaw and Belle were fourteen and ten.

Belle's doctors did have one other reference book, *The Care and*

Management of Elephants in Burma, published in Rangoon. This work contains such information as, "From the twelfth to the sixteenth month a pregnant female can do light work, but should on no account be made to *aung* in streams during rises as she may be struck by floating logs."

On January 18, one week after the first reports of Belle's impending delivery were made public by Portland's papers, the baby's kicking became more violent and visible. Belle had also begun an intermittent weaving and rocking motion which Dr. Maberry speculated might be an instinctive attempt to loosen the bones of the pelvic girdle, as well as aid in moving the fetus into position for birth.

From that date until the morning of April 14, Maberry and one or more of his aides maintained a day-and-night vigil which became known as The Great Portland Elephant Watch. Headquarters was the vast, concrete-walled back room of the zoo's elephant house. Besides fodder, medical equipment, and men, this room contained two extraordinary wild animals. Caged against one wall was an Abyssinian ground hornbill, an enormous, black, evil-looking bird with a beak like an iron banana and the appetite of a vulture. Periodically it shuffled around in the remains of its dinner and ran its beak along the bars, making the sound of a policeman's nightstick. Portland's hornbill was temporarily not on exhibition because the public found it too boringly revolting to look at.

The other wild beast was the unfortunate Thonglaw, 8,000 pounds of furious elephant inside a maximum security stockade. Thonglaw's temporary insanity had no relation to his impending fatherhood. He was in *musth*, a periodic affliction of male elephants which is not well understood, possibly because it renders the bulls unapproachable by human beings. *Musth* is so dangerous to man that zoos and circuses over the years have found it expedient, though not always easy, to eliminate all adult male elephants from their herds. Snyder, for example, had to be dispatched in Salina, Kansas, in 1920, but it took twenty-five high-powered rifle bullets and twenty-five grains of cyanide to do the job. All circus pachyderms billed today as "bull elephants" are really ladies of large girth, and mostly middle-aged. Since the external characteristics of male and female elephants are not readily distinguishable to humans, the deception is not difficult to pull off, and it removes the likelihood of a berserk bull menacing a crowd of spectators, an event which happened with some regularity back in the heyday of Alice and

Snyder. There are now only thirteen male elephants left in the U.S., most of them serving out their captive lives in lonely desperation, and observing the change of seasons only when they are winched back and forth from summer to winter quarters. This sad state of affairs accounts in part for the dearth of baby elephants, though it is by no means the whole story.

Musth subsides in a few days or weeks as mysteriously as it comes on, and the animal can then be rebroken, like a wild bronc. Using an electric cattle prod, Morgan Berry has successfully rebroken Thonglaw four times in the ten years since acquiring his unruly pet. But each time he has to wait until Thonglaw's galloping hormones settle back to normal. Meanwhile, the only control is stout bars and a slim diet.

At the start of their vigil, participants in The Great Portland Elephant Watch were a group of healthy, alert, eager animal experts and reporters. They lounged in the hay pile swapping elephant tales; they read avidly through. the scant elephant literature available; they catnapped occasionally, and rose often to poke, fondle, and feed the female herd. Sometimes they played poker; Belle's liver pills and antibiotic capsules made excellent chips. They dined on one hundred pounds of peanuts which a Portland nut merchant had sent to Belle, drank innumerable half-cups of coffee (the second half invariably was saved for the expectant mother) and watched TV.

The zoo switchboard was swamped with more than 500 Belle calls a day. Many callers were people in betting pools seeking hot tips on the likeliest day and hour of the birth. Others were amateur obstetricians offering hot tips to the zoo men. Fill the enclosure with teak logs, suggested one, so Belle "would feel at home in the jungle." Another affirmed that all elephant babies are stillborn, but come to life if the rest of the herd is allowed to toss the infant back and forth with their trunks. A number of callers said it was well known that the gestation period of an elephant is three, or six or nine years, so the Elephant Watch might as well go home. This particular suggestion soon came to have a strong attraction for the Watchers. They grew irritable, groggy, emotionally strung out, itchy from the hay, and sickest of all of the overpowering smell of elephant. After a few hours in Belle's snugly warmed maternity ward, each heavy lungful of air seemed to weigh on the diaphragm like another rancid dumpling.

A private 20-by-20-foot concrete maternity chamber was in readiness for Belle, if necessary, but Maberry preferred to leave her with the other pregnant females. Elephants are herd animals by nature, and the doctor believed that the companionship of Belle's ladies-in-waiting would reassure her. He suspected that Alice's murderous frenzies almost a half-century before had been stimulated by the fact that, each time her labors began, she was isolated from her herd and chained and staked.

"Preservation of the young is the greatest instinct of all wild animals," Maberry says. "But if you interfere, they'll often switch and try to destroy the young. The best procedure is to keep your mouth shut and your eyes open." Nevertheless, Maberry felt a certain amount of human intervention was essential.

On the afternoon of Thursday, January 18, Belle had a sudden seizure. She moved away from Rosy, Pet, and Tuy Hoa to the opposite end of the enclosure. The seizure lasted two and one half minutes, then subsided.

That night Belle's temperature remained steady, but the temperature outside the elephant house dropped to 20° and an icy wind swirled snow along the deserted pathways of the zoo. Inside, Maberry, his aides, and the waiting press sipped black coffee and walked the floor. So did Belle. From time to time, Thonglaw charged the bars of his cage with a force that shook the building. Once he trumpeted so fiercely he roused the guard at the zoo gates a quarter-mile away. At 5:10 A.M., Belle moved off alone again and squealed in the grip of a mighty spasm. This one lasted four minutes. Half an hour later, she had a third attack. An elephant in labor exerts about four times the force of a horse, and Belle's pains must have been gargantuan. Every time Belle squealed, the other elephants crowded close to Belle's flanks and petted her with their trunks.

By morning all was quiet again. When there was absolutely no change in Belle's behavior throughout the rest of the long day, the six-man team decided to seek the advice of the one man on earth known to have delivered an elephant in captivity, Dr. Eremanno Bronzini of the Rome zoo. The Portland phone company eagerly agreed to put through a conference call gratis. A high school Italian teacher was rushed to the zoo to translate. Then it turned out that Dr. Bronzini had no telephone. Finally, in London, the frantic callers roused Dr. Emmanuel Amoroso of the Royal Veterinary College. Dr. Amoroso had seen many elephants born in African jungle compounds, and he said that Belle's labor might last twelve hours, since this would be her first baby. He added that the cord would break automatically, and he told Maberry not to worry about tying the umbilical knot; Belle would do that job herself, with her trunk. He warned the Portland team to remain on the *qui vive* because, once Belle got into high gear, "it will be a rather precipitous birth."

Alas, it was about as precipitous as a glacier crossing the polar ice cap. On Friday, January 19, Maberry and Metcalfe ran the first electrocardiograms ever reported on an elephant. Belle's great fifty-pound heart was thumping steadily at about thirty-eight beats per minute; fetal heartbeat was eighty-five. On Monday, at 2:20 P.M., Belle trumpeted loudly twice. It seemed as though she had entered the acute stage of labor at last, but in retrospect Maberry feels that these early symptoms were false labor stimulated by the unsettling presence of so many pop-eyed journalists.

For some reason, Belle always suffered most on Thursdays. After the first pains on Thursday, January 18, she slept little, ate little, drank little, and spent most of her time executing a curious, three-legged rocking motion. She kept her left rear leg half-cocked—whether to fend off meddlesome medics or just to relieve the well-known leg cramps of pregnancy, no one but Belle knew for sure. Blood tests showed that Belle was becoming slightly anemic, so her diet was fortified twice daily with a pailful of diluted molasses. Belle took each dose with a single slurp of her trunk and downed it with the ecstatic expression of a child swallowing cough medicine on a TV commercial.

The next Thursday, January 25, Belle suffered several unusually severe contractions and for some hours stopped eating and drinking altogether. When Maberry and Metcalfe attempted to obtain a second blood sample, Belle bellowed and charged. The doctors ducked back outside the steel bars just in the nick of time. "She snapped three steel chains just as if they were thread," Maberry said later.

The following Thursday, February 1, Belle had her worst night yet. She rocked and walked the floor all night long. One of her elephant midwives always paced alongside and kept the miserable beast company, while the other two lay down and slept, snoring loudly through their trunks.

The next night, Maberry put down his bedroll just outside the bars. When Belle's pains appeared to become especially severe, she lay down flat and little Pet knelt beside her and gently massaged Belle's belly with her knee for fifteen or twenty minutes. During the massages, both elephants made odd snorting sounds. Pet even tried half-sitting on Belle's head. Later Belle half-sat on Pet. Nothing seemed to help. When the pains were sharpest, all four elephants crowded close together and cried in unison. Sometimes the muscles between Belle's eyes knotted into a tremendous bulge, and tears rolled down her trunk. Though Maberry could see very severe muscular contractions, the baby's kicking was no longer apparent. The doctor thought the baby probably couldn't kick because he was now holding in a vertical position, almost directly head down.

By then, the assembled newsmen were also bellowing loudly. In a rout of journalism by science, the reporters were banished from the elephant house and armed guards were posted to assure Belle's privacy. Maberry wanted to do everything in his power to prevent having a premature baby elephant on his hands.

On the evening of Friday, April 13, all was quiet in the elephant house of the Portland Zoological Gardens. At midnight, Dr. Maberry made his regular check on bulging Belle and, noticing nothing at all unusual, he bedded down in the massive pile of hay which had served him as his uneasy and tickly resting place for three months. At 12:45 A.M., the veterinarian was roused by an urgent telephone call: across town a pet poodle was gravely ill. Leaving the regular night guard on duty at the elephant house, Maberry drove to the stricken dog's bedside. As he was reviving the poisoned poodle, the zoo guard telephoned and reported that Belle had suddenly begun thrashing around in her cage. She was throwing water over her head with her trunk, and her three elephant midwives appeared greatly agitated. Maberry got back to his outsize patient by 2 A.M.

This time there was no question that acute labor was under way at last. Belle was bellowing oddly, her eyes were wide and bulging, she was continually straining and pushing against the walls and bars, throwing her head from side to side, alternately kneeling and standing. The veterinarian quickly telephoned Zoo Director Jack Marks and summoned two more keepers to help him control the three rambunctious midwives. By 5:30 A.M., these excited females were still squealing shrilly, but Belle had quit bellowing and was busy rapidly crossing and uncrossing her hind legs. While all this was going on, the human observers thought it the better part of prudence to remain watching from outside the bars.

At 5:56 A.M., Belle suddenly began spinning rapidly and silently in circles, pivoting on her forefeet. After two solid minutes of this dervish-ing—abruptly at 5:58 A.M.—hind feet first and backside front, Belle's 225-pound infant quietly dropped in a heap to the floor and gazed about with bright red but wide-open eyes. As he lay huddled under Belle's great belly, the mother swiftly knotted or clamped the umbilical stump with her trunk. When Pet and 5,000-pound Tuy Hoa strolled over and tried to sit down on the newcomer, the guards quickly prodded all three of the ponderous ex-midwives outside to their open-air patio.

Belle gave her newborn son a couple of swift kicks in his fuzzy flanks. Slowly but firmly, he rose up on his stout legs. Gently shoving him with her trunk and forelegs, Belle nudged his head around to her breast. At 6:30, the baby took his first swallow of elephant milk, a thin liquid which is said to taste like diluted coconut milk. He much enjoyed his first breakfast, though part of it was lost dribbling down the fringes of his hairy chops. Occasionally his tiny, flabby, pink-tipped trunk seemed to quiver with gourmet appreciation, and he emitted high squeals of delight.

At 7 A.M., excited Zoo Director Marks was on the telephone, pro-claiming the blessed event to reporters, when he collapsed to the floor in a dead faint. He was rushed to the hospital, put to bed for a couple of hours, and then sent home to rest. On the way home, he insisted on stopping at the zoo to see how Belle was doing.

A few hours later, a brilliant spring sun was shining over Portland, a blue elephant flag fluttered from a shopping center flagpole, and the city's children were trooping to the zoo grounds to view the newborn elephant child, and also to take part in the annual Easter egg-rolling contest on the zoo lawn. Inside the elephant house, the newcomer was alternately nursing and stumping sturdily back and forth through his mother's legs. Belle's owner, Morgan Berry, finally dashed in from Seattle, clutching a tape measure. His baby elephant, he reported proudly, stands thirty-five inches high, measures forty-six inches at the chest, fifty-three inches at the abdomen, and eight inches at the trunk. Later he announced that Belle and the little fellow could be purchased for $30,000, and the people of Portland immediately started a fund-raising drive to meet the price.

At 10 A.M., Keeper Tucker forked Belle her morning meal of hay, bread, apples, and so forth, and she devoured the mess with gusto. After twenty-one months of pregnancy, she appeared within four hours to have returned completely to her old, sweet-tempered, high-spirited, gentle-hearted self. So indeed had Dr. Maberry. The lines of fatigue and tension from attending a 6,000-pound female through three months of on-and-off labor had vanished from his face. As Maberry, Belle, and baby lounged amid the hay wisps regarding one another with an air of total contentment and fulfillment of a job well-done, the director of the egg-rolling contest poked his head through the doorway. He suggested that Belle, as Portland's first lady, should have the honor of stepping out onto the lawn and rolling out the day's first Easter egg.

"I don't think so," said Maberry. "Belle has already rolled her egg for today."

Life—May 11, 1962

3

An Elephant Condolence

Woodland, Washington
April 17, 1975

Dear Shana:
Look forward to seeing you on TV Sun. nights. As you are always in print or on TV I am able to keep track of you.

I have been single since 1970 and live alone here on the farm. I do have a partner who trains animals for fairs and the circus. Have an act of 5 male Indian elephants and one of the 3 African elephants. My partner has an act of 6 bear, 3 lions, 2 tigers and a leopard in Puerto Rico.

Thought you might be interested in knowing that the elephants at the Portland zoo are not doing too well. Thonglaw the male after fathering 15 babies died just before Christmas. Everyone at the zoo from top to bottom are new. There was not the interest in the breeding that there used to be. From standing in his own droppings, Thonglaws feet almost rotted off and his feed was cut from 2 bales of hay to 1/4 bale a day and before he died he looked like a skeleton.

Would like to see you next time you are out this way.

Your friend

Morgan

4

Kids' Country

Children are a relatively modern invention. Until a few hundred years ago, they did not exist. In medieval and Renaissance painting, you see pint-size men and women wearing grown-up clothes and grown-up expressions, performing grown-up tasks. Children did not exist because the family as we know it had not evolved. In the old days, most people lived on the land, and life was a communal affair.

Children today not only exist; they have taken over. God's Country has to an astonishing degree become Kids' Country—in no place more than in America, and at no time more than in the period Halloween-to-New Year's Day. It is during the frantic family skedaddle from pumpkin to holly that Kids' Country runs in its jumpingest high gear.

But it is always Kids' Country here. Our civilization is child-centered, child-obsessed. A kid's body is our physical ideal. Weight-watchers grunt and pant. Sages jog from sea to shining sea. Plastic surgeons scissor and tuck up. New hair sprouts, transplanted, on wisdom's brow. One way or another we are determined to "keep in shape," and invariably this means keeping a kid's shape—which we then outfit in baby-doll ruffles, sneakers, blue jeans.

The food we live on is kids' food: pizza, hot dogs, fried chicken, ice cream, hamburgers. This bizarre diet is the reason we have such trouble maintaining our kids' bodies. The stuff we now drink has thrown the beverage industry into turmoil. Our consumption of soft drinks has risen 80 per cent in a decade. Americans not only are switching *en masse* from hot coffee to iced tea, and from bitter drinks to sweet. The popularity of alcoholic soda pop—the so-called "fun" wines like Thunderbird and apple wine—has jumped 168 per cent in five years.

Children hate spinach, vitamins, and *haute cuisine*. They like their food kooked, not cooked: you pop, thaw, dissolve, or explode it into eatability. To buy it you push around a wire perambulator, and at the end of the supermarket line you get prizes of colored stamps.

In Kids' Country, every day must be prize day. Miss America, Miss Teen-Age America, Miss Junior Miss America, and probably Miss Little Miss America trample each other down star-spangled runways. Volume mail-order giveaways will shortly silt up our postal system entirely. All day long TV shows like *Concentration, Dating Game, Hollywood Squares,* and *Jackpot* hand out more toys: wristwatches, washing machines, trips to Hawaii.

The rest of the world may be in fee to the Old Boy Network, carried on to the point of senility, but here there are no elder statesmen left. Seniority in an American politician no longer denotes wisdom, only power or tenure. The old age of the present Congress is a major hindrance. No one considers the Heberts and Eastlands to be Athenian men.

Our contemporary heroes are a series of golden boys. A direct line links Charles Lindbergh to Billy Graham to the astronauts to John F. Kennedy—and to his kid brother.

The philosopher-kings of Kids' Country are professors like Erich Segal and Charles Reich, who saw in Woodstock and the flower children a new golden age of innocence he called Consciousness III. The totem animal in Kids' Country just now is a talking, philosophizing sea gull who soars on vast updrafts of hot air, and the Kids' Country bogeyman is a wicked movie mafioso with a heart of gold.

The ideal of American parenthood is to be a kid with your kid. Take him to Disneyland, take him fishing, take him out to the ball game. Our national pastimes are kids' games, and we are all hooked. When the Redskins are blacked out in Washington, the President holes up in New York so as not to miss the big game. Bobby Fischer, the quintessential smart boy of every school, turns the whole country on to chess. *The Boys of Summer* becomes a best-seller. In nostalgia's golden haze, we disremember the poet's full line, "I see the boys of summer in their ruin."

In Kids' Country, we do not permit middle age. Thirty is promoted over fifty, but thirty knows that soon his time to be overtaken will come. Middle-aged man must appear to run, even if it is only running in place. Often the big kid outruns his heart. In our over-sixty population, there are ten widows for every man.

Like a child's room, Kids' Country is a mess. New York City seems about to disappear under its load of litter, graffiti, and dog droppings. How is it that China can eliminate the house fly, and we can't even clean up Central Park?

In Kids' Country, not so ironically, Mommy and Daddy are household gods, and so we have two immense national holidays, elsewhere virtually unknown, called "Mother's Day" and "Father's Day." Without them, the American small businessman would be in even worse shape than he already is.

Ours is the first society in history in which parents expect to learn from their children, rather than the other way around. Such a topsy-turvy situation has come about at least in part because, unlike the rest of the world, we are an immigrant society, and for immigrants the only hope is in the kids. In the Old Country, hope was in the father, and in how much family wealth he could accumulate and pass along to his children. In the growth pattern of America and its ever-expanding frontier, the young man was ever advised to Go West. The father was ever inheriting from his son; the topsy-turviness was built-in from the beginning. A melting pot needs a spoon. Kids' Country may be the inevitable result.

Kids' Country is not all bad. America is the greatest country in the world to grow up in *because* it's Kids' Country. We not only wear kids' clothes and eat kids' food; we dream kids' dreams, and make them come true. It was, after all, a boys' game to go to the moon.

The stirring spoon has done its job. As a people we thrive. By the time they reach sixteen, most American kids today are bigger, stronger —and smarter—than Mommy and Daddy ever were. And if they are not precisely "happier," they may well be more "grown up." But because this is a civilization with no clear rites of passage, life in Kids' Country seems to me to be in many ways the exact opposite of medieval and Renaissance life. If in the old days children did not exist, it seems equally true today that adults as a class have begun to disappear, condemning all of us to remain boys and girls forever, jogging and doing push-ups against eternity.

Newsweek—December 11, 1972

5

Getting Old in Kids' Country

The news of radical mastectomies performed on Mrs. Ford and Mrs. Rockefeller has put the mysteries of modern medicine much on all our minds. I am reminded that my own first brush with futuristic medicine was not reassuring. It happened twelve years ago in Seattle when I was investigating the then newest new medical miracle, the artificial kidney machine. In theory, the machine could save—and since has saved— hundreds of thousands of lives, though the treatment could be harrowing physically and psychologically, and the cost appalling (in the intervening years, both the pain and the cost have been dramatically reduced). But in the long run, what was most troubling about this incredibly delicate and expensive machine was that it really did work. The age of artificial organs had arrived.

What sort of a world would we have, a young doctor asked me then, when huge stockpiles of other man-made replacement parts—hearts, lungs, livers, even brains—crowded the hospital shelves? When half the population—the healthy half—spent their days operating these delicate machines to keep the other half, the weak and sick, alive? The question has haunted me ever since.

Today we have about one million sick people in hospitals, and another million or so elderly people living in nursing homes. But the balance is shifting. The end of the postwar baby boom, plus cuts in Medicaid, means fewer hospital patients; meanwhile, improved general medicine allows old people to live on longer than ever. This week, or the one after for sure, a very important statistical collision will occur: the two population curves will intersect, the nursing-home population will overtake the number of hospital patients, and that Seattle doctor —if he is still practicing—will believe his old nightmare has inched a little closer to reality.

For now, we will not concern ourselves with the vast profits made from those million nursing-home beds, nor the scandalous living conditions that frequently prevail there, but only with the mental and physical health of the people who inhabit them. Elderly people—sixty-five and over—constituted 4.1 per cent of our population in 1900. They are now 10.3 per cent, and will soon be 15 per cent. Officially speaking, we do not know a great deal more, because here in what I have called Kids' Country, we worship youth and prefer our old people to remain invisible, out of sight *and* out of mind. In all of Kids' Country, there is not a single university or medical-school chair of geriatric medicine, nor any related chair in psychiatry. Less than 3 per cent of National Institute of Mental Health funds are spent on geriatric problems.

If it is not hacked to bits, a federal bill now before Congress will provide much-needed money for education, training, and research in such geriatric commonplaces as mental depression and organic brain disease. At present, geriatric medicine abounds with myth and misperception. It is not true, for example, that hardening of the arteries is an inevitable part of aging. Preliminary studies indicate that some of what is called "senility" may be in fact be "auto-immunity," or a heightened sensitivity to one's own proteins.

The mental health of the elderly is an even gloomier uncharted sea. Depression and anxiety states are commonplace. People over sixty-five account for more suicides than any other age group. Twenty-five per cent of total suicides is the usual figure given, but it is probably higher.

Many such suicides can be classified as "rational" in the sense that as people grow older they have more and more to be depressed about. Continuing loss of loved ones, grief, increasing isolation, fear and anxiety about doctors and disease, financial worry, and reluctance to see one's life savings dissipated on one's own prolonged demise are entirely realistic reasons to despair.

Female readers—if any are still with us—may now prepare to become even more depressed. The average woman marries a man three years older than she, and lives seven years longer than he, so she can expect to spend the last decade of her life alone and in decline. Under age sixty-five, it may be more stressful to be a man in our society, but after that, a statistical flip-flop occurs. There are more women than men in mental hospitals at all ages, but after sixty-five, the percentage escalates dramatically. Our nursing-home population is 80 per cent female.

I sought some answers from Dr. Robert Butler, psychiatrist, authority on aging, and a consultant to the U.S. Senate Special Committee on Aging. His first answer terrified me. "The main reason is because most men over sixty-five have a living wife. Most women end up taking care of a dying husband. Say she's sixty-three when he dies. Twenty years later she's eighty-three; economic erosion has eaten up thirty or forty per cent of her capital; she's probably used the rest to help pay for her son's heart attack and her grandchildren's education. Some people say it's her fault that she didn't manage or invest more wisely, but society never taught her to manage money. If her son dies, her daughter-in-law may not take her in, not necessarily through malevolence but perhaps because she herself has remarried."

In this instance, the aging widow is apt to be stuck living in the inner city. One-third of all elderly people do live in the inner city, where old women especially are very vulnerable to crime.

As nursing homes fill up, what is to be done? Dumping out older patients back into the so-called community is no favor, Dr. Butler says. "It just takes them out of the mental-health system and puts them into the welfare system, where they get even less medical or mental-health aid."

As I typewrite, dawn is rising over New York City, the rubble heap Dr. Butler has told me is now the home of one out of twenty old people in the United States. He has also supplied the answer to the question raised twelve years ago by the doctor in Seattle: geriatric medicine is not just the science of keeping organisms alive; it is the business of maintaining vigorous people. It can be done. The elderly themselves will be the first to help, if we let them.

Looking down from my window in the new dawn, I think for the first time in years of a true and wonderful short story by Anzia Yezierska, a once-famous writer who was also my great-aunt. When Anzia was about seventy-five and feeling restless, she volunteered to help out at the Home for Aged and Infirm Hebrews on 106th Street in New York City. One day she attended a birthday party there. My aunt described with gusto and delight the parade of guests on sticks, crutches, and wheelchairs tottering into the dining hall. The birthday presents were humble—an apple or an orange saved from last night's dinner. But the air was festive. "We are gathered here today to celebrate the one hundred and ninth birthday of our oldest resident, Sadie Solomon," said the toastmaster, raising his water glass high. Three dozen other glasses lifted tremblingly skyward.

"Long life to you, Sadie Solomon!" they cried.

Newsweek—November 11, 1974

6

Why Children Like to Pick Up Beer Cans

The three most overused words in the language right now are "pollution," "ecology," and "recycling." The hullabaloo in media and marketplace about the havoc we are doing the planet, and the dirt we are spewing around us, has increased in volume to a point where it practically constitutes "noise pollution" in its own right, to employ still another overused term.

While I am all for cleaning up the mess, and preserving the little bit of virgin nature that is still left, I wonder at the sheer ferocity of feeling these overused words can arouse. The hue and cry about ecology seems to be shrillest among the very young. Schoolchildren have become hordes of tiny, avenging angels swarming over the littered landscape with gunnysacks and trash barrels to gather up the rubble left there by their elders. Even seven- and eight-year-olds now have become such fanatic ecologists and demon recyclers that woe betide the mother who temporarily sets aside her half-drunk soda bottle, or the father who leaves unattended his partly-smoked cigar. It used to be that adventurous kids made off with your beer or cigars in order to sample their forbidden delights; now they do it to depollute your happy home. To these children, lugging their hoards of salvaged garbage off to school on Recycling Day, the recycling plant seems to loom as a new kind of unappeasable Minotaur whom no amount of cans, bottles, and other refuse can possibly satisfy.

I submit that our children's wildly exuberant response to the much-advertised perils of pollution is due to something more than their natural energy, and the wonderful rebuke to Daddy and Mommy that each salvaged bottle and butt implies. It seems to me that all the elaborate talk about dirtying up the environment is really such a simple, neat concept, or rather a simple and messy concept, that it must have great appeal to a child's mind. Compared with some of the other issues of the day—how to get the economy working right again, what to do about prison reform, or about busing, or nuclear disarmament—ecology has great appeal. If we can't figure out how to keep the planet from blowing up, we can at least police the place, sweep the paths, and tidy the flower beds, while we continue going round and round in the holding pattern that began at Hiroshima, the holding pattern with the unthinkable end. Rather than grapple with that one, any kid would rather go around picking up beer cans. And so would I.

CBS "Spectrum"—October 15, 1971

7

The Rich Kid: Tony Curtis

Once upon a time—but not so long ago that you couldn't look it up —there lived in the Bronx a poor tailor's son named Bernie Schwartz. From earliest memory, Bernie knew he was different from the other youngsters playing along the gutters of his humble neighborhood. It wasn't that he didn't like stickball or marbles or that he couldn't spit and swear as royally as any of his eight-year-old friends. It was just that from the time his bright blue eyes could focus on a movie screen and his well-shaped ears could make sense of dialogue not delivered with his native Bronx accent, Bernie was entranced and obsessed by a single idea—the sort of way-out cockeyed dream most humans give up the first time anybody laughs at them.

But Bernie Schwartz didn't. Inflamed by hope and nourished by the elixir of Hungarian blood coursing through his veins, he clung to his dream of glory. Every afternoon he journeyed to a neighborhood shrine, the RKO Fordham Theater, to burnish his dream to a still higher luster. Inside that dark and delicious cavern, it was Bernie's daily ritual to gaze upon his shadow heroes—Gable, Cagney, Flynn, Fairbanks, and especially, Cary Grant—and plan his future. Someday he, Bernie Schwartz, would be a movie star, live in Hollywood, and have the best of absolutely everything.

One day in the much more recent past Tony Curtis—for indeed Bernie Schwartz was he—was tooling his $24,000 silver Rolls-Royce convertible down Sunset Boulevard in pursuit of nothing more than fresh air and the joy of driving. He spotted a busload of sightseeing tourists ahead of him. Instead of fleeing down a side street in the manner of most high-carat movie stars, Curtis overtook the bus, blew his horn, and threw the tourists a cheery wave.

"Hiya, Tony! How's it going?" shouted a passenger.

"Are you *kidding?*" the famous Bronx voice boomed from the silver chariot. "It's bee-*yoody*-ful!"

It is not surprising that Curtis finds life beautiful these days. By every Dream of Glory standard he forged in the Fordham Theater, he has it made. He not only drives a movie star's motorcar, he lives in a movie star's house (a $250,000 mansion loaded with modern art and marble bathrooms). He has a movie star's income (something over a million dollars a year), and he has a movie star wife of his very own (Janet Leigh in living Technicolor). Incredibly, it still seems to him, Bernie Schwartz has become the most dazzling, flamboyant, wondrous personage the movie-struck mind of a poor tailor's son could possibly conceive.

That Bernie's boyhood fantasies came true, that he is not now a middle-aging Bronx butcher with thinning hair and a fat wife, is the result of three things. Schwartz/Curtis was blessed with a truly stunning naivete which made it possible for him never completely to grow up. In Hollywood a childlike state of mind can be invaluable. (As Kirk Douglas says, "How in hell can a grown man pretend to be a cowboy all day long?") Second, Curtis pursued his fantasy with fanatic zeal, relying not on toughness but on guile. Where other men might use their growing power crudely, Tony conned his way to the top. In the opinion of one who knows both men well, Curtis spent much more time and energy trying to become a movie star than John F. Kennedy did seeking to become President. Then there was pure gypsy luck. Curtis was one of the last pretty boys to hit Hollywood while the old star-making machinery still operated. In thirteen years under personal contract to a major studio, Universal-International, he had a now-vanished opportunity to learn his trade. With the advent of television, Hollywood became a scientific, impersonal film farm, raising a limited crop of supercolossal movie melons between endless rows of TV corn.

Above this dreary landscape, Tony Curtis blooms like the last rose of summer, with much the same old-fashioned, innocent charm. Curtis has reached full flower as a movie star at a time when his, and America's, old shadow heroes—Gable, Garfield, Power, Flynn, Cooper—have all faded from view. In fact, Hollywood now has only two home-grown, full-blown, under-forty leading men left. The other one is Rock Hudson, who was nurtured in the U-I greenhouses right alongside Curtis.

According to which poll you read, Curtis is either the fourth- or sixth-ranked movie star (of either sex) in America. At thirty-six, he lives in a constant glow of amazement and delight. His public loves him; they prove it by writing 10,000 fan letters per month. The movie bankers love him; no Tony Curtis picture has ever lost money. Even high-brow critics are finding kind words for him. The *Saturday Review* recently called Curtis that rare "phenomenon, an authentic screen personality who, through hard work, has made himself into an actor ... of considerable subtlety and some breadth." Curtis' life is filled with the many odd perquisites of major movie star rank. He lectures to university dramatic students. He charters yachts. Last January, after the J.F.K. inaugural, Curtis and his wife spent two weeks in Florida as the house guests of the President's parents.

Curtis is having so much fun being a movie star that he cannot bear *not* working, even at a standby salary of $20,000 a week. Last spring, Curtis was idle for ten weeks while M-G-M wrestled with script troubles on its proposed movie version of *Lady L.* By the time he was $200,000 richer for doing nothing at all, the star had developed an aching back, a churning stomach, and severe insomnia. The symptoms cleared up rapidly as soon as his threatened lawsuit against M-G-M released him from his intolerable status as the best paid unemployed actor in history.

Thereafter Tony made the best of a dull summer by hiring writers and working out four possible screenplays and one short-subject project; planning a restaurant; opening a men's wear shop; setting up a record company; painting two dozen large oils (he's an accomplished amateur who has progressed to abstract expressionism); visiting his psychoanalyst; teaching his daughters, Kelly, five, and Jamie, three, to swim; and designing the new offices of Curtleigh, Inc., the independent production company which looms importantly in his future plans. Nonetheless, the strain of not acting often was too much to bear. By September, he was occasionally inclined to spring suddenly from behind his enormous desk, fling an arm at the expensive paneling and cry, "All these walls are cardboard sets! Put a sword in my hand! I wanna *work!*"

Tony is now cheerfully marooned in the middle of the Argentine pampas, 700 miles from Buenos Aires, with the location company of *Taras Bulba,* a fifteenth century Ukrainian western based on the Gogol novel. When the big color cameras begin to roll, he flourishes his sword and gallops over the wheat fields at the head of 2,000 Argentine gauchos dressed up like Cossacks. He is doing what his destiny intended. He is a movie star at work. He is happy.

When Tony Curtis arrived in Hollywood thirteen years ago, his chances of lingering one moment longer than his six-month contract appeared remote to everybody, himself included. His acting ability was nil, and even the talent scout who discovered him said his voice suggested "an immigrant taxi driver with a mouthful of hot bagel."

"I was a million-to-one shot, the *least* likely to succeed. I wasn't low man on the totem pole, I was *under* the totem pole, in a sewer, tied in a sack," Curtis says now. The saga of Curtis' climb out of the sewer, up the totem pole, and into the Rolls-Royce is the sort of illogical folktale that sometimes happens in the movies—embellished by magical dream-sequences and a rousing musical score—but never to a kid in the audience. Though true, the Curtis saga is best enjoyed as a simple fable, a modern Hollywood *Just So Story; How the Bronx Boy Got His Rolls-Royce.*

If the greatest pleasure of the eight-year-old Bronx kid was moviewatching, his second greatest pleasure—being a nimble, quick-witted, daring little devil of modest means and pure Hungarian ancestry—was acting out his romantic dreams of adventure. Often the boy was able to combine both his passions in a single afternoon. After four or five hours curled up in his dark movie seat of dusty plush, he emerged as, say, Douglas Fairbanks. To perfect and sustain his new identity, he then stole rides on trolley cars, brandishing a wooden sword. Once, as the Black Pirate, he commandeered his own trolley car in a car barn and piloted it eight blocks before it was boarded by the forces of law and order. As Errol Flynn, he stole apples off pushcarts. As Jimmy Cagney, he defied a bully on a rooftop and earned a terrible belt in the teeth. While recovering, he bravely smoked in the subway, being George Raft.

As plain Bernie Schwartz, he joined a neighborhood gang whose chief delights were playing hookey from school and organizing elaborate pilfering raids on the local five-and-ten. But fortunately, when Bernie was eleven, an understanding settlement-house worker saved him from what he is now convinced would have been a life of delinquency by sending him off to Boy Scout camp. There Bernie worked off his excess imagination by spinning tall tales of his city exploits to fellow campers.

At sixteen, he got his first real acting job, a bit part playing an idiot in a settlement-house drama. He eagerly prepared for his debut by shaving his head. When he got home, his mother burst into tears, sobbing that she had enough trouble without a son who was the only completely bald boy in the Bronx.

After Pearl Harbor, Bernie quit high school and joined the Navy. The day after the movie-struck boot saw Tyrone Power in *Crash Dive*, he applied for submarine duty. One fateful night about two years later, many fathoms deep in the Pacific, an accident befell Bernie comparable, in cinema history, to the apple falling on Newton's head. The only movie available for showing aboard the submarine was *Gunga Din*, and the crew finally learned the sound track so well that they could turn the sound off and supply all the *Gunga Din* noises themselves. Roles were chosen by lot, and several crewmen soon developed highly special skills. One could bellow an elephant love call. Another could sound exactly like a cracked bugle. A third reproduced rifle fire—nineteenth century British rifle fire. Bernie Schwartz became a whiz at impersonating Cary Grant. Furthermore, he found being Grant so exhilarating that he was hooked for life. Even today, when Bernie Schwartz feels uneasy being Tony Curtis, he will metamorphose instantaneously into Grant. This odd habit unnerves some of Tony's Hollywood friends, especially Cary Grant.

In New York, a few months after the war ended, Bernie discovered that Comedian Larry Storch, a Navy acquaintance, was working in a stage show with Perry Como. Bernie attached himself to Storch like a barnacle, massaged his head, hustled sandwiches backstage, did anything to sustain this one frail link with show business. One night after the show, autograph-seekers surged around Como like sharks after a chunk of meat, and some in their blind frenzy even asked Bernie Schwartz for his autograph. When Como shouted, "Hey kid, what are you doing? You're not even *in* show business!" Schwartz yelled back, "I'm trying, I'm trying!" and kept scribbling furiously.

First Bernie begged Storch for acting lessons. Storch tried, but after a series of disastrous coaching sessions he called it quits. "The kid," he says, "was hopeless." When Bernie then enrolled in an acting school, the proprietors swiftly reached the same conclusion. He was assigned to crouch behind a backdrop and pull the ropes attached to the revolving stage. "I used to sweat like a galley slave," he recalls, "and think —what a thrill it must be to be *on*stage, to *say* something!"

Bernie got his chance to say something the following summer, when he landed a $15-a-week job in a traveling theatrical company, but the thrill was diminished because he did not understand a word he was saying. The troupe performed in Yiddish, and although Bernie's folks were Jewish, it was Hungarian he spoke at home. He read his Yiddish dialogue phonetically from prompting cards hidden in the wings. Adding to his feelings of unreality on tour was the fact that he was billed as "Bernie White." The company impresario feared that chauvinistic patrons, hearing such miserable Yiddish spoken by an actor named Schwartz, would feel they were being hoodwinked; that the speaker was really an Italian or Irish kid who was faking it—instead of a Jewish kid who was faking it.

He tried next to fake his way into a Tarzan role. The producers took one look at the 5-foot 8-inch would-be Ape Man and suggested he grow eight inches before coming back.

Finally an impoverished off-Broadway group doing *Androcles and the Lion* needed somebody with a loud roar to fill a middle-sized lion suit. In this manner, Bernie caught the ear of an aspiring theatrical agent, who arranged an interview with Robert Goldstein, eastern head of Universal-International Pictures.

Bernie prepared for his big opportunity by buying a pair of high-heeled boots. He increased his stature still further with a deck of cards, which he cut in half—keeping the ace of hearts on top for luck—and stuffed inside each boot. Then he hobbled into Goldstein's office. When he finished auditioning, the producer remarked, "The kid looks good, but he oughtta get his feet fixed."

Goldstein was appalled at the reading, but at least, he recalls, "it proved the kid could read." Bernie was given a stock contract, a new suit, and a plane ticket to Hollywood.

In his Dream City, Bernie's new life was a nightmare. The camera terrified him. He survived his first movie assignment, a three-minute sequence as the dancing partner of Yvonne de Carlo in *Criss Cross*, by keeping his back to the camera the whole time. When the picture was released in 1949, he discovered that his new movie name, as listed at the bottom of the credits, was "Dancer—Jimmie Curtis."

He stormed into the studio casting department. " 'Jimmie Curtis' sounds like a *schnook!*"

"You got a better idea, kid?" the casting director asked.

Bernie did. Diffidently he suggested Anthony Adverse. The casting chief demurred. "Sorry, kid, there already *is* an actor named Anthony Adverse." Bernie compromised on "Anthony Curtis."

His take-home pay was $43 a week. He lived in a room furnished only with a mattress on the floor, and he subsisted chiefly on milk and pie. His eager-beaver personality made him the butt of endless practical jokes around the studio. Wags dissolved sleeping pills in his milk, and some days he staggered around the lot like a wounded buffalo. Evenings, before going out on a date with a promising starlet, he would find himself inexplicably locked in the steam room. The morning after a date with Wanda Hendrix, the then estranged wife of Audie Murphy, the war hero challenged Tony to a fast-draw contest. Their guns were supposed to be unloaded, but somebody in the crowd on the set gave Murphy a gun loaded with blanks. At the "draw" signal, Tony felt a gun muzzle ram into his stomach. Then he heard a loud explosion and saw blue smoke curling up past his belt buckle. He fainted dead away.

Though at least dimly aware that he was the laughing stock of the studio, Curtis preferred ridicule to obscurity or, worse, banishment back to the Bronx. If he couldn't be king or prince or even page, he decided, he would be the court jester. All young actors at U-I had to attend the studio talent school. Tony's classmates included Rock Hudson, Jeff Chandler, and Hugh O'Brian, and in this fast company he felt he was still low man. "Where I came from, being good-looking was a passport out of a garbage can. But at Universal there were fifteen guys who looked just as good as me, all waiting for me to break a leg."

In self-defense, Tony took to cutting classes. When the teacher berated him, the frustrated young actor exploded. As he remembers it, he rose, vaulted over the desk "with a perfect Errol Flynn leap" and grabbed the teacher's head. As the startled man crashed to the floor, Tony burst into tears. "I always cry when I really fight," he explains now. "I can't stand blood."

A studio press agent found Tony several hours later at Union Station waiting for the first eastbound train, but at length was able to persuade him to come back. However frustrating his performance in other departments, Tony always had an instinctive rapport with the publicity boys. "We found him delightful," says veteran press agent Frank McFadden. "He was plenty naive, but smart enough to be colorful. In six months the fan magazines were giving him star-type treatment, even though he was still only a bit player."

Fan magazine readers, in turn, deluged the studio with mail. No Curtis role was too trivial to evoke a scented paper blizzard from teenagers. In one bit part Curtis spoke only two words, "Woo, woo!" But he got more letters than the star of the picture, a talking mule. Of this unsettling period, Curtis recalls, "I was a big star in movie magazines, but I couldn't get arrested in pictures. They even had contests —'Win Tony Curtis for a week.' Alluva sudden, I was a *prize!* One week a woman in Terre Haute won me, and when we got there she said, 'I really wanted the gas burner.' "

Tony's big break finally came when his fifth picture, *Sierra,* opened in San Francisco and the cast went along to ballyhoo the premiere. As each actor walked out onstage, the spectators applauded warmly. Then, near the end of the parade, Curtis appeared. The audience of teenage girls, preconditioned by massive doses of fan magazine publicity, exploded into a stomping, shrieking near-riot. "It was like walking into an open furnace," says Curtis wonderingly, "like touching a hot nerve."

The riot touched a hot nerve at the studio too. Their new woo-woo boy had stolen the show from its star, Audie Murphy, one of the greatest war heroes of modern times. The awed U-I moguls began a frantic search to find Curtis a starring show of his own, and finally blew the sand off something called *The Prince Who Was a Thief,* a preposterous adventure piece requiring a maximum display of supple beefcake and a minimum of thespic skill. At one point, the well-oiled hero emerged from a crocodile-filled moat, removed a dagger from between clenched teeth, flung out a dripping arm toward an imposing heap of Arabian papier-mâché, and declaimed, "Yonduh lies de castle of my fadduh, de caliph," in accents of purest Bronx. Connoisseurs of cinematic goulash remember the scene with reverence.

The studio bigwigs gave their new star his first private dressing room in which to dry off in between takes. Curtis appropriated the necessary materials from the studio art department to make a sign for his door —"The Rich Kid" spelled out in Christmas tree spangles. He was beginning to feel his oats in all departments. One night he crashed a party, and suddenly found himself gazing upon "a chick like nothing I had ever seen in my whole life. She had a sparkly dress and hair fixed like earphones and—well, she was the wildest." This was Janet Leigh, a star of far greater magnitude then than Tony. Her steady beaux, Louella and Hedda reported breathlessly, were two of the richest, most powerful bachelor moguls in Hollywood. The Rich Kid proceeded with caution. "I did not want anything to interfere with my objective, which was of course to steal her for myself," he says now. He avoided meeting the chick at the party, but a few days later, openly disguised as Cary Grant, he called her and made their first date. Thereafter, Tony spent many long evenings spying on Janet's house from a clump of bushes across the street. When she attended premieres with her other beaux, Tony hid in the crowds. When she returned home from dates, she found notes stuck in her door: "Do not kiss him good night. Big Brother is watching." For some unfathomable reason, these tactics gradually caused Janet to see less of the other men and more of the note-writer.

U-I considered Tony's offscreen love life his own business. But when Curtis suddenly announced that he and Janet had decided to get *married*, the studio turned on the pressure. For three days and nights, a battle raged as executives strove to protect their million-dollar woo-woo boy from poisoning himself at the box office. But despite bitter recriminations, even threats of banishment back to the Bronx and assurances that his movie career would be *kaput*, Tony and Janet eloped.

If anything, the marriage spurred the Curtis career. *The Prince Who Was a Thief* cost $230,000 to make, and grossed over $2 million. A sequel, *Son of Ali Baba*, was rushed into production at once. For over a year his working clothes were gold lamé pantaloons and a large earring. "I was the male Yvonne de Carlo," says Curtis. Then he graduated to velvet doublet and fencing foil. Says one director, "Every young fellow that comes out here, they break him in the same way. First they teach him to fence. Then at least they can put him in a sword thing while they're teaching him to talk." When U-I ran out of sword things, they put Tony in boxing things. Altogether, Tony starred in fourteen sword, boxing, cowboy, and gangster things in the next five years—all cheap, all wildly profitable, all dreadful. But they consolidated Tony's position as a star. For five years—gracefully slashing, leaping, punching, shooting—he was visible, and more or less audible, on the bottom half of every double bill in America.

Then Tony signed with Hollywood's all-powerful talent agency, Music Corporation of America, and his career took still another leap upward. The Boys (movie patois for MCA's black-suited legions) had been keeping a careful eye on Tony for years, and when Curtis joined them, he fastened his own careful Hungarian eye on the Big, Big Boy, Lew Wasserman, MCA's president. Tony embarks on new relationships with the warmth of a puppy falling into a bowlful of kibble, and his confidence in Wasserman and his Boys was so complete that even today he carries with him printed cards which read, "To whom it may concern: This is to advise you that I have no authority to make any decisions, oral, or in writing, or in any other way regarding my career. Thank you for talking to me. If lost, please return me to MCA, 9370 Santa Monica Boulevard, Beverly Hills. (signed) Tony Curtis."

In 1955, when Curtis' original seven-year contract with U-I was about to expire, Wasserman gently told his client the facts of Hollywood life. "Tony, you can carry a U-I picture alone, but you can't carry a first-class picture. So let's look for outside pictures where Burt or Kirk or Frank or Dean has to carry the load. Okay?"

"Crazy," said Tony, and the Boys went to work. Over the next few years, Tony co-starred with Burt in *Trapeze;* with Kirk in *The Vikings;* with Frank in *Kings Go Forth;* and with Dean in *Who Was That Lady?* Again Tony stole the spotlight or, as he now puts it, "The big movie stars took the pressure off me. I had the best roles. The big fellows knew it, but they didn't care because it gave them a chance to relax. And to protect their money—because they knew the kids liked me. At the same time I educated my own fans. They began to say to themselves, 'Well, Burt Lancaster don't play scenes with bums.' "

After three years of this, Wasserman called Curtis into his office and said, "Now it's time to look for a picture *you* can carry." They found *The Defiant Ones,* and Tony's performance as a chain-gang fugitive won him an Academy Award nomination. The honor arrived at a time when Tony was in sore need of all the comfort he could get. That same year he had made *Some Like It Hot,* a hugely successful farce which provided him with the most disturbing professional experience of his career. Tony's agonies were both physical and emotional. To prepare for the scenes in which he and Jack Lemmon dressed as women, they had to arrive at the studio at 7 A.M. Their hair was twisted into tiny pin curls so it would lie flat under hot, heavy wigs. Their legs were shaved. They were buckled into special tight-fitting underwear, squeezed into women's dresses, plastered with makeup. "By nine o'clock they had us trussed up like astronauts," says Curtis. "We had to lie back with our feet in the air and rest our heads on little pegs so we wouldn't get our wigs mussed. We couldn't even go to the bathroom." Marilyn Monroe, who was also in the picture, rarely showed up before lunchtime. She then often required thirty or forty takes to do one brief scene. When the time came to shoot Tony's love scene with Marilyn, the actress' eccentricities had so enraged and unstrung Curtis that he could barely bring himself to tackle the job. He found nuzzling Marilyn "like kissing Hitler."

Jack Lemmon says, "Tony had to learn to act *after* he was already a star. That's doing it the hard way. Tony can still get flipped like a little kid. He's about as blasé as a steamroller. He's susceptible to anything, and his openness frustrates him because, when he gets hit, he gets hit so hard."

The frustrations of *Some Like It Hot* were more than made up for by the multiple joys of Tony's next assignment, *Operation Petticoat.* His old dream had come completely true. He was back on a submarine, now as a star, and as an officer, and the sub's skipper was none other than Cary Grant.

"Out of my way, McChesney! . . . I do believe I've got a pebble in me left boot! . . ." Curtis greeted his co-star, in letter-perfect mimicry of the original *Gunga Din* dialogue spoken by Grant twenty years before.

"At first, Cary was kind of at a loss about Tony," says Director Blake Edwards diplomatically. Actually, Grant was appalled. But despite certain tensions during shooting, the combined appeal of Grant and his fervent disciple proved to be so potent at the box office that *Operation Petticoat* became the highest-grossing comedy U-I ever made. Of Tony's strange obsession, Grant now admits mellowly, "Every young actor, I suppose, needs to find his own ideal of elegance. Mine was Noel Coward. For years I kept one hand in my pocket and one eyebrow in the air."

Tony's present ideals have not developed much since his Fordham Theater days, but his dramatic ability has improved and Curtis has finally found an acting style of his own. In his two most recent pictures, he carries the ball alone . . . and does it well. In *The Great Impostor,* he plays the marvelously gifted phony, Ferdinand Demara. "When they told me about this part, I said, 'Great!' I didn't even have to read the book. There's something *honest* about a guy who likes to lie." In *The Outsider,* to be released in December, he plays Ira Hayes, the Pima Indian Marine who helped raise the flag at Iwo Jima. "I didn't need any acting coaches to teach me how Ira felt," says Curtis. "To Ira, the white men were the savages. When I met Ira's mother, I realized that his mother is all mothers and Ira Hayes is Bernie Schwartz. All kids are Outsiders until they get Anglo-Saxonized. That character poured out of me like out of a garbage disposal."

When he was still a studio rookie, Tony heard a director remark that the ideal movie star is composed of one-third intellect, one-third sex, and one-third heart, so he drew up a huge chart listing every male star in the business, nailed it on the wall above his mattress, and kept batting averages on each man. "I figure movies is a lot tougher than baseball, where .300 is a good average," he explains. "In Hollywood you gotta bat at least .850 or .900 to make it. Cary Grant I gave .900, but it was not all in balance. He had more than a third of sex, and less than a third of heart. Gable had two-thirds sex, one-third heart, very little intellect. I gave Cooper more soul than Gable; more heart, but less sex. John Garfield had two-thirds heart and one-third sex—he was like an open wound."

Tony Curtis still keeps up the graph in his head. He thinks three actors are now batting a perfect 1.000: Brando, Lancaster, and Sinatra. He sets his own current batting average at .850. But like the eight-year-old boy in the Bronx, he still dreams of supreme perfection, of becoming the Compleat Movie Star.

A visitor to the Curtis household today sometimes feels he has stumbled by mistake into de castle of de caliph, but it is for a time a weirdly wonderful place to be. A plane flies overhead towing a sign: "Happy Birthday Janet!" Tony kneels in the middle of an acre of white carpeting, wearing a wet bathing suit and practicing the flute. A new painting arrives for the living room; it is twenty-five feet long. Janet glides past in a leopard sari and a foot-long cigaret holder; in a minute she glides back in a baby's pinafore; a minute later in even less. The phone, one of six, rings. Tony answers as Cary Grant. But it *is* Cary Grant! Confusion. Joy. The French teacher arrives. Janet and Tony remember that their tenth anniversary is coming up soon and decide to throw a really big wingding. "Let's have an Arabian party, with horses dashing through the living room, and belly dancers!" says Tony. "For *Schwartz?*" says Janet. They decide instead on a Hungarian gypsy party. Tony's mother will make potato pancakes for 200 people. Janet orders a tent, candles, red carpets, ribbons, tambourines, strolling violinists, private detectives, and a stunning $1,500 gypsy costume dyed in colors to match her tent. The Sinatra Clan flies in from location by chartered plane. Nobody falls in the pool. Success!

Many years ago Curtis stole an enormous movie still of Cary Grant out of a New York theater lobby. Now elaborately framed and authentically autographed, this object hangs above the black fur couch in Tony's study. Recently, sprawled under the portrait of his guru, Curtis told a visitor what it feels like to be the caliph at last. "I often ask God: why me? Am I gonna have to pay for all this? How much better can

I live? How much more do I want? It's like Lew Wasserman said, 'How much more you gonna steal?' Some day I may wanna pull a Gauguin and disappear, or go to Paris and paint. I may wanna study medicine, or spend time at sea. Things are swinging now, but I got my big hairy foot out the door. . . . I live in this big, beautiful mansion, but some days I wanna yell, 'Stop! Lemme get off!' Sometimes I think about the one hundred scars I'll have to show my grandchildren. The cut on my knee, from the fight in *Flesh and Fury* . . . the cut on my cheek from the fencing in *The Purple Mask* . . . the épée furrow in my eyebrow from *Son of Ali Baba* . . . the mark on my wrist where the drawbridge fell on me in *Prince Who Was a Thief*. I love to come home all busted up and hurt at the end of the day. It makes the screams and aggravations you get all worthwhile. It shows you really worked.

"Today, I'm adjusted as a man, and as a star, but in a way I'm still doing the same thing I did when I was seven or eight—looking in the gutter for money. But now it's not the gutter, and it's not money. It's just looking. . . .

"That little Hungarian kid crying inside of me—he must be paid attention to. You know what that kid would really like to be doing right now? Standing on the deck of a ship, with a sword in his belt, kind to his men, commanding the ship in the teeth of a storm. A beautiful highborn chick comes on board, and she's not scared of him, and he's not scared of her. The big scene is on—and that's *it*. But he walks away, from the girl, from everything, back to the melancholy, lonely life at sea.

"The little imaginary kid inside used to be big. Then when *I* became the big guy, I started to retire him. I don't need to call on him very often these days. But he's always there when I need him. Sometimes he can't give me the answer. Sometimes he says, 'Don't ask *me*, Charlie!' For example, he don't know *nothing* about women. But he has a good life today. Sometimes I'd still like to be *him*. And I think he'd like to be *me*."

The visitor asked Curtis to name the era in which ideally he would have chosen to live his life. "That of Heathcliff," he answered dreamily. "Only I'm the young duke of a Hungarian castle. When the evil king tries to take my land away, I rally up my peasants and fight. They all love and admire me. The castle has a big hall with a fireplace where I sit and brood. I also have a hunting lodge in the mountains with a beautiful mistress. There are very sad problems with her, much sorrow, because I don't want to leave my wife and beautiful children. . . ."

Next day Curtis said he'd been talking this idea over with a friend, who had come up with an even better idea: "He said I should have been a monk. I live my whole life in silence in a bare, whitewashed cell with nothing in it but an autographed picture of me and a string of beads that spells out t-o-n-y-c-u-r-t-i-s. Ain't that bee-*yoody*-ful!"

Life—November 17, 1961

8

Motherliness

"Motherly" to most of us, means gentle, open, warm, uncritical, and adoring. By these lights, some of the most motherly people I know are fathers.

Take a look at any beach in summertime. Here the motherly fathers are out in force. They help build the sand castles, they rub on the sun creme, go for the ice cream, and carry the toddlers into the surf. For this is the height of America's custody season and these are the weekend fathers. The bright summer sunshine reveals all the new patterns in part-time parenthood which our soaring divorce rate has forced us to devise.

About a third of all American marriages now end in divorce. In some communities, like Southern California, the divorce rate has passed 120 per cent, which means that the mythical "average citizen" has been divorced one and one-fifth times. Divorce, here, is considered a normal part of marriage, much the same as death is accepted as a part of life.

But what of the children? What does a man do with a four-, or a six-, or an eight-year-old child, or perhaps all three of them, when "Daddy's Day" rolls around? Visits with the new wife or girl friend are difficult; Disneyland is expensive. Every spare cent Daddy has already goes for alimony and child-support. So it comes down to a choice of the beach—or visiting your children in your ex-wife's living room.

One stretch of California coastline has become so chockablock with weekend fathers and their offspring, it is known as Alimony Beach. The regulars here do not greet each other by name, but by number— "two-two-five," or "three-five-oh," according to the amount the divorce is costing them per month, in cash. One day across the sand lurched a lone man festooned with beach towels, umbrella, hamper, and thermos jug, and followed by five small children. "That's seven-five-oh!" someone whispered.

I watched seven-five-oh all the long day—finding lost sneakers, settling fights, and brushing sand out of the peanut butter—and I have never seen a more gentle, more patient, and—well—more motherly parent.

That qualities like "motherliness" or "fatherliness" are not inborn, nor God-given, but are really states of mind, is something men and women both must remember as drastic changes in patterns of marriage and family life tug at the fabric of our society.

CBS "Spectrum"—August 3, 1971

9

Down With Motherhood?

Social scientists say the world is now turning so fast that it's the young people who must teach their parents. So what wisdom do the young wish to impart to us across the generation gap? Well, here is what a columnist called Ellen Peck has to say. Mrs. Peck is the author of a book extolling the virtues and joys of not having children, a book called *The Baby Trap.* And in honor of Mother's Day, she has composed an obituary to motherhood, which was duly published by *The New York Times.*

Now I would not at all object to abolishing Mother's Day. This seems to me mostly a sales device to foist on Americans more candy and sentimentality than is good for them. But it seems to me crazy to talk about abolishing motherhood. Yet, according to Mrs. Peck, that is exactly what lots of young women in today's generation propose. She quotes with approval the valedictorian of Mills College, who recently announced "The best thing I can do for mankind is never to have children." I, too, recognize, and deplore, the evils of the population explosion, but the valedictorian's forever-unborn child will not do one thing to abate the population explosion she fears, not even if multiplied a thousand or a million times.

What are we to make of the midwest doctor, also quoted in *The New York Times*, who says that pregnancy, today, represents a state of pathology, not a state of health? It seems to me this man is setting himself up not only in opposition to woman's deepest biological nature, as developed over thousands of generations, but also against the most profound instinctual drive of the human race. The pathology here is in the physician, not in the patient.

Other, still sillier arguments are set forth, such as the statement that so-called "planned nonparenthood" shields the might-be-born from an uncertain future. Everyone has an uncertain future, for heaven's sake! These abstract intellectual exercises seem to me foolish, sentimental, and at bottom profoundly cynical. Silliest of all is the claim that today in America it costs a minimum of $23,800 to raise one child to age eighteen. Even if this figure were correct, what better way is there to spend money than on raising the next generation to realize the full human potential that is in them? What else is it all about?

CBS "Spectrum"—May 16, 1972

10

And Now . . . Infants' Lib!

The advancement of science was never as orderly as scientists would have us believe. Human knowledge has always moved forward by a process of epiphanies, sudden leaps of logic that make the discoverer shout "Eureka!" as he bounds from his tub. In the case of Dr. Frederick Leboyer, fifty-seven, a distinguished French obstetrician, the epiphany arrived not in the tub but on the psychoanalyst's couch, when the obstetrician reexperienced the trauma of his own birth. Born in Paris at the end of World War I, when anesthetics were not available for pregnant women, he was a first child and three weeks overdue. His mother, held down by four people, labored more than thirty hours.

By the time he was psychoanalyzed, Dr. Leboyer had delivered some 10,000 babies in the traditional way. Now he began to reflect on the needless agony that modern medical techniques might inflict on the newborn: why the harsh noise and blazing lights? The spine-jerking dangle upside down? The instantaneous cutting of the umbilical cord? The result of these ruminations was a European best-seller, *Birth Without Violence,* which has just been published in the United States, and which sets out a simple but revolutionary new approach to childbirth.

The newborn child, Leboyer argues, is not an "it" to be dangled upside down, spanked, roughly wrapped, and put aside. Rather, *because* he is new and raw—the baby is the most exquisitely sensitive, "feeling" human being in the room. Leboyer has now delivered 1,000 more babies in the manner his book describes: in a hushed room, under dim light; placing the newborn instantly on the mother's warm belly for a few moments' rest, and only then cutting the cord; using a gentle massage; bathing the child in a tepid bath—all simple, commonsense aids intended to calm the infant after the excruciating agony of birth, and to cushion the terrifying contrast between its new life and the quiet, rocking watery darkness of the womb. There is nothing much new in *Birth Without Violence.* It in fact describes the way in which all infants used to be born, and in "uncivilized" parts of the world, still are: quietly, by lamplight, at home.

Months ago, I saw a photograph of a just-delivered Leboyer baby. His utterly blissful smile has haunted me ever since. Is radiant happiness possible in the newborn? "In sorrow thou shalt bring forth children," says the Bible. Leboyer interprets the Scriptures to mean the pain and suffering of the child as well as the mother, and he would simply like medicine to give the baby's pain and suffering equal attention. Certainly I know that I was born that way, not only from what my mother has told me, but from certain forceps scars on my neck and face. All of us bear similar marks on the unconscious mind, psychiatrists say. *Everybody* does, since birth is the one universally shared human experience.

Leboyer is a small, shy, nut-brown man who is uncommonly serene and radiant himself, and was especially so the afternoon we talked. That morning he had met with doctors at New York Hospital, where, only a few days earlier, the first Leboyer-style delivery had been performed in the United States. Very soon, one suspects, the "radical" Leboyer technique will be the accepted way of childbirth in our so-called civilized world, as it always has been elsewhere, before the technocrats of medicine got their hooks, so to speak, into the baby business.

Leboyer is that rare modern combination of scientist, mystic, and poet who can be entirely serious without losing his twinkle. When I asked about prenatal consciousness, so-called womb-memory, he said that in his opinion and by his definition the child is conscious from the moment of conception. "And possibly before," he added with a grin, "although I myself have not gone back that far."

Leboyer's convictions about the universality of the birth trauma have led him to other, wider conclusions about mature human behavior with which I also find it difficult not to agree. The awful struggle to be born imparts to many people the belief that life is a merciless battle in which only the aggressive can survive. But aggression is the opposite of strength. "Aggression and violence are the masks of weakness, impotence, and fear," says the doctor. "Strength is sure, sovereign, smiling."

Leboyer describes the dreadful law of reprisal, which makes people believe that only a hard life builds character. "Really what they are saying, without admitting it, is: 'I've suffered. Why shouldn't others suffer too?'. . . The cult of suffering isn't new with us. It leads directly back to the stake, to the Inquisition, to all the massacres committed in the name of King or conscience. There is no sin involved here . . . only error and ignorance. This kind of suffering is without point. It serves no purpose. It springs from a failure of intelligence."

It is brave today to dare to be poetic. It takes courage to resist the wonders of a technology that exists chiefly for technology's sake, and listen instead to one's own heart, to Eliot's "trilling wire in the blood." For a scientist, it must be especially difficult. Leboyer's book, with its wealth of human and medical insights, has been criticized for a rhapsodic literary style. But if rhapsody has no place in the delivery room, where does it belong?

When Leboyer rented a sound studio to work on his birth film, technicians in the corridor overheard the laboring mother's breathing on the sound track and assumed it was an erotic movie. "And why not?" the doctor asks. "Childbirth is also passion. This is why giving birth should be an ecstatic experience. Because it is of the same nature."

At a Leboyer delivery, all the sophisticated equipment of modern medicine is at hand. But the prime concern of the attending adults is not for apparatus and procedure but for the comfort and serenity of the newborn. Leboyer does not discard science. He merely puts it in its place. He merely wishes to offer the infant the nicest possible welcome, to say: come on in. The world is a wonderful place. Trust me.

Newsweek—March 31, 1975

11

Children of Vietnam

The American prisoners of war continue coming home. Each night on TV they recapture the national imagination: a parade of lean, grinning men seized up in wild family embraces. These repeating images of rejoicing and reunion have immense symbolic weight. They help appease the insatiable appetite all Americans feel just now to somehow come together as a nation once again.

Yet in the midst of great national rejoicing, agony over amnesty tears us apart. Some of us demand "justice" in the name of Vietnam's thousands of injured and dead; others urge forgiveness and reconciliation. Parent is set against parent, son against son. Some cannot forget, some cannot forgive, and all our sensibilities are rubbed raw.

We all make mistakes, says the President magisterially. But we must be made to pay for those mistakes. Evenhandedness is perceived in the White House as next-to-Godliness; mercy is a sign of weakness.

Vice-President Agnew blames the hue and cry over amnesty on the antiwar people's need for "a new issue to shout about." The Vice-President accuses the news media of magnifying this shouting disproportionately. But to blame the media for the amnesty uproar makes no more sense than did the ancient practice of killing the messenger who brought the bad news to the King. It is not the media but our own sandpapered sensibilities to morality and justice that make the amnesty issue feel so raw. If anything, the media have attempted to soothe these sensibilities.

The other day, CBS canceled the telecast of *Sticks and Bones,* a fine, bitter play by David Rabe about the homecoming of a blinded Vietnam veteran, on the ground that Rabe's subject matter might be too "abrasive" just now. It is this playwright's talent first to make you smile at Middle America's family foibles, and then to ram that smile down your throat, and I wish that *Sticks and Bones,* which a year ago won a top prize on Broadway, could receive the broad national audience it deserves. Good drama *should* sandpaper the mind. Still, the network is right that the nation's attention is "emotionally dominated" just now by the images of returning POW's and others who have suffered the ravages of war.

In thinking about amnesty, it helps somewhat to remember the meaning of the word: not to forgive, but to forget. It is a plea not for absolution but for amnesia. My dictionary calls it "an act of oblivion . . . reconcilement and passing over that which is passed."

I'm not sure whether 100 per cent forgiveness is any more possible to achieve than 100 per cent forgetfulness, but still one must try. The difficulty is that at the same time one longs for universal healing and forgetting, it is impossible to deny the bewildered rage and impotent anguish of those other Americans who grope the ashes of war seeking some "fairness" and "justice" at long last.

While I agree that it may have taken as much or more courage to resist this war on moral grounds as it did to fight in it, I also agree that to now invite home the tens of thousands of men who have fled the country or gone underground seems to mock those thousands of others who sacrificed all their freedom and even their lives. Finally, as a practical matter, even supposing all the draft dodgers and deserters could be rounded up, how could we possibly sort out the idealists from the opportunists, the brave from the cowardly?

It helps, too, in thinking about amnesty, to weigh another responsibility, another sad legacy of war. While we struggle to forget, or to forgive our older children for what they did or failed to do, we might turn our attention to the other children whose only crime is to have been born. These others are the children fathered by American soldiers in Vietnam. Are there 15,000 or 100,000 of them? Nobody seems to know. Some relief officials appear to inflate the figures to inflame world sympathy. Whatever their numbers, these children, too, are assuredly prisoners of war, as well as its casualties and accidents. But these prisoners will never come home. They have no homes to come to.

Journalistic old hands in Vietnam warn newcomers away. They call it "the unwritable story." A British journalist reports: "Even a 'relatively good' orphanage is chaotic, filthy, stuffed with children so starved of adult contact that the moment you step inside the courtyard your whole lower body and legs are covered with small, exploring hands."

Soldiers always leave children behind, in every army. The occupation of Germany and Japan produced thousands of such children, the Korean War thousands more. Yet our government has never devised any legislation to provide for them. Rather we appear to go to some pains to deny that these children are our responsibility.

The French, too, fought a bad war in Vietnam, but in the end they made some injustices of that war just. They allowed the illegitimate children of their soldiers to be brought to France to be educated, fed, clothed, and raised. The spawnings of the French Army were recognized, cared for, and given citizenship. U.S. policy toward such children, by contrast, appears to be one of benign neglect at best. They receive less than one-tenth of 1 per cent of the relief funds sent to Vietnam. Thousands of them have been abandoned, left in city slums, herded into primitive, unfunded orphanages, used as servants, or just left to die. Less than 5 per cent are adopted, due to the intricacies of Vietnamese law and to political, religious, and racial bigotries. In Southeast Asia, black is not considered beautiful at all.

Pearl Buck, who died last week, left most of her estate to the foundation for American-Asian children which she had herself established long ago. The novelist was raised in China by missionary parents, spoke Chinese before she did English. To the end of her life, she sometimes dreamed in Chinese. Because she was the product of two cultures, and felt somewhat an outsider, a curiosity, in each, Pearl Buck once referred to herself as "mentally bifocal"—a quality more people should cultivate in themselves. She said she was drawn to the plight of these children not primarily by maternal feelings, but by some acute sensitivity to "disorder" which compelled her to try to set it right.

While we struggle to repair the disorder at home, most Americans surely would welcome some gesture of fatherhood and responsibility to the part-American children of Vietnam.

Newsweek—March 19, 1973

12

Operation Baby Lift: A Sentimental Binge

I read this scene in a novel long ago: a small boy walks out alone into a blowing wheat field. Overhead, clouds scud swiftly by. "Clouds, I command you to blow to the east," shouts the power-mad little boy. The clouds continue to blow as before, so the little boy yells, "Clouds, I command you to blow to the west," and struts off, fulfilled.

In its attitude toward the war in Southeast Asia, the U.S. government has often reminded me of that little boy. The necessity to feel *in charge* was overwhelming. The forces at work always had to be something we intended, never something that just happened. As the chaos worsened, the illusion of control became more urgent.

The latest and most wretched appearance of this *take charge* attitude was the ill-named and ill-advised Operation Baby Lift, the mass deportation of thousands of children from their homeland in which we became so hastily and—I believe—irrationally involved. Operation Baby Lift is a perfectly terrible idea for all sorts of reasons. Nobody really knows how the children actually were rounded up, how many were truly orphans, how many abandoned, how many lost, how many fathered by Americans, how many ill, how ill they were, how many wanted to come, how many had suitable homes awaiting them, how or whether the legal problems had been overcome. Nobody even knew how many children there were.

Sick babies should not be moved. Children already in orphanages are surely safer than children on the loose in the ravaged countryside, being pushed aside and fired upon by retreating mobs of demoralized troops. In the panic to get the children out, no one seemed to ask what they were being rescued *from*. If we know one thing about the government founded by Ho Chi Minh, it is that its social services are excellent: good health care, day-care and educational programs abound, especially for the poor.

When the U.S. interrogated Viet Cong deserters, or prisoners, and asked what is "good" about being on the Viet Cong side of that civil war, the inevitable answer was "security." They meant that the North Vietnamese regime promises security in old age, security for children, security for the sick, for the poor farmer and peasant especially. In this context, the "Ferry to Freedom" concept which turned up here overnight in newspaper fund appeals was particularly absurd. THE MORE MONEY WE RAISE, THE MORE CHILDREN WE CAN RESCUE AND FERRY TO FREEDOM. IT'S THAT SIMPLE, the copy said. But it is not that simple, and it never was. You cannot ferry such children to freedom any more than you can ferry freedom to children. In fact, you can't ferry freedom at all. If we have learned one lesson from our twenty-year involvement in Vietnam, it is that freedom doesn't export. It grows out of the ground, like grass.

The baby lift may not turn out to have been a humanitarian act, but it was certainly a political one. On the one side, it seemed an attempt to snatch honor from the jaws of dishonor. To the degree that this was conscious government policy, I find it abhorrent. One can only recoil at the cynicism and stupidity of our ambassador in Saigon who is supposed to have said he hoped the baby lift would "help create a shift in American public opinion in favor" of South Vietnam. Cynics on the other side, cynical doves if you will, called Operation Baby Lift one last rape of Asia before going home, and compared the children to export souvenirs or war mementos like porcelain elephants.

I am afraid there is some truth to this, as well as some truth to the bitter charge by many South Vietnamese that we are carrying off their children to assuage our war guilt. There is also "survivor's guilt" to consider, a particularly bitter crop which takes a long time ripening. But studies of Hiroshima and Hitler's concentration camps have shown that survivors feel an almost unbearable anguish at having been not just spared, but randomly spared. The Ferry to Freedom is a one-way ticket which I think we will almost certainly one day regret having handed out so rashly.

Please do not misunderstand. I do not argue the biological mystique.

"Natural parents" are no better per se than so-called "adoptive parents"; more often, they are worse. It takes no skill to have a baby. It can take everything you've got, and sometimes some you haven't, to raise a child.

Nor am I opposed categorically to all adoptions of Vietnamese children. If adequate care is not available in Vietnam; if the child's family wishes him to leave; if the child's health permits the trip; if the child has a good home guaranteed in the new land; if the child himself *wants* to go; or if for any reason the child has no future where he is, of course he should go.

But the Thieu government, which we tried so long to keep standing, was not only a house of cards, it was a house of marked cards. Corruption was built-in. So it was scarcely surprising to find that the baby lift was not only disorganized but dishonest. When the planes unloaded here, a number of the children turned out to be not orphans, but members of wealthy families who had bribed their way aboard. Far less advance planning seems to have been devoted to Operation Baby Lift than Operation Gold Lift—the secret transport to Switzerland of the $70,000,000 private fortunes of Presidents Thieu and Lon Nol.

But though one hopes the baby lift is now mercifully almost over, it is still worth reflecting on how and why we could have embarked on such an ill-advised and sentimental binge in the first place. The real trouble was that the airlift did not begin with the consideration of what was best for the children. Rather, it was the product of a fundamentally decent urge, shared by military personnel and relief workers alike, to *do something* in the face of growing chaos, despite mounting evidence that there was in fact nothing to be done. It is normal and human to want to put a good face on disaster. In that sense, the baby lift was more emotional than rational, reflecting the same need to *do something* that moves firemen to take heroic measures to rescue a kitten from a burning building. The baby lift was chiefly a symbolic act, designed less to assist the helpless children than to ease our own sense of helplessness in a time of horror. At such moments, some atavistic and irrational dread of the massacre of the innocents arises from a primitive level of being. We respond by filling the sky with orphans.

Perhaps every war gets the epitaph it deserves. A skyful of babies—what a symbol for the end of this war! We cannot and will never wave a white flag. Instead, we fill the skies with innocents, tiny human peace symbols borne aloft in the same planes that flew the bombs that made them orphans in the first place.

This baby lift is not *only,* nor entirely, symbolic, of course. But to deny its irrational component is, I think, to reject an aspect of that primitive common humanity which we and the children share.

Newsweek—April 28, 1975

SECTION 6
Deep-water Diving, Unbuttered Truth

1

Diary: 1976

Although one feels compelled to dive in and attempt to deal with the heavyweight ethical questions of our time, I find such pieces especially difficult to do, unburdened as I am by any professional or systematic study or background in history, philosophy, military affairs, foreign affairs, economics, art, law, or politics. (This information may be less than mind-boggling to certain readers, and editors, but truth compels.) True, I always read a lot, always studied literature, poetry, mythology, a smattering of science—but the rest is blank. In the years when most schoolchildren get their basic education in American and European history, our family must have been moving around a lot, and I must have just missed out every place. In any case, I can remember studying nothing between Rome and repeal. Later, at Vassar, I did not elect to take courses in art, history, or philosophy, because I already felt so far behind. As for choosing a major field of study, economics mystified me, and sociology bored me. Then I discovered the joys of anthropology and, in my final year of college, felt something like a scholar at last. End of education, except for the subsequent thirty years' field work in the world's news vineyards.

Considering the time span, I am not exceptionally well-read or traveled. Now that I think of it, my only true fields of expertise are cookery, needlework, mythology, and show biz. But somehow it has worked out. I think I write the way I cook and sew, stirring and stringing things together a little bit at a time, slowly, with many false starts. As a commentator, I approach deep-water issues like a timid swimmer on a cold day. I just stand there, frozen, until the deadline pushes me in.

What makes me approach a particular subject in the first place is mysterious but not obscure. Certain subjects in the news oblige one to deal with them. Failure to deal with these subjects feels like a cop-out. Not being an expert is no excuse for not using your head. Thinking about and writing about something you don't know much about is tough, but good exercise. More people should try it. The stress is comparable to the Outward Bound program of physical survival. A week of hard, solitary thinking about the abuses of the CIA, for example, is the mental equivalent of spending a week in the wilderness armed with nothing but knife, matches, and compass. A nervy time, but one emerges with a feeling of confidence, strength, and well-being.

I don't know why I've chosen the particular subjects I have—and in fact deep-water topics are scattered throughout this scrapbook. It would have been risky, if not tendentious, to load them all into one section. Anyway, common to all the hard choices was some sense that the press, or the pundits, or the public was not really confronting these issues head-on and unbuttered. My Outward Bound system is not fail-safe. Frequently I've had to be assisted out of the wilderness by a wise editor who, assaying the rubble of foggy ideas, damaged phrases, and false starts, utters the magic words, "It seems to me, Shana, what you're really trying to say here is . . ." Or sometimes, even more mercifully, "Forget it, kid."

But when it does work, I feel like Marco Polo. Here are some hard ones I liked.

2

Prisoners of Peace

World War I had the Rainbow Division. World War II had Iwo Jima and the Bulge. Even Korea had the men of Changjin Reservoir. But until last week the longest and most dismal of all America's wars had victims, casualties, and the faceless brutalities and braveries common to all wars, but it had no heroes. Well, we have them now.

One of Melvin Laird's last and finest acts as a Washington bureaucrat was to scrap a monstrous mouthful of Pentagonese—Operation Egress Recap—and retitle it Operation Homecoming. The new label for the prisoners' return gave one a faint foreshadowing that some measure of grace might also be about to return to American life.

When the first batch of prisoners came bounding down the airplane steps in so much better shape than anyone had been led to expect, joy was universal. Even press and politicians wept. Then other feelings trickled out. The procession of smart salutes, recruiting-poster grins, radiant wives, near-identical statements of gratitude to Commander in Chief, God, and the American people—all this made one feel we were watching a carefully prepared TV commercial on behalf of the Administration.

Of course we were. Operation Homecoming was meticulously stage-managed by eighty military public relations men, one for every two prisoners. The PR men had an awesome assignment: not only to welcome the men, not only to prepare them for "reentry" into American life, not only to coach them in how to act and what to say, but most importantly to shield them from direct contact with the American public. The PR men set up an inviolate DMZ between prisoners and press, and escort officers were warned that they personally would be held responsible if this zone were breached.

The first excuse for this shield of protection was said to be concern for the prisoners' health. But as one spokesman at Clark Air Base put it, "Their health is so good that in some cases we've had to assign two escorts per returnee."

Then we were told that the shield was necessary lest something be said that might jeopardize the POW's still held captive. Most important, the shield was necessary because men who had suffered, in Mr. Nixon's words, "the most barbaric handling of prisoners of any nation in history" faced a very difficult psychological readjustment now. As Operation Homecoming roled on, it became apparent that the U.S. public was also being asked to readjust its thinking. The Pentagon planners had reason to believe that this adjustment too would go smoothly. We have been asked to adjust our thinking about this war many times before. First they told us our troops were there to help South Vietnam hold back the Viet Cong. Then we were there to help repel invasion from the north. Then we were there to stave off the Chinese. By the time Mr. Nixon became President, we were there to defend our national honor. Finally we were there *in order to* get our troops out and get our prisoners home. The self-justification had come full circle, and the consequences of the war had become its causes.

Unlike newly-released POW's in war movies, these men did not ask: "Who won the World Series?" Instead they asked: "Who won the war?"

Of all the high-flown phrases cranked out about Operation Home-coming, none was sadder and more revealing than the military's care-fully prepared reply,"South Vietnam didn't lose, and North Vietnam didn't win." This is the language of Alice in Wonderland, the logic of Kafka, and the voice of *1984*. I think these first-returned men deserved a straight answer, not another riddle. Surely what they really wanted to know when they asked who won was "Did *we* win or lose?" Why else save to win had they been there so long, and given so much? It is also doubtful that men whose professional duty had been to drop bombs from airplanes cared much whether northern peasants had beat southern peasants, or vice versa.

Nothing more cruelly exposes the hollowness of America's own posi-tion in the war than this tragic question and answer. For if nobody lost and nobody won, which is what this official reply says, then the war becomes officially meaningless. More than 46,000 Americans died for a circular sequence of justifications. And Captain Heck, the bomber pilot who after flying 156 missions refused to fly the 157th, was right when he said, "I have come to the conclusion that no war is ever worth what it costs to win it."

Still another way to answer the question "Who won?" is to say, "Nobody won because the war isn't over." Since the "cease-fire," the level of combat has increased. No wonder, despite Homecoming's joys, that the old Egress Recap label continues to haunt the mind. The egress part is clear enough, but what does "recap" mean? Is it some-thing like tire recapping? After hearing nearly identical statements of loyalty and patriotism from each man, one wondered if they had not been brainwashed more in twenty hours on the plane home than in all the years in camp; as if what had been recapped were the prisoners' heads. These POW's often seemed to be offering only name, rank, and serial number to the American public.

Our joy in having the prisoners back goes beyond relief at their safety, and the surprise of their excellent physical and mental health. Part of what we feel comes from our admiration for their personal character. One of the many ironies of this meaningless, disastrous war

—disastrous *because* meaningless—is that these POW's, having sat out the permissive sixties in the skies and jungles of Vietnam, now appear to us to embody precisely those moral qualities of honor, patriotism, discipline, and purpose which have otherwise largely disappeared from American life. The penultimate irony may be that no one suffers this disappearance more keenly than Mr. Nixon himself.

A nation cannot long sustain a war its own people don't believe in. The South Vietnamese themselves long ago reestablished the truth of that old cliché. But Americans, too, have needed something to believe in. Many who found the Communist-containment line insufficient also reject the peace-with-honor gambit. Operation Homecoming has at last given those Americans something to pin their beliefs on.

As heroes of the Vietnamese war, these POW's are precious to us in a most special way. If it is not possible to hail them as conquering heroes, then we will hail them as survivors. For hail them we must, lest the entire episode in Indochina be seen as the national disgrace it is. The final irony may be that after eight cruel years as prisoners of war, the men have now become hostages of propaganda, prisoners of peace with honor.

Newsweek—March 5, 1973

3

Showcase Trials

The announcement this weekend that a bulletproof, Plexiglas shield has been securely bolted in place in anticipation of the next California courtroom appearance of San Quentin's Soledad brothers has set me to thinking about some of the implications of holding glass box trials.

The most memorable image of a man in a glass booth was the Eichmann trial in Israel, when one pale and pinch-faced bureaucrat was convicted of responsibility for the deaths of ten million people in

Hitler's Germany. Eichmann's glass box dramatized the showcase aspects of the trial itself. When monstrous crimes are committed, some-one human has to pay. The inhuman must be made flesh, so that we can comprehend it. The Nuremburg trials were similar in intent, though guilt at Nuremburg was assigned more on a national, and less on a personal, level.

In a showcase trial, the glass box is metaphorical as well as real. There was actual Plexiglas at Nuremburg, but none at the court-martial of Lieutenant Calley—a trial which, in the minds of many Americans, combined aspects both of the personal guilt of the Eichmann case, and the national guilt of Nuremburg. But on this occasion no box was necessary. Lieutenant Calley has no natural enemies. No one wishes him personal harm. Vengeance need not be anticipated—from the ditch at My Lai, nor from Hanoi.

In the upcoming trial of Angela Davis, I imagine the metaphorical glass box to be a prism through which pass three of the most powerful light rays or lines-of-force of our era. One line stretches from white-to-black; another from right-to-left; another from girl-to-woman. In my mind's eye, the figure of the beautiful young woman is far less distinct than these three intersecting beams.

In another upcoming courtroom battle—the Daniel Ellsberg case—it seems to me that what we will really be judging is the way in which the government of this country works, and in particular the relationship between its executive and military establishments. Not Ellsberg but the United States will be up for scrutiny in the protective custody of a glass box.

To me there is something vaguely upsetting, even disturbing, about all of these trials. Justice does not seem to be the sole point—or at least not the exclusive concern—of any one of them. In a showcase trial, perhaps, it never is.

CBS "Spectrum"—August 10, 1971

4
Diary: 1976

Others could take it or leave it, but for some reason I always had a special fondness for this piece. In retrospect, its psychology—final paragraph in particular—strikes me now as eerily on target in its anticipation of Watergate.

5
Eagleton's Saintly Revenge

When the state was in crisis in ancient times, the priests used to sacrifice an animal and study its entrails for signs and portents. The all-star sacrificial goat of our own state and times seems to have been Senator Thomas Eagleton. A close study of the Eagleton sacrifice, however, reveals more than the downfall of an honorable Presidential candidate and a great political party. In those bloody guts, one may read many signs and portents of what we as a people have become.

The one advantage that George McGovern had over his opponent from the beginning was his aura of rocklike integrity. McGovern's handling of the Eagleton affair destroyed that advantage, and destroyed himself as well. It was probably the most shattering blow to any Presidential candidacy in America's 200-year history. But even more interesting than the two men themselves was the American public's strange, intense, visceral reaction to the brief encounter of these two flawed politicians.

Consider apathy. When the entire campaign period has been characterized as a demonstration of nationwide don't-give-a-damn, it is odd to realize that the one politician this country was not apathetic about was Tom Eagleton. Although he was only a candidate for eighteen days, by every measure of success we believe in—lecture fees (highest in the nation); fan mail (60,000 letters, all but 200 favorable); decibels of applause—noncandidate Eagleton ended his eccentric election year the most popular political figure in America. "Tom *Who?*" he loved to call himself before the cheering crowds that everywhere turned out to huzzah each modest, self-deprecating public appearance, so appealingly shaky-but-staunch. But Eagleton is not "Tom Who?" any more. Rather, he is the Tom who stuck in his foot and pulled out a plum. Somewhere along the long, grimy political track, "Tom Who?" became The Man Who: the man who turned defeat into victory, humiliation into triumph, liability into asset, and mental instability into immense political clout.

What makes us love him so? There are many good reasons. He is the little guy who met the dragon and survived. He has overcome his flaw. He has come back from madness. Rising from the ashes of his defeat, he seems as much a phoenix today as Teddy after Chappaquiddick. Such survival tells us something good about ourselves: we have moved beyond the tribal mentality. We don't have to scapegoat, to cast people out into the desert. Perhaps it will never again be acceptable in our society to do to a man what the French did to Dreyfus. One may hope.

But the near beatification of Eagleton also has its dark side. The chief virtue in a politician is candor; at least we used to think so. Yet the fact that Eagleton's lack of candor at a crucial moment brought down his man, his ticket, and his party went largely unperceived by the American people. I find his lack of candor striking, and his explanation —that he didn't regard the hospitalizations and the electrodes as "skeletons in his closet"—unconvincing. The first time he was hospitalized, he had put out a story that he was suffering from "a virus"; the second time, it was "a gastric disturbance." These are scarcely the statements of a man unaware that mental illness in a politician is a skeleton to rattle the house down. But the funny thing is that when the press brutally yanked open the closet door, it was not Tom Eagleton's house that fell down, but rather George McGovern's!

In a most curious inversion of moral accountability, people seemed to feel that it had not been Eagleton's job to volunteer the perhaps damaging information about himself, but rather that it was McGovern's responsibility to ferret it out. The weird emotional mix of scorn (for McGovern) and sentimentality (for Eagleton) thickened as people watched the Democratic presidential candidate respond to the delicate situation.

It is useful to observe the contrasts of character and instinct between McGovern and President Eisenhower, who also had to handle a sudden, unexpected whiff of scandal in connection with his choice of Vice-President. In 1952, when the Nixon slush fund was disclosed, Ike said that his running mate would have to be "clean as a hound's tooth" to survive. Ike swiftly distanced himself from any potential taint, to await public reaction and keep his options open. Only after the desperate ploy of the Checkers speech had worked did Eisenhower say to Nixon, in effect: OK, you're my boy.

McGovern, by contrast, when confronted with a crisis whose importance and dimensions he did not and could not yet know, immediately painted himself into a corner, and backed Eagleton "one thousand per cent." By committing himself to a course of action he later had to revise, McGovern made himself look like every other cheap politician. And the public in their infinite folk wisdom figured that if McGovern wasn't smart enough to handle that one, he wasn't smart enough to run the country. I believe McGovern when he says he made the "one thousand per cent" remark out of compassion, as a moralist. But Americans want their leaders to make decisions rooted more in practicality than morality, and they are probably right.

From then on, Eagleton's continuing, saintly loyalty to McGovern became a kind of kiss of death. To watch the victim stumping the country for the man who had dumped him was to see in action the classic martyr's revenge: licking the feet of the man who had kicked him, every speech a new reminder of the cruel rejection he had suffered, every speech doubtless turning off a few more precious McGovern voters.

Eagleton on the stump turned out to be as glib in the techniques of engaging self-mockery as he had been tongue-tied in speaking blunt truth. The man's crowd-pleasing tendency to put himself down was evident from the moment he strode onto the national stage calling himself "Tom Who?" He said he was writing a book on his eighteen days as a candidate. He suggested himself as a subject for *Newsweek*'s

"Where Are They Now?" section. The skeleton was out of the closet, cracking jokes.

It strikes me that another spontaneous outgush of national sympathy happened recently. Then the object of unreasonable affection was Lieutenant William Calley. I have been wondering what the two situations could possibly have in common—for of course the two men have nothing. I think the answer may be that in each instance a highly charged, dramatic episode pilloried a man for something that people see as fundamentally *not his fault,* even though he was the central actor in the play. We reserve unbearable compassion these days not so much for the altogether guiltless victims—of war, poverty, or riot—as for those guilty ones whose sins can be blamed at least in part on the situation in which they find themselves.

In some way, Tom Eagleton's strange psychological state—the piety, the lack of candor, the tinge of self-pity, and the refusal of personal accountability—seems to mirror the psychological state of the country in 1972.

Newsweek—November 13, 1972

6

A No-Fault World?

Last year, California adopted what is called a "no-fault divorce law." This means that when a marriage breaks up, the court is no longer obliged to assign the blame to either partner. Or to put it another way: no matter what went wrong, both husband and wife are to some degree responsible. The point about no-fault divorce is that by removing the concept of guilt, the judge is free of the need to impose punishment. On either party. He can decide matters in the way he thinks will be best for both—and for the children.

Another good idea is no-fault insurance, which has just become law in Massachusetts. This means that when my car hits your car, or vice versa—and can some actuarial genius explain to me, by the way, why it is the vice versa that always, inevitably happens?—neither one of us is to blame. Our insurance companies simply pay each other off. No more lengthy litigation. No more lawyer's fees. Just the cash, please.

But whereas no-fault divorce and no-fault insurance are both obvious giant steps forward in social progress, I am getting edgy about where all this blamelessness may be leading us. To what extent can we bleach the stain of fault from the fabric of our lives and at what peril?

In big business: is a dismal failure on the scale of the billion-dollar Lockheed disaster really nobody's fault?

In the prisons: does our obvious inhumanity to prisoners leave them no choice but bloody revolt? Or guards no choice but to shoot them down?

What about drugs? Is it true that the vast numbers of new drug addicts are merely and only "sick"?

Finally, and most ominous of all, I think: we have now been told officially, more than three and a half years after the massacre, that My Lai was not really anyone's fault either.

It's getting so that the only fault one can count on in this country is the San Andreas Fault, the deep-down crack underneath California which causes all those earthquakes. Incidentally, that primal fissure has begun to rumble ominously of late . . . I'm scared, but I'm not surprised.

CBS "Spectrum"—September 28, 1971

7

Diary: 1976

Poverty is something nobody ever wants to write about. The subject is not "box office," and I didn't write about it especially well, but I'm glad to have published this particular piece. A few months later, Dr. George Wiley, the remarkable and dedicated organizer of the poor people's lobby, was drowned in a tragic accident.

8

The Crime of Poverty

Way down upon the Old Miasma, most Americans are in a trench of deep gloom stretching from apathy to zombie. The one truly jubilant man I have run into in many months is the head of the poor people's lobby, Dr. George Wiley, executive director of the National Welfare Rights Organization. This gentle brigade of marching militants, mothers, and others insists that poverty is not a crime. George Bernard Shaw made the same point in *Major Barbara* when he observed that there is one "irresistible natural truth which we all abhor and repudiate: to wit, that the greatest of our evils, and the worst of our crimes is poverty, and that our first duty, to which every other consideration should be sacrificed, is not to be poor."

Shaw wrote this in 1905, but identical ideas float through our minds today. They are the nightmare side of the American dream. They drive us to ignore the poor, or regard them as shiftless swindlers. They are a deep-down reason why most Americans prefer Mr. Nixon (whom they perceive, correctly or not, as the candidate of the rich) to Mr. McGovern, whom they see as the candidate of the poor. They blind us to the truth that this richest nation on earth rests on a foundation of the hardship of nearly one third of its people (twenty-five million Americans live below the poverty level of $80 a week for a family of four; another thirty million to thirty-five million live just above this). But we won't face it, and this is the root of our "welfare mess." This is why in 1969 the President named welfare reform his "Number One domestic priority." It is also why the Ninety-second Congress, in its twilight hours, scuttled the single most important provision of Mr. Nixon's domestic program—his Family Assistance Plan. So much for Number One priorities. How the old playwright would have chuckled in his beard!

By the time the original bill emerged from the Congressional shredders, it had been killed in the Senate, reborn in the House, and finally had mutated into a cruel travesty of its former flawed self. Who was responsible? HEW Secretary Richardson accused Senator Long of locking up the legislation in the Finance Committee. Long claimed he deserved gratitude for keeping the dangerous thing off the floor. Senator Ribicoff, the leader of the so-called liberal forces, blamed the President. "He killed his own child," Ribicoff said.

But there is no question who really killed FAP. The poor killed it themselves, in self-defense. That is what Dr. Wiley was so happy about. "The sweetness of this victory is that we got the whole cancer in one scoop," he says. *Sweetness? Victory?* How can he use these words when the "welfare mess" remains riddled with inequity and inefficiency, and the only prospect is four more years with, so to speak, no relief in sight?

To perceive this situation as a victory, you must look at it from a poor person's point of view—an experiment well worth making. One cannot see poverty clearly from above. But the perspective flips completely when you stop looking down *on* it, and begin looking up *from* it. What both the President and the liberal reformers in Congress saw as bountiful and orderly, the poor people saw as cruel and punitive. For example, the original FAP would have established one uniform federal floor of payments, nationwide. In principle, excellent—but the floor was only $1,600 a year for a family of four, much less than most states already were paying!

Each time the legislators rewrote the bill, they made it worse. They raised the floor to $2,400, and took away the food stamps. They made provisions for minimal day care, then forced the mothers of small children to go to work at substandard wages. They even proposed social security numbers be issued at birth to welfare children to check cheating, and blood tests given to fathers to check paternity. In the end, it was a very bad bill indeed, and one must congratulate NWRO for shooting it down.

The victory over FAP was historic in the annals of the poor because, for the first time, through extensive lobbying, the poor spoke with their own voice instead of relying on reformers, liberals, or social theorists to speak for them. Welfare reform must be led by the poor for the same reason that abortion reform must be led by women: nobody else is going to do it right. Taxpayers demand tax reform. Parents and teachers lobby for educational reform. Property owners clamor for cleaner streets. Only welfare has heretofore lacked a vocal constituency. That is one fundamental reason we have the welfare mess. The other is that we still cannot see the crime of poverty as Shaw saw it. We still blame the poor for being poor, which makes as much sense as blaming the sick for being diseased. Now that we have accepted no-fault auto insurance and even no-fault divorce, surely it is time to accept no-fault poverty as well.

The poor ought not be punished for being poor. Access to food, clothing, shelter, and medical care are basic human rights. When lawmakers attempt to convert welfare into workfare, which is essentially what happened to FAP in the Congress, and what is happening in California now under Governor Reagan, this is less conversion than perversion of that basic idea. Workfare assumes that people on relief don't really want to work. It overlooks the fact that more than half the people on welfare are children; and that the rest are mothers, blind, disabled, or too old to work; and that many of these people *do* work but cannot earn enough in low-paying jobs to support themselves and their families. HEW reports that less than 1 per cent of the people on welfare are able-bodied men. And to dispel yet another myth, most people on welfare are white.

But the real perversion is the assumption that any class of people is shiftless and must be forced to work. The truth is that one's sense of personhood compels all people to want to participate in society. "The rich are different from us," said Fitzgerald. "Yes, they have more money," Hemingway replied. The same logic, in reverse, applies to the poor.

NWRO's long fight against FAP has achieved more than reprieve from cruel and repressive legislation. The years of lobbying have helped to define the rights of poor people. It has made the poor more aware of their rights, and less fearful of asserting them. This may not sound like much, but, like Alice in Wonderland, the poor must often run very hard just to stay in one place.

Newsweek—October 30, 1972

9

Attica

If you regard news events as contemporary theater, and can see one news event in terms of another, sometimes both dramas come into perspective. Consider first the Attica Prison rebellion last fall and, in particular, the refusal of Governor Rockefeller to come to the prison during that desperate five-day siege. Despite urgent pleas both from the prisoners and from the committee of outside observers who were attempting to negotiate a settlement instead of a shoot-out, Rockefeller, like his famous namesake, Admiral Lord Nelson, chose to turn a blind eye.

Certainly this governor is a firm, inflexible man. In his testimony the other day before the state commission which is investigating the tragedy, Rockefeller disclosed for the first time that even his own State Corrections Commissioner suggested, to no avail, that the governor come to Attica.

It turns out now that Rockefeller's refusal was based only partially on legal and practical grounds. He says he also had a deep conviction that his personal appearance in the Attica drama would create, "a worldwide theater . . . (for) revolutionary forces." So the builder of Lincoln Center, the patron of the arts, medicine, the humanities, decrees: no play.

Now, consider a second dramatic confrontation: this time it is anti-war Columbia University students who are barricaded for a five-day siege. Buildings occupied. Assault forces drawn up. Ambulances waiting. Kent State in the memory. Situation very tense. The students refuse to talk to the administration, the administration won't talk to the students. Now, enter a little man: his name, Anibal Archilla. He is a dormitory security guard. The guard enters upstage, dramatically

—his head sticking out through a window of one building. He shouts across to the barricaded students in the next building, and one of them comes out onto the roof to see who is yelling. They begin to shout back and forth. They talk . . . and finally, as a result of all the talk, a violent clash does not take place.

Maybe Nelson Rockefeller was right in avoiding Attica. He doesn't seem to have the talent for this sort of theater; which is to say, he doesn't have the humanity. It is a pity he couldn't even have sent Anibal Archilla as envoy to Attica. The dormitory guard is not only a better negotiator than the governor. He also appears to be a more human human being.

CBS "Spectrum"—May 3, 1972

10

Alimony

Alimony is as American as apple pie. As a surefire comedy character, the alimony-poor ex-husband ranks just behind the battle-ax mother-in-law. But alimony is no joke to the women who live off it, any more than to the men who pay it. Both, it turns out, are victims of what might be called The Alimony Mystique. The gold digger ex-wife driving her husband into the poorhouse is just another myth figure to support the subtle sex discrimination in American life.

The evidence is contained in a new Labor Department report on how our present alimony and child support laws actually function. The report is a by-product of women's protracted and really quite incredible struggle to get the Equal Rights Amendment passed by a male-oriented, male-dominated Congress. One of many arguments that have been used to oppose the Amendment is that constitutional guarantee of equal rights for women would weaken men's obligations to support the family, and would thereby weaken the family itself. This argument is based on the assumption that under present law men are required to support their wives without regard to their wives' ability to support themselves.

The Labor Department's research reveals that, in practice, the rights to support of women and children are extremely limited anyway; much more so than is generally known. As the report states, "A married woman living with her husband can in practice get only what he chooses to give her." To force him to support her and the children, she generally has to sue him for separation, or divorce. Furthermore, courts actually grant alimony in only a tiny percentage of cases, and if the man fails to make his alimony, or child-support payments, they are notoriously difficult to collect. In most divided families, it is working mothers, rather than absent fathers, who provide for the children.

Alimony is a humiliating concept at best, and a degrading one—both to men and women. But we can't improve upon it until we at least acknowledge how it does—and does not—work.

CBS "Spectrum"—February 18, 1972

11

America the Ugly

The other day a fragment of an old cockney song ran through my head. "Ain't it a bleedin' shame. They're shifting daddy's bones to build a sewer. Ain't it a bleedin' shame." I was standing on a New York street in the sunshine, watching a steel ball batter a fine old brown wall, and doing it great hurt. We were once again demolishing ourselves.

Now, I'm not against change. A great part of the American genius has been to sell its old timbers to pay for new hardware. We are, after all, the greatest consumer society the world has ever known. And the metabolism of a consumer society requires it continually to eat and excrete, every day throwing itself away in plastic bags.

But what I do object to is the violence done to the quality of life by all the wrapping and unwrapping. We allow some things to last, but very little to mature. That fine hundred-year-old wall in New York will be replaced by—what? Probably another parking pyramid. A ziggurat of stacked-up automobiles. Ain't it a bleedin' shame.

Tied to the question of waste is the question of taste. Contemporary culture seems to worship a freakish goddess. We have made waste and taste into Siamese twins, joined at the pocketbook. When something ugly comes down, something uglier nearly always rises in its place, and the explanation is always money.

Must we be forever re-creating ourselves as ugly America, battering down the cities and ploughing up the countryside to sow ever-more-freakish crops of gas stations and Laundromats? We have zoning laws, fire laws, earthquake laws. But we have no eyesight laws. An eyesight law might not have preserved my fine old wall . . . perhaps it had to come down. But it would preserve us from things like plastic pizza parlors. The public should also be protected from really overpriced tastlessness, such as the marble arrogance of the new Kennedy Performing Arts Center, in Washington.

What we may need is a Ralph Nader of America the Beautiful, someone to regularly question this cash-registering but consumer-consuming society of ours, that tears down to put up to tear down. Someone to ask, bravely and openly: why should *we* reshape *our* lives to fit *your* new hardware?

CBS "Spectrum"—October 18, 1971

12

Diary: 1976

Shortly after Jerry Brown won the California gubernatorial election, he appointed Raymond Procunier, former chief of prisons, to serve as the new head of the Adult Authority, the state's name for its parole board. It was a good appointment, but California's prisons are still overcrowded human stewpots of violence, race war, and despair. Another Attica is still a very real possibility, though it would not be handled with the brutal stupidity exhibited by New York's Governor Rockefeller and his "correctional" staff at the time of Attica.

I accompanied "Pro" on several of his official tours of his vast and seething realm, as part of my background research on the origins of the SLA, and two impressions linger strongest in my mind: the eerie, menace-laden sense, in every prison, of interlocked necessity between convicts and their guards. Neither population could exist without the other; it is a genuine symbiosis. The other memory is of the awful, permeating stink, a compound of sweat and fear and punishment and hopelessness that hangs in the air of every prison, crummy old rock pile or modern green-painted pen.

The best prison news out of California is the recent federal court decision that solitary confinement, the wearing of chains and manacles, and the other routine deprivations of prison life themselves constitute *cruel and unusual punishment and thus are violations of prisoners' constitutional rights.*

13

Under the Rock: California's Prisons

"Why do you think they stuck the prisons way out in the countryside in the first place? So people don't have to see them, don't have to think about locking up men in cages," said Raymond Procunier, chief of California's vast prison system.

California is once-and-future America, and much that is newest and biggest in this country, both its best and worst, is concentrated along our western edge. California's prisons are best, worst, *and* biggest: today they house 23,953 convicts, the third largest incarcerated population in the Western world.

What is liveliest in America, most energetic, most dissatisfied with things-as-they-are, most ardent for things-as-they-might-be has always tended to pile up along our Pacific shore. It is no accident that the prison-reform movement and such champions of prison reform as Eldridge Cleaver, George Jackson, and Angela Davis emerged here. The accident is that an Attica—so far—has not.

The citizens of California are of two minds about the criminal world: recently they voted overwhelmingly to restore the death penalty for a variety of offenses; yet California is also worldwide center of the drive to reform, empty, and even tear down the prisons altogether.

For a decade, California's prisons have rocked with increasing violence—hundreds of stabbings and homicides in recent years—and the maximum security wings of Folsom and San Quentin have now been in various degrees of lock-down for eight months.

The increasing unrest behind prison walls is exacerbated by racial tensions inside, a growing climate of violence outside, a shift in the kinds of criminals who get sent to state prisons, a rising public demand for law and order, and the fact that as one young lawyer expressed it, "prisons contain not one but two gangs of terrible people—criminals and guards—each hating and fearing the other."

Looking into prisons is like looking at the underside of society's rock. Save for a few hot-eyed reformers, nobody wants to turn the rock over. But someone has to, and probably no one today knows that dark and ugly underside better than "Pro," Raymond Procunier, the stocky, blue-eyed, chain-smoking career corrections officer whom Governor Ronald Reagan picked out seven years ago to run California's Department of Corrections.

It was a fine appointment, and there is much unspoken hope here that Pro can be persuaded to stick around when a new governor takes office next year. Two who must share that hope most fervently are the state's rival gubernatorial candidates, Democrat Edmund G. Brown, Jr. and Republican Houston Flournoy. They may not care to look under the rock any more than the rest of us, but when I called on each of the candidates to discuss their prison policies, it turned out that each of them already had privately—and one may assume anxiously—consulted Pro. He had advised that "no prison policy" was the best policy, at least until after the governor takes office. By that time, Mr. Procunier himself has said he intends to resign. A delicate matter, evidently, in many quarters.

When I consulted Mr. Procunier myself, I found him affable, voluble, and paradoxical. All of California's immense prison problems ultimately come to rest in his lap, or would if he had a lap. But he rarely sits down long; the only place he seems uncomfortable is behind the huge, bare desk in his Sacramento office. Frequently he sprints across the room to chalk circles on a blackboard, to diagram the cornerless, Mobius-strip shape of human systems: left rounds into right, good to bad, authority to permissiveness, punishment to crime.

"The prison world is a world all its own," he told me, "yet without understanding it you can't understand the rest of society, because the whole issue of blacks and browns, radical movements and social change, all that hate and fear ties in with the prison things and the way our society handles those kinds of people."

The basic change in the prison population, says Pro, is that until a decade or so ago, "every inmate I've ever known accepted that he was a bad guy and that ultimately he had to change." Today rebellious inmates claim that an unjust and racist society must change, and one of the thousand ironies of the world beneath the rock is that Pro, of all people, agrees with them.

As people in California are fond of saying, "Pro is a real pro," both a shrewd bureaucrat and a supreme realist. "Prisons are only good for punishment," he believes, "to keep the bad people away from the good people." They don't rehabilitate anybody. They don't deter crime; they teach crime.

Who is in prison today? They are mostly losers, mostly poor and black. Their chief crime, in Huey Newton's memorable phrase, is practicing "illegitimate capitalism." They are unemployables whose only hope of enjoying some of the good things of life is in ripping off the system.

The most hardened wardens agree that 80 to 90 per cent of these people could be released without constituting any menace to society. As for the 10 per cent who are a menace, who will commit violent crime, the trouble is that nobody, not even the most brilliant criminologist, can positively identify who they are. "Given the right circumstances," says Pro, "it could be you, or me."

When I ask what's to be done, he replies, "There are no answers. There is no solution. Everything I do around here, at least half the people get pissed at me. The right wing wants me to gas everybody, and the left wing wants me to blow up the prisons.

"I believe if a guy violates the law he should be punished. Quickly. The judge sentences him quickly, and for a short period of time, and the guy knows exactly what he's doing time for; not to be rehabilitated, nothing else but 'Buddy, we're just sick and tired of you.'"

Newsweek—July 8, 1974

14

Bail

One fringe benefit of the uproar over Mr. Nixon's disastrous appointments to the Supreme Court has been to compel us ordinary citizens to think about our own personal concept of justice, however naive or unscholarly it may be. To me, it comes down to the question: whom would I want to judge me? Well, I think I have found him. His name is Bruce McMarion Wright, and he is a justice of the Bronx Criminal Court. Judge Wright is a night court judge, which means that mostly he processes the city flotsam: petty criminals, disturbers of the peace.

But last week, Judge Wright broke the dismal court routine in a dramatic and humane way. Of fifty-four prisoners who appeared before him, he paroled forty-five on their own recognizance; that is, he sent them home without demanding bail.

Judge Wright is black, and most of the prisoners he meets are black and poor. When he paroled them, Judge Wright remarked that blacks and Puerto Ricans seem to be unusually "visible" to the police, who are mostly white. And he refused to continue sending people whose crimes are drug-related into prisons which have no facilities for treating addicts.

Our Constitution speaks of equal protection under law, but rich and poor are not equal. This I think is the point Judge Wright was making. Why should a man, who is innocent until proved guilty, spend months in prison for want of money, when anyone who *has* the money can take a taxi home?

We impose the heaviest punishments of any civilized country today. This obsession with punishment, plus our antiquated court system, has perverted the law itself. The intent, at the criminal court level, is not to dispense justice, but to clear the docket.

Judge Wright was having lunch recently with some fellow judges who boasted that they had disposed of 60 per cent of their cases. "Yes, but do you get sixty per cent justice?" Judge Wright asked.

I would feel confident of getting more than 60 per cent justice in Judge Wright's courtroom. And I would respectfully suggest to the many individuals in the White House, the Justice Department, the FBI, the American Bar Association, and the United States Senate who have been so busy of late examining judicial credentials, that they drop in and take a look at the quality of justice and mercy being dispensed in Bronx night court.

CBS "Spectrum"—October 22, 1971

15

Breast Cancer and News Overkill

The tone and volume of reportage on Mrs. Nelson Rockefeller's second operation for breast cancer compel one to shout: enough! Enough medical detailing of private matters for public scrutiny. Enough of lymph nodes and lesions held up for inspection by Dr. John Q. Public and Betty Boop, M.D. Enough of hospital press conferences and operating-room stakeouts. This is *news?* What is going on in there, a mastectomy or a hijacking?

I do not object to the medical bulletins themselves. The stunning coincidence of breast cancer striking first Mrs. Ford and then Mrs. Rockefeller threw a valuable media spotlight on a feared and neglected subject; this in turn may save thousands of lives. I do protest a certain harshness of language, and obsession with clinical detail. To take a tiny example, whereas one network says "an operation for breast cancer," a rival network calls it "an operation for the removal of her cancerous left breast," hard-edge wording that strikes me as unnecessarily specific and unnecessarily unpleasant. If Mrs. Rockefeller wants to say it that way herself, fine, but I have come to feel strongly that she is entitled to make her own medical announcements.

I do not of course speak as Dr. Alexander, merely as citizen Alexander, even prospective patient Alexander if I read the statistical probabilities right. Breast cancer is the leading killer of women in the United States. But at this point I would like to yield the podium to a very new friend, Dr. Max Cutler, seventy-five, who has been a cancer specialist and breast surgeon for half a century. He was the first Rockefeller fellow at the Memorial Hospital cancer clinic in New York; he founded the Chicago Tumor Institute, and he brought radium therapy to the United States. Fourteen years ago, Dr. Cutler was among the first American surgeons to introduce the less-mutilating, so-called modified radical mastectomy procedure, in which the chest muscles are left intact.

The good effects of the recent publicity about breast cancer are well-known. Dr. Cutler dares to speak out about the bad side within the medical profession. "Tremendous confusions now exist among doctors, as well as the public," he says. "Doctors are overdiagnosing; surgeons are afraid *not* to operate. I'll tell you why. The public doesn't understand and doctors don't speak about the tremendous gray zones that exist in medicine. People think mammography [X-ray diagnosis of the breast] is one hundred per cent accurate, but it isn't at all." The error factor is from 10 to 20 per cent.

Yet patients now come to breast surgeons not because of suspicious lumps but because of suspicious-looking X rays. An ambiguous shadow compels the surgeon to operate; it *may be* cancer. Of the last twelve such exploratory operations Cutler has felt compelled to do, not one proved to be cancerous. He has decided henceforth to wait three months and X-ray such patients again before picking up his scalpel. The nerve to wait, the nerve to risk error, the nerve to say "I don't know," the nerve *not* to cut is too rare among surgeons today.

Now that cancer can be mentioned aloud, thanks to heroic figures like Mrs. Ford and Mrs. Rockefeller, it is time to clear up some public confusions, too. The most serious one in Cutler's view is the false and dangerous idea that the greater the extent of the surgery, the greater the likelihood of cure.

A related misconception exists in my own field. Is saturation news coverage of a "good story" always a good thing? The media's stunning capacity to distort both public and professional judgment is no surprise. Understanding this special ability—even inevitability—of journalism is essential. Unless we learn to reckon with it, we are stuck with the kind of news overkill, maxi-peel, and mega-strip in the name of clinical candor that characterized last week. I oppose opening one's own life to popular scrutiny for almost any reason. Beyond a certain point—and last week we were way beyond it—medical disclosure becomes mutilation of feeling on all sides.

That this happened is not the fault of the press, nor of the press advisers to the stricken families. Full disclosure just now is everywhere out of control. Everyone is confessing everything—medical records, bank accounts, psychiatric despairs, sexual kinks, all manner of bleeding wounds and running sores of the spirit are on show or on sale. Some mass urge to confess, to display, to fling off aprons seems to be epidemic. Decorum, seemliness, all respect for privacy of person appear to have been tossed aside in the mania to take it *all* off, to tell it like it is, to—most hideous usage!—let it all hang out.

Were I to let my own inmost feelings of outrage hang out, I would suggest that this time we have been witness to a grotesque displacement of Mr. Rockefeller's political woes onto Mrs. Rockefeller's helpless body. Mr. Rockefeller had been humiliated and chivied for many weeks into making full financial disclosure of his enormous wealth. Little by little, he was forced to open bankbooks, checkbooks, the whole vast library of accounts to public scrutiny. And when doctors found the crab growing in one of his wife's breasts, Rockefeller opened up his wife's hospital and medical records in the same way. In the matter of Attica, Mr. Rockefeller now says his mistake was not to be hard-nosed and decisive enough to crush the prison insurrection at once. It seems to many people, doctors included, that Mrs. Rockefeller's husband and her doctor made just that kind of fast, decisive decision when the tiny pinhead of precancerous cells was found in her other breast. But a human body is not a battlefield, and war on cancer is a faulty concept in every way.

Perhaps we have reached a point in this stressed democracy where persons contemplating public office should demand assurance of personal privacy in advance, some written guarantee that "in the event any medical, psychiatric, spiritual, or other purely private trauma should

befall me or any member of my family during my term of office, it shall
be none of the public's damned business."

Those six words, "or any member of my family," may be the crux.
While it can be argued that the public has a right to know every bodily
frailty of its Chief Executive, from President Eisenhower's bowel
movements to President Johnson's belly scar, does that right extend
equally to the wife of the Chief Executive? And what about the rights
to privacy of the wife of someone who is a once and possibly future
Chief Executive, but who is at present chief of nothing but a vast
amount of wealth, of sorrow, and—it would seem—all manner of bad
advice.

Newsweek—December 9, 1974

16

Real Gardens, Real Toads: Some Speculations on Secrecy and the Dark Night of the CIA

The letter was forwarded to me by CBS News. Underneath a demurely
garlanded *O*, traced in Wedgwood blue, it said:

June 8, 1975

Dear Ms. Alexandria:

There was indeed a conspiracy in November 1963 in which my
young son Lee Harvey Oswald was allowed to take the blame.

Sincerely,

Marguerite C. Oswald

How swiftly she swam up from the depths of my memory—a pathetic, clownish eccentric in glasses and a funny hat. A publicity seeker
and flinger of wild charges. A nutty, slightly sinister, big-nurse type.
Not a woman to be taken seriously.

But that was twelve years ago. Today one feels differently. Twelve years ago I believed the Warren Commission Report, believed that President Kennedy had been killed by a single, deranged assassin acting alone, believed that this man in turn had been killed by another deranged assassin acting alone—Jack Ruby. I do not necessarily believe that now. But my belief survived for a dozen years—survived the assassinations of Robert Kennedy and of Martin Luther King and the shooting of George Wallace, survived Vietnam and Cambodia and Chicago '68 and Jackson and Kent State, and lasted even through much of Watergate. My belief held steadfast much longer than most people's.

Three years after President Kennedy's assassination, the Gallup and Harris polls reported that two-thirds of the American people refused to accept the conclusions of the Warren Commission. But like most professional journalists, I did accept them. I wrote off the skeptics and doubters as a pack of conspiracy nuts, assassination buffs, loonies, and paranoids babbling about a second gun, a third Oswald, conjuring up James Bond plots and secret links between Cuba, the CIA, and Cosa Nostra—flaky people, like Mother Oswald, not to be taken seriously.

Then the CIA revelations began to surface, leading first to the formation of the Rockefeller Commission and later to the inquiries directed by Senator Frank Church and Congressman Otis Pike. This was different. I took the spook stuff seriously from the very beginning; and as time passed I began to wonder why.

What was I looking for? I knew the intelligence establishment was overgrown and overblown. I knew it tapped phones, read mail, engaged in dirty tricks; that it mixed in the internal affairs of other nations, propped up "friendly" governments, and tried to "destabilize" others. I knew that for a generation or more Congress had preferred to look the other way rather than exercise the appropriate and necessary control, and I knew the dangers to democracy when police power is allowed to range unchecked.

In short, I knew that there was little in these new CIA headlines that we didn't already know. So why the eagerness for the morning paper, the thirst for the nightly news? At first, it was the magnetism of the subject matter, the pull toward secrecy itself. To think the unthinkable, discuss the unmentionable, poke around the untouchable, is a pleasure very hard to come by in these days of bared souls, spread-eagled account books, full-political-disclosure laws, and full-frontal-nudity barmaids.

Very few forbidden subjects remain. The secret world of the secret agent is the last taboo place left.

Marianne Moore once described poetry as the art of creating imaginary gardens with real toads in them. The secret agent lives in exactly the opposite landscape—real gardens, imaginary toads. What can it be like in there?

As the year wore on, I found myself temporarily distracted from these speculations about gardens and toads by new doubts about the Warren Commission Report. More accurately, I found myself wondering why it was that so many "rational, responsible" reporters like myself, including nearly all my professional colleagues and friends, had so long refused to listen to the assassination nuts and conspiracy freaks. Who and what were *we* afraid to take seriously? Ourselves? I voiced my doubts to James J. Kilpatrick, the syndicated newspaper columnist who is my opponent in our weekly "Point-Counterpoint" exchange on the CBS-TV program *60 Minutes*. It was these comments that triggered the instant response from Lee Harvey Oswald's mother.

Admittedly, my new doubts were based on old and circumstantial evidence: suggestions that Oswald may at one time have been an undercover FBI agent, that a so-called "second Oswald" may have been operating in New Orleans and Mexico City, that more than one set of fingerprints had been found in the Texas School Book Depository; evidence that at the time of the President's murder the CIA was already heavily into the assassination business in Latin America and elsewhere, sometimes with the helping hand—the Black Hand—of the Mafia; evidence that some original information about Lee Harvey Oswald had been hushed up by the Dallas police, and that other information about him had been deliberately withheld from the Warren Commission by the FBI and the CIA.

I was not the only person with newfound doubts. The recent CIA revelations had convinced even a member of the Warren Commission staff, Ohio Judge Burt Griffin, that back then the country had been told something less than the truth.

The climate of sheer puppy-dog belief that existed ten years ago in America is almost inconceivable today. In 1965, *Life* magazine had headlined an insider's account of the Warren Commission's findings: MOTHER'S MYTH: OSWALD WAS A PAID U.S. AGENT. Implying that Marguerite Oswald was in fact a 100-per-cent nutball, the writer boasted that the commission had "the sworn denials . . . of men like FBI

Director J. Edgar Hoover and Secretary of State Dean Rusk. We quizzed personnel from the U.S. Embassy in Moscow," the article continued. "We sent our own men into the agencies involved to study their old personnel files. We were, and we are now, convinced that Oswald was never an agent for the U.S. government." The author of these staunch reassurances was Michigan Congressman Gerald R. Ford.

In the past bloody decade, the FBI, the CIA, the White House, and government itself have lost credibility. Recent history forces one to consider that maybe the conspiracy buffs were right. Personally I'd hate to discover that last year's paranoid nut is next year's Pulitzer Prize-winning investigative reporter, but that's a chance recent history forces us to take. Ten years ago, it was difficult to doubt the conclusions of the Warren Report. Now new studies of the Report are under way in both the House and Senate. The very same items we were once unable to doubt we are now unable to believe.

Read the Warren Report again.

• It is difficult today to believe that all fifty-two witnesses were mistaken who testified that at least some of the shots came not from the Texas Book Depository behind the car in which the President was riding, but from the grassy knoll in front of him.

• It is difficult today to believe the so-called magic bullet theory: that one single shot struck President Kennedy in the back, came out his neck and hit Governor John Connally in the back, smashed through Connally's rib, came out his chest, struck him in the wrist, wound up in his thigh, and was later conveniently discovered on the governor's stretcher in the hospital.

• It is difficult today to believe Oswald could have hit the moving target at all from the book depository window. He had been a poor shot in the Marine Corps. He was right-handed, and the clumsy old single-shot, Mannlicher-Carcano rifle had a left-handed scope. None of the three National Rifle Association marksmen hired by the Warren Commission to re-create the shooting was able to hit even a level, stationary target within the required 5.6 seconds, the interval that movie films proved had elapsed between the first and the third, fatal shot.

• It is difficult today to accept that within three years of the assassination seventeen witnesses to the murders of Kennedy, Oswald, and Dallas Police Officer Tippit would die under curious circumstances. Five died of "natural causes"; twelve were victims of murder, suicide, or fatal accidents. The actuarial odds against this happening have been reckoned at 100 *trillion* to one!

● It is difficult today to accept that the President's brain, removed after autopsy and preserved in formalin because the pattern of its wounds was crucial to proving the "magic bullet" theory, has innocently disappeared from the National Archives building.

● It is difficult today to accept that the two photographs of Oswald holding a rifle, which the Dallas police say they found in his garage the day of the shooting, are photographs of the same man, or even photographs of Oswald at all. The man in one picture is six inches taller than the man in the other.

● It is almost impossible today to accept the Commission's murder timetable: that Oswald was able to rearrange the shield of boxes he had set up around the sixth floor window from which it was said he shot, wipe his fingerprints off the rifle, hide it, run down four flights of stairs to the second-floor Coke machine, and be found there by the police calmly sipping Coke only eighty seconds later.

The truth is, today it is difficult to accept *any* FBI or CIA testimony or evidence at face value. Remember, the Warren Commission had no investigative staff of its own; all its field work was done by FBI or CIA agents. Remember that J. Edgar Hoover admitted withholding certain files from the commission. Remember that while then-CIA Director Allen Dulles claimed he was telling the truth when he denied Oswald had ever been a CIA agent, he also admitted that, yes, he would lie under oath to protect the CIA. So indeed would any CIA man. So, then, what was truth? Real gardens, imaginary toads.

Marianne Moore's toads are truths, of course, which is why the world of the secret agent must be just the opposite of the poet's. The spy lives in a real garden with imaginary toads—a world of double agents, dealers of doubt, smugglers of truth, speculators in rumor, hoarders of dirt, spendthrifts of lies. It is a garden whose only signs read KEEP OUT, NO ENTRY, BEWARE THE DOG! The public is emphatically *not* invited. Nor are the public's representatives welcome—that is, the Congress—save to rubber-stamp what's going on anyway.

Inside this garden, the gardeners make their own rules, sit in judgment on their own crimes, write and break their own laws with no accountability to anyone save to their one god: "national security." But even this god is at least sometimes false. The recent nose-to-nose confrontation between Congress and the White House questioned the value and competence of secret intelligence reports, notably on the eve of the Tet offensive and later the 1973 Yom Kippur war, when the President was wrongly assured that there was no danger of attack.

It seems obvious here that former CIA Director William Colby was struggling to protect not national security but the CIA cover-up of its own incompetence, as well as various abuses of power by intelligence officials. Deadly poisons were stockpiled in the garden in direct contravention of Presidential orders; frightening, sometimes-fatal drug experiments were carried out; mail was opened, phones were tapped, civilians were spied on illegally and in wholesale batches; underworld liaisons and assassination plots were commonplace—and all this has been kept continually watered with billions of dollars of uncounted and unaccountable taxpayer dollars.

Looking back at the Warren Commission Report from this CIA-conditioned vantage point, one finds there such a volume of evidence to contradict the conclusions of the Warren Commission that one can see the Report itself as a kind of conspiracy by the government and its investigative agencies to suppress or ignore any evidence of a conspiracy by assassin or assassins unknown. Not evidence that in any way linked the FBI or the CIA with the assassination of President Kennedy, but evidence of numerous shadowy links that appeared to exist between these agencies and Lee Harvey Oswald, and between the FBI and Jack Ruby.

Whether these links did in fact exist is no longer of major importance. What is new and important is not the evidence but the doubts about it. What has changed is the climate. What has cracked here is belief itself—belief in all institutions, not just in the thoroughness and —yes—*honesty* of the 888-page Warren Report, handsomely bound in baby blue and reassuringly stamped with the trusty U.S. seal.

From its inception, the purpose of the Report was double. First, it was necessary to find out exactly what had happened. Second, it was necessary to reassure the nation that the moment of danger had passed. This two-fold purpose was always the flaw, the crack in the credibility of the report: one document could not reasonably be expected to be both a thorough job of police work and a giant security blanket for the nation.

The crack that began in 1963 had widened and become a chasm by 1975, a Grand Canyon of doubts. At the bottom of a tangled bone yard of shattered beliefs lay the decade's news events: the assassinations of the President's brother Robert Kennedy and of Martin Luther King; the attempts on the lives of other leaders, from George Wallace to President Ford; increasing doubts about the wisdom of the Vietnam war, doubts that finally forced President Johnson to give up his office, doubts that led directly to the massive disaffection of the people, and especially the young, and helped the "turn on, tune in, drop out" drug culture to flourish; doubts that led to active revolution—the Weathermen, the bombings; the urban despair that became riots in Watts, Newark, Detroit, Boston; the outbursts of psychopathic violence such as the Manson murders and the Symbionese Liberation Army's hokey, confused politics of idealistic anarchy, which began with the murder of School Superintendent Marcus Foster, accelerated with the kidnapping of Patricia Hearst, triggered the assault by the Los Angeles police against the SLA holdouts in a burning house, and will end God knows where. By the time the Vietnam war had "wound down" through Cambodia and the Christmas bombing, the national honor itself seemed to teeter on the brink of the chasm. With Watergate it fell in. From then on, everything was poisoned, nobody could be believed, anything was possible.

I think it no accident that the politician most popular today among his constituents is California's Governor Edmund G. Brown, Jr. Brown is an austere, icy figure who seems to me to understand the national illness better than any other politician. He understands that the fundamental problem in this country is that the people have lost confidence in all the institutions that traditionally nourish and protect them, including that overarching institution called *government.* He understands that the only way to restore that necessary measure of equilibrium which will permit our institutions to function again is to recover the regard of the major political constituency in this country—all those people who have become so turned off, they don't even bother to vote; that crucial majority (56 per cent in the last California election) which Brown calls "the constituency of no confidence."

There is only one way to regain that confidence, and that one way is through truth. Turn over every rock, ask every question, examine every toad. Don't just reopen the investigation of President Kennedy's death. Test the "second gun" theory in the Robert Kennedy assassination. Look again into the killing of Martin Luther King, and ask anew where convict James Earl Ray got his money and how he could have acted alone. Ask how it was that dim and dippy Arthur Bremer was able to shoot down George Wallace. Find out how Lynette "Squeaky" Fromme, who appears to be everybody's next-door psychopath, could creep so frighteningly close to President Ford; how Sara Jane Moore, a woman of some concern to the San Francisco Police Department, could be free in a crowd to fire a pistol at him. Ask every question. Open up the garden; examine all the toads. Ask *yourself* what you can believe.

A member of the Senate Foreign Relations Committee once told me that whenever a witness testifying in closed session told the senators he had the information but couldn't reveal it, he was automatically assumed to be either faking or lying. This is a pretty solid assumption, too seldom made by most of us. We are too easily cowed by self-proclaimed experts. "If *you* only knew what I know," they murmer, and we nod gravely. "Ah, if *we* only knew what *they* know . . ." (about Vietnam, about the atom bomb)—*we* being the public and *they* being the experts, the Secretary of Defense, the Joint Chiefs, the CIA, the President.

Except that the hindsight of history tells us that they didn't, entirely, know. As one comes to realize that most executive command decisions of necessity are made on the basis of incomplete or inaccurate or misleading intelligence information, the more one dares to question, to turn over toads.

"Secrecy itself frequently gets in the way of rational examination of our intelligence," says Representative Otis Pike, drawing on his fourteen years' experience on the Armed Services Committee. It gets in the way at every level, top to bottom. Secret organizations are run on a "need-to-know" basis. Each man knows only as much as he needs to know to carry out his bit of the operation. But when the spooks apply the need-to-know rule to the man at the top, to the President, to protect him from knowing the dirty work his own men are up to, that's trouble.

The man at the top has an overriding need and duty to know everything because he's in charge. The buck stops here, as President Truman said, or one faces the horrifying prospect that it doesn't stop anywhere, that free-lance assassins are loose, mad dogs out of their masters' control. Something like this may already have occurred in the Caribbean, Latin America, Africa, perhaps elsewhere. Though, of course, one doesn't know.

What does the secret life do to the man? Isn't the secret a terrible burden to have to carry? Sometimes I imagine the man as a kind of stone urn or stoppered jar, and the secrets as a powerful liquid that eventually must corrode and eat away at the jar itself. On TV, the CIA's Colby, Helms & Co. looked to me like men who have contained the acid too long. And in the tight face of James J. Angleton, the former head of the CIA's counterintelligence group, one saw a man not only self-contained but also self-embalmed.

When a man becomes an initiate, part of a select company chosen to serve a select cause, he acquires certain privileges not accorded outsiders. He is removed from ordinary accountability. He can lie and the lie is morally justified. He can assassinate. Membership in the secrets society becomes so compelling that people who are not evil in themselves begin to do bad things to stay in the inner group. Acceptance of the group's methods is the price of belonging, and that price keeps rising.

The weight of forbidden secrets can warp a man's loyalties. We are told that Dr. Nathan Gordon, a former "middle-level CIA employee," decided "on his own" to preserve a deadly medicine cabinetful of shellfish toxin, cobra venom, and heaven knows what other horrors. Richard Helms, then chief of the CIA, says well, yes, he did give an "oral order" in 1970 to destroy the stuff, as President Nixon had directed. But it appears obvious that the real reason the deadly vials were preserved was that a man in Dr. Gordon's position can come to believe that the highest authority is neither the law of the land nor the President of the United States. It is the Secret Organization itself— and that is very bad news indeed, because it means there is no authority at all.

Presidential Aide John Dean told his boss Richard Nixon there was a cancer growing on the Presidency. Recent CIA revelations suggest that for years a cancer has been growing on this whole country. The intelligence community was a secret, dark garden, and what appears to have been growing there under cover of such rubrics as "national security" was nothing less than the roots and tentacles of a genuine police state. Of course, we need to keep some secrets. Of course, we need to maintain an intelligence capability—though far less, I suspect, than the present intelligence community and the White House would have us believe.

Once you set up something so secret that nobody else can look at it, nobody else can oversee it. You no longer have to ask yourself: how dirty a trick is "too dirty"? You can use any damned trick you want.

One is free to lie. One is also free to cheat, embezzle, or steal without fear of ordinary criminal prosecution. This is the very antithesis of our system of checks and balances. What were the CIA's and FBI's own punishments for murders, attempted murders, botched murder plots? No way to tell.

Another thing about secrets: they don't seem to last as long as they used to. They ooze; they leak; they degenerate and decay into history almost before our eyes. The official secrets closet today, I suspect, is a threadbare place full of obsolete codes, moldy disguises, broken ciphers, bulging files on plots long dead. It was in recognition of this modern truth that Congress recently amended the Freedom of Information Act, over President Ford's veto. This amendment provides the public with a tool to pry no-longer-critical information out of the government.

What is to be done? It is all so massive and so sinister, one is tempted to make the radical suggestion to abolish the CIA altogether. Or at the very least, cut the monster into two pieces—surveillance and operations —and put each one under separate government control. Or if the CIA has grown too fat in its thirty-year history, too hydra-headed to be cut in two, or if the dirty tricks have been too dirty too long to clean up now, perhaps we should let the dear old monster go the way of the brontosaurus. Consider it obsolete and start over. Only time and vigorous continuing congressional investigations will tell. I hope they tell plenty.

I think we need to hear a lot more about the value and durability of secrets in the post-Vietnam, pan-nuclear age. We also need to give some thought to the distinction between "data" and "intelligence." The Warren Commission Report, in hindsight, appears to be mostly data, and incomplete data at that. But what is the nature of "intelligence" in a world where, as someone in Washington recently testified, "the lead time on World War Three is fifteen minutes"?

I don't know the answers—only that we all must begin to ask ourselves these questions. We all must pick up toads and handle them. Self-government in the dark is not possible. The central secret of democracy may be that there *can be* no enduring secrets, that the people must know, that to opt for the democratic form of government is to forfeit forever one of life's sweetest comforts: the right not to know.

Redbook—January 1976